ELSPETH HUXLEY
A Bibliography

by Robert Cross
and Michael Perkin

Foreword
by Elspeth Huxley

ST PAUL'S BIBLIOGRAPHIES · WINCHESTER
OAK KNOLL PRESS · NEW CASTLE · DELAWARE
1996

First published in 1996 by St Paul's Bibliographies,
West End House, 1 Step Terrace, Winchester, UK
as part of the *Winchester Bibliographies of 20th Century Writers Series*

Published in North and South America by
Oak Knoll Press, 414 Delaware Street,
New Castle, DE 19720, USA

© 1996 by Robert Cross
© 1996 in Foreword by Elspeth Huxley

A CIP catalogue record for this book is available from the British Library

Library of Congress Cataloging-in-Publication Data
Cross, Robert S.
　Elspeth Huxley: a bibliography/by Robert Cross and Michael Perkin: foreword by Elspeth Huxley.
　　p. cm.—(Winchester bibliographies of 20th century writers)
　Includes bibliographical references and index.
　ISBN 1-884718-17-5 (alk. paper)
　1. Huxley, Elspeth Joscelin Grant, 1907–　—Bibliography.
2. Women and literature—England—Biblography. 3. Women and literature—Kenya—Bibliography. I. Perkin, Michael. II. Title.
III. Series.
Z8430.C76　1996
[PR6015.U92]
016.829'91209—dc20　　　　　　　　　　　　　　　　95-26301
　　　　　　　　　　　　　　　　　　　　　　　　　　　CIP

ISBN (UK) 1-873040-06-7—ISBN (USA) 1-884718-17-5

Printed in Great Britain by Henry Ling Ltd, The Dorset Press, Dorchester

Contents

List of Illustrations	*page*	vi
Foreword by Elspeth Huxley		vii
Publisher's Note		ix
Introduction		x
Acknowledgements		xii
Abbreviations		xv
Chronology		xvi
A. Books and Pamphlets by Elspeth Huxley including translations		1
B. Books edited or with Contributions by Elspeth Huxley		104
C. Contributions to newspapers and periodicals		110
D. Radio and television appearances		154
E. Miscellanea		173
Index		177

List of Illustrations

		page
I	Elspeth Huxley CBE	frontispiece
II	Page one of her prize-winning essay *Royal Commonwealth Society Collection, Cambridge University Library*	xvii
III	Dust-jacket of first edition of *White Man's Country* vol. one	xx
IV	Dust-jacket of *Murder at Government House* first edition	7
V	Binding of *Murder at Government House* first US edition – *Harry Ransom Humanities Research Center*	8
VI	Dust-jacket of *Red Strangers* first US edition – *Harry Ransom Humanities Research Center*	18
VII	Dust-jacket of *African Poison Murders* first US edition – *Harry Ransom Humanities Research Center*	21
VIII	Covers of *Colonies: a Readers Guide* – *Royal Commonwealth Society Collection, Cambridge University Library*	33
IX	Dust-jacket of first edition *The Walled City* designed by Edward Bawden	35
X	Covers of *What are Trustee Nations?* – *Royal Commonwealth Society Collection, Cambridge University Library*	47
XI	Dust-jacket of *The Red Rock Wilderness* – first edition	49
XII	Dust-jacket of *The Red Rock Wilderness* first US edition – *Harry Ransom Humanities Research Center*	51
XIII	Dust-jacket of *The Flame Trees of Thika* first US edition, Apollo series	57

Foreword

No eager truffle-hound rootling in the woods for tubers could rootle with greater determination, skill and perseverance than Robert Cross has brought to the task of digging out every fact relevant to the literary output of a long lifetime; and to have been the object of this exercise is a great honour. Indeed, Mr. Cross has surprised me by digging up titles long buried in the compost of time that I had forgotten all about; mainly short books and booklets written half a century ago to provide reading matter for a newly literate generation then emerging in colonial Africa, before that gap could be filled by African writers themselves.

A bibliography not only sets the seal on a writer's career, it invites him to look back on his output not, of course, in judgement, but to review motives and objectives he or she set out with, and how far the latter have been realised. I started as a freelance journalist, insofar as I was trained at all I was trained as one, and it was as a freelance journalist in its widest sense that I approached my craft. Today, journalism of any kind commands a pretty low rating in public esteem, but in my youth it was a much more respectable profession. My mentor in my first job was Patrick Ryan, who had learned his trade on the old *Manchester Guardian* in the shadow of the great C. P. Scott – he who coined the phrase "Facts are sacred, comment is free" – and went on to become deputy editor of *The Times,* whose editors still dined with prime ministers and prelates and whose front page was still devoted to classified announcements. The principal lesson, I think, that I imbibed had been summed up about a century and a half ago by Matthew Arnold: "Have something to say and say it as clearly as you can: that is the only secret of style".

Curiosity, I suggest, is the driving force that motivates the serious journalist: curiosity not only about when and where the murderer battered his victim to death but why he did it; not only when and how one country invaded another, but what drove its leaders to give the command "Go bid the soldiers shoot"; in short, the mainsprings and vagaries of human nature. And here the cub reporter covering Town Hall elections and the Nobel prize-winner for Literature join forces in exploring the measureless caverns of human behaviour, even if they do so in different ways and at a different level.

The principal criticism levelled at the journalist, however responsible, is that his approach is superficial. He cannot, like the good shoemaker, stick to his last, but must cobble up all sorts of footwear. I have laid myself open to this charge by trying my hand in a number of genres: biography, memoirs, letters, travel, novels of several kinds – crime, documentary, farce, straightforward – as well as diaries, agriculture, wildlife and anthology, instead of concentrating on one or two. A long life isn't long enough fully to master the craft of even one of these categories, let alone nearly a dozen. In spreading one's energies, one risks diluting them; the wide-angled lens must lack the definition of its long-angled brother; yet a wider perspective may have its advantages. I remember, years ago, seeing at a photographic exhibition an enlargement labelled "Three hairs on the leg of a bee". The whole bee, or even the comings and goings in the hive, might have held more interest.

I was fortunate enough to have enjoyed a childhood and adolescence in an African country just before the tide of Western customs and values swept away the cultures of its indigenous peoples. The imprint of a child's surroundings on mind and character can never, as we all know, be quite obliterated, so it was inevitable that memories of those surroundings, those experiences, should have worked their way into much of my writing. It was in the hope of pinning down on paper some of the sights and sounds, dreams and realities, of a bygone Africa that I hammered out inexpertly on an obsolete manual typewriter my African books. Perhaps, like flies in amber, they will remain to commemorate some of the characters, adventures and perceptions of a corner of Africa that saw, in a very short space of time, the rise and fall of the colonial experiment, the birth and death of many expectations, the playing out of many dramas, and the opening of a new chapter in a long story of uncertain direction that can have no journey's end.

Elspeth Huxley
Oaksey
8 August 1995

Publisher's Note

Building up the Winchester Bibliographies of 20th Century Writers has not been an easy matter, especially as compilers of author bibliographies, who are prepared to commit themselves to 4 or 5 years of study for scant financial reward, are few and far between.

This, unfortunately, comes at a time when many publishers' records have never been at greater risk, due to the indifference towards archival material shown by the present owners of many historic imprints.

If this situation continues, we are in danger of leaving scant records about 20th-Century writers to those who follow us.

It is for this reason that with the help of Michael Perkin and others, I decided to compile a bibliography myself: if I had hoped to complete one faster than some of my bibliographical authors, I was mistaken. I chose Elspeth Huxley as my subject because it would give me access to a superb author/publisher relationship whose correspondence is held in the Reading University archive, and because I had always intended that my series should include a good proportion of women writers. It has also been a joy to get to know Elspeth Huxley and to have the benefit of her help and advice.

Nothing daunted, I am now moving on to Vita Sackville-West.

R.S.C.

Introduction

Titles in *Section A. Books and pamphlets by Elspeth Huxley,* include those whose concept was Mrs. Huxley's. They are arranged in chronological order of first publication, and under the first published title (cross-references to American or alternative titles are given in the Index). A running-number is assigned to each book; all subsequent editions, issues or re-issues given a separate entry for whatever reason are assigned a lower-case letter after the number. Evidence or information concerning the parent-setting of type in the case of reprints, re-issues, new impressions, paperback reprints, etc., is given in the *Notes* section, together with details of textual changes.

Titles in *Section B. Books edited or with contributions by Elspeth Huxley,* are also arranged in chronological order of publication. The main entry is the title of the book, followed by a full catalogue description, and a transcription of the contribution with page references. Notes on their printing history are given where obtainable.

Information under each entry in *Section A* is given in the following order:

(1) In the *transcription of the title page* in Section A the quasi-facsimile method is used in that line-endings are noted with a slash, capitals, lower-case, roman, gothic, decorated or italic type faces are distinguished, and the punctuation of the original is preserved.
(2) The *collation statement* includes the register of signatures where present; where signatures are not present no attempt has been made to provide a register unless the sewing is clearly visible and it can be deduced. The pagination statement follows with page numbers not present before and after the text supplied in square brackets. Page-size by height and width is given in millimetres.
(3) The list of *Contents* follows by page numbers with all matter transcribed within double quotation marks.
(4) A more detailed note on *Illustrations* then follows, when relevant.
(5) *Binding cases* are briefly described; their colours are assigned the number of the nearest matching colour in *ISCC-NBS Colour-Name charts Illustrated with Centroid Colours,* Inter-Society Color Council/US National Bureau of Standards, 1965 (in some cases the match is not very close).
(6) The *Dust-Jacket or Wrappers* is then described. It has not been possible to obtain complete consistency in the descriptions because of their haphazard survival and because information has been derived from a variety of sources. The names of designers are always recorded when present.
(7) A description of the *Paper* used is given whenever obtainable from production ledgers.
(8) The *Copy (Copies)* used for the description are identified.

(9) Finally *Notes* are given on printing history, the number of copies printed, author's agreements, prices, textual changes, cancellations, etc., from archival sources. Brief notes are given of translations and serialisations in journals or on radio or television which are keyed to Sections C and D.

(10) *Reviews:* a brief note of these has been included where the information could be found.

Section C. Contributions to newspapers and periodicals contains the articles in chronological order written by Elspeth Huxley in newspapers and periodicals from 1921 to 1995: in cases where their dates or provenance are unobtainable, they are listed in the Appendix.

Section D. Radio and Television appearances: contains all radio and television appearances by Elspeth Huxley from 1929 to 1991: the index separates them.

Section E. Miscellanea is divided into five parts
 1. Articles where the date and/or provenance is uncertain
 2. Prize (Empire Essay Competition)
 3. Radio programmes written but not necessarily transmitted
 4. Report on East African Literature Bureau and Seminar at LSE
 5. Introduction by EH to book not yet published

The index consists of names of book titles, authors (except EH), publishers, designers, photographers, printers, binders, newspapers, periodicals, reviewers, radio and television channels and interviewers; it also contains other references relating to the books described.

We are well aware that information may have been missed and that mistakes may have been made in this bibliography: we welcome comments from users.

Acknowledgements

It would have been impossible to tackle this bibliography without the unstinted help of librarians and Michael Perkin and I extend our thanks particularly to Alan Bell, until 1993 Librarian of Rhodes House, Oxford, who encouraged me to start studying Elspeth Huxley's papers deposited there, and to Clare Brown, their archivist, and Mary Bull, who have guided and helped me over the past 4 years: then Michael Bott, archivist at Reading University Library, who has patiently helped us over the years, with the correspondence between Mrs Huxley and Chatto and Windus amounting to many hundreds of letters often spiced with humour, and also their production ledgers up to 1980 which contain so much important detail. My steps took me inevitably as an alumnus to Cambridge University Library where their help has been unbounded and my thanks go to David Hall for making everything possible and to Terry Barringer the librarian of the Royal Commonwealth Collection there who opened a Pandora's Box for me on yet more periodical articles by Mrs Huxley; my sincere thanks go to Professor Tom Staley, the Director of the Harry Ransom Humanities Research Center, Austin, whose collection of 20th-century literature must be unrivalled, and whose help and encouragement not only to this book but for the Winchester Series as a whole has been most generous, and that includes Cathy Henderson and her staff. My special thanks too go to Mrs. E. H. Owako, the lady librarian of the invaluable records in the Basement of the McMillan Library, Nairobi. There have been many other librarians who have helped me and they are included later under periodicals.

The help of publishers has been crucial except for those whose records have sadly been dispersed: I must mention first Chatto & Windus whose managing Director was then Carmen Callil, who allowed us to look through the correspondence held at Reading and John Charlton who helped me interpret them: and then a chance meeting with Sophie Arditti at a beach party in Kenya brought me in touch with Barry Featherstone, head of Chatto's production department, who introduced me to the ledgers after 1980 and was able to answer many important questions, leading on to Chatto's senior publisher Jonathan Burnham, who accepted my list of the records. John Handford who is in charge of Macmillan's archives at Basingstoke gave generously any information I required and treated me as if I was still his colleague, showing me too the correspondence between Harold Macmillan and Elspeth Huxley on the subject of *Red Strangers;* also my thanks are due to Elizabeth James who helped me find the production details of this book in that part of the Macmillan archives which is in the British Library. I am very grateful to Peter Carson and Miranda McAllister of Penguin who by providing me with their invaluable print-outs of the last 15 years gave me instant information on print numbers and published prices, and also Nick Lee, Librarian of Special Collections, Bristol University. Lord Weidenfeld provided important information on the books he published of Mrs Huxley, as did the archivist at

Orion Books, Simon Cobley. I owe to Professor Richard Smyer the discovery of the vanished production records of Methuen, which are now looked after in the Manuscript Department of the Lilly Library by the distinguished bibliographer, William R. Cagle, at Indiana University. I am very grateful to Michael Carney who gave me guidance, before his excellent book *Britain in Pictures* came out, on the early history of this series and of Adprint, later Aldus Books, and the founders. This included putting me in touch with Joyce Howell, Wolfgang Foges' secretary and Peter Cook who also helped me greatly over *The Challenge of Africa*. Dr Huelin, archivist of SPCK and Sheldon Press, has been most helpful and patient in unearthing copies of Elspeth Huxley's *English Women* in Swahili, and *Brave Deeds of the War* which no one seemed to have heard of. My grateful thanks too go to Mr Charles G. Richards, the first Director of the East African Literature Bureau from 1948, for his advice on *Settlers of Kenya*, and about the Bureau itself; and to Dr Prosser Gifford, Director of Scholarly Programs in the Library of Congress, for his ready help; and to Cathe Giffuni for her help.

I want to thank the following among other publishers who have supplied us with information: Philip Attenborough, Rayner Unwin and Julian Shuckburgh, Batsford, Jonathan Cape, Century, Evans Brothers, Collins-Harvill, The Folio Society, Longman, Orion Books, Pan, William Morrow (USA), University of Nebraska Press, Greenwood Press (USA), Radcliffe Press, Fulcrum Publishing (USA), Reed Publishing, Clive Bradley of the Publishers' Association, Severn House Publishers and also to Books on Tape Inc., and Frank Popeley, a specialist dealer in African books who has given me enthusiastic help. James Oliver, working at the Centre for the Study of Propaganda at Kent University, also gave me invaluable information on IRD and Background Books.

We have many people to thank who have helped over the numerous articles in periodicals and Mrs Huxley's TV and radio appearances, and the following should be named: Jabu Maphalala of Anglo American Corporation of South Africa, the librarians at Associated Newspapers, Jacqueline Kavanagh of BBC Written Archives, and Simon Rooks and Andrew Whitehouse in Broadcasting House, the Bibliographic Information Service and the Newspaper Library of the British Library, the librarian at the British Library of Political and Economic Science at LSE, Alexandra Erskine at the Daily Telegraph Library, Jane Dunlop of the *Geographical Magazine*, Blossom Martis of *Homes and Garden*, Sarah Howes of The Institute of Commonwealth Studies Library, the Director of the South African Library, Cape Town, Deborah Gibbs of Masterpiece Theater, WGBH Boston, Len Witcher of Thames TV, the archivist of Unilever, Nigel Begby and the Editorial Librarians at Reader's Digest, the US Information Service at the American Embassy, London, and Amanda Ballard of the World Wide Fund for Nature, the librarians at the Hampshire County Reference Library in Winchester, and to Katharine Wilson who did much valuable research for me; David Bradbury, former Director of the Document Supply Centre, Boston Spa; and to the Librarian of Special Collections, Cornell University.

My thanks too are extended to Virginia Morgan-Grenville who has wrestled with my handwriting as she transferred it on to her computer.

Finally Michael and I want to express our gratitude to Elspeth Huxley who has shown us unfailing helpfulness, kindness and hospitality over four years, and for her permission to quote from her letters; and also to Sara Dick-Read without whose generous help this bibliography would never have been finished.

R.S.C.

Abbreviations

BL	British Library
caps.	capital letters
CIP	cataloguing in publication
C&W	Chatto & Windus
dec.	decorative
d.j.	dust-jacket
EH	Elspeth Huxley and her collection
EMB	Empire Marketing Board
f. and c.	folded and collated sheets
Hants CL	Hampshire County Library
HM	Harold Macmillan (Macmillan & Co.)
HR	Harold Raymond (Chatto & Windus)
HRHRC	Harry Ransom Humanitites Research Center, Austin, Texas
h.t.	half-title
illus.	illustration(s), illustrated
inst.	instalment
JGW	John G. Willey (William Morrow)
L	left
LC	lower cover (book, dust-jacket)
LF	lower flap (dust-jacket)
LW	lower wrapper
ndk	no date known
npk	no provenance known
NS	Norah Smallwood (Chatto & Windus)
orn.	type ornament
pbk	paperback
R	right
RC	Robert Cross
rev/d.	reviewed
RH	Rhodes House
rom.	roman
RUL	Reading University Library
Times	The Times Newspaper
Tiptree	Chatto & Windus archive at Tiptree
tp	title page
tr.	translated
UC	upper cover (book, dust-jacket)
UF	upper flap (dust-jacket)
UW	upper wrapper

Chronology

1907   Elspeth Josceline Grant born in London on 23rd July.

1913   Joined her parents, Josceline and Eleanor ('Nellie') Grant at Kitimuru Farm, Thika, Kenya.

1915   Returned to England with her mother.

1919   Back at Thika.

1921   Her first anonymous article at the age of 14 'Country Sport – Makuyu Hunt and Polo Club. Mr Swift's Accident' was published in the *East African Standard* on 10th December 1921.

1922   On 17th September Nellie Grant began working on a new farm which she called Gikammeh Farm at Njoro, where Josceline and Elspeth joined her after the sale of Kitimuru.

1924   Won the Empire Essay Competition with her essay entitled 'Improved Communication as a Factor of Imperial History', later published in part in *East African Standard*. Wrote in the *East African Standard* the last of her articles on polo and hunting listed in Section C and in the Appendix.

1925   Left the European School in Nairobi and went to Reading University where she studied agriculture

1927   Obtained her Diploma in Agriculture in Summer 1927. Studied at Cornell University, Ithaca, where she continued her agricultural studies until Summer 1928. She wrote about her Cornell experiences in the Reading University student magazine, *Tamesis*.

1929   Employed as Assistant Press Officer at the Empire Marketing Board until the Depression closed it down in 1932. She wrote many articles during this period in many British and Commonwealth newspapers. Started writing regularly for *The Times*.

1931   Married Gervas Huxley who was then Secretary to the Publicity committee of the Board. In 1932 he became Director of the Ceylon Tea Propaganda Board which later became the International Tea Market Expansion Board.

1935   *White Man's Country: Lord Delamere and the Making of Kenya*, was published by Macmillan and Co. on 17th May.

1937   *Murder at Government House*, her first crime novel, 22nd April, Methuen (who only published her crime books).

1938   *Murder on Safari*, 24th February, Methuen.

1939   *Red Strangers:* this novel was rejected by Macmillan due to editorial disagreement with Harold Macmillan; published by Chatto &

Class A. II.   Praesentia confer praeteritis.

Improved Communications as a Factor of Imperial History.

"Transportation is civilisation" is an aphorism whose truth becomes plain on examination. Civilisation, as we understand the word, has been spread abroad chiefly by colonisation, since to found an empire is an attempt to civilise distant peoples by bringing them under a civilised government. The commander of an invading army aims first at securing his communications, and this also is the object of the colonist; if the communications were cut off, the colony would perish as surely as would the army. Since transport has hitherto been, to a large extent, identical with communications, these latter play a very large part in the civilisation of distant countries.

All previous empires in the history of the world have been ephemeral because they have failed to consolidate their conquests. Conquest outstripped the slow and insecure methods of communication which they were forced to use for lack of better, and the empires became too large, and scattered to admit of centralised government; further, settlement was too risky to be undertaken by the civilian, so that colonies were held by the sword alone, and so were bound to revolt eventually. Alexander the Great, for example, marched for thousands of miles defeating all whom he met in battle, till his empire stretched from Greece to the Indus, from the Caspian to the Nile; but he paid no attention to communications, built no roads, had no regular sea transport, and for this reason his dominions disintegrated immediately on his death. His empire lasted little over twelve years.

The Romans, on the other hand, held their empire for longer than any previous nation had done because they paid more attention to communications. Whenever they annexed a country they built roads, the quality of which may be judged from the Roman roads existing in Britain today after eighteen hundred years' use. The saying "all roads lead to Rome" illustrates their system: a centralised government conducted from Rome. The empire fell because it outstripped its communications; it became too wide, and its outposts lost touch with the capital, so that it gradually dissolved.

II. Page one from EH's essay entitled 'Improved Communications as a Factor of Imperial History' which won the Empire Essay Competition in 1924.

xviii   *Chronology*

Windus, 1st June, when her close relationship began with Harold Raymond and subsequently Norah Smallwood. *Death of an Aryan*, on 19th October, Methuen; entitled *The African Poison Murders* in the American editions.

1941/4 Worked for BBC News Department on war propaganda for British Commonwealth and USA; later became Liaison Officer between BBC and Colonial Office.

1941 *East Africa*, March, Penns in the Rocks Press and William Collins; *The Story of Five English Farmers*, Sheldon Press, commissioned by Foreign Literature Committee of SPCK for use in African schools. *Atlantic Ordeal*, 15th December.

1942 *English Women*, Sheldon Press.

1943 *Brave Deeds of the War*, Sheldon Press, taken from Elspeth Huxley's broadcasts to Africa. Started writing regularly for *Time and Tide*.

1944 *Race and Politics in Kenya*, jointly with Margery Perham, 5th May, Faber & Faber. Charles, her only child, was born.

1945 Invited to submit a report on the formation of the East African Literature Bureau which was finished in 1946 (see Appendix).

1947 *Colonies: A Reader's Guide*, December, Cambridge University Press.

1948 *The Walled City*, 22 March; *Settlers of Kenya*, 3rd May, Longmans; *African Dilemmas*, 1st November, Longmans: *The Sorcerer's Apprentice*, 4th November.

1950 *I Don't Mind if I Do*, 25th September.

1954 *Four Guineas*, 11th February; *A Thing to Love*, 11th October; *Kenya Today*, 30th November, Lutterworth Press. Member of BBC Advisory Council until 1960 and was a regular broadcaster on Africa and took part in 'The Critics' up to 1962 (see Section D).

1955 *What are Trustee Nations?* Batchworth Press.

1957 *Red Rock Wilderness*, 16th May; *No Easy Way*, June, East African Standard.

1959 Member of the Monckton Commission to advise on the Central African Federation. *The Flame Trees of Thika*, 2nd March.

1960 *A New Earth*, 30th June.

1962 Awarded the C.B.E. *The Mottled Lizard*, 10th May.

1963 *The Merry Hippo*, 4th April.

1964 *Forks and Hope*, 6th February; *A Man from Nowhere*, 11th June; *Suki*, 22nd October; *Back Street New Worlds*, 12th November.

1965 *Brave New Victuals*, 11th November.

1967	*Their Shining Eldorado,* 11th May.
1968	*Love Among the Daughters,* 12th September.
1971	Gervas Huxley died. *The Challenge of Africa,* Aldus Books.
1973	*The Kingsleys,* an anthology, Allen & Unwin.
1974	*Livingstone & his African Journeys,* 29th April, Weidenfeld & Nicolson.
1975	*Florence Nightingale,* 27th March, Weidenfeld & Nicolson.
1976	*Gallipot Eyes: a Wiltshire Diary,* 4th May, Weidenfeld & Nicolson.
1977	*Scott of the Antarctic,* 7th November, Weidenfeld & Nicolson.
1979	*Nellie: Letters from Africa,* 6th March, Weidenfeld & Nicolson.
1981	John Hawkesworth serialisation of *Flame Trees of Thika* on Thames TV. *Whipsnade: Captive Breeding for Survival,* William Collins.
1982	Alistair Cooke introduces 'The Flame Trees of Thika' film in Mobil Masterpiece Theater in USA, the start of its great success in North America. *The Prince Buys the Manor,* 4th October.
1984	*Last Days in Eden,* Harvill Press.
1985	*Out in the Midday Sun,* 7th November.
1990	*Nine Faces of Kenya,* an anthology, 20th September, Collins-Harvill.
1993	*Peter Scott: Painter and Naturalist,* 25th October, Faber & Faber.

Note: the publisher was Chatto & Windus unless stated otherwise.

III.   *Dust-jacket of the first edition of* White Man's Country: Lord Delamere and the Making of Kenya *published in 2 volumes by Macmillan & Co. in 1935.*

A. Books and Pamphlets by Elspeth Huxley including Translations

A.1 WHITE MAN'S COUNTRY: LORD DELAMERE AND THE MAKING OF KENYA   1935

(a) First edition

WHITE MAN'S COUNTRY | *Lord Delamere* | *and* | *The Making of Kenya* | BY | ELSPETH HUXLEY | VOLUME I [II] | 1870–1914 [1914–1931] | MACMILLAN AND CO., LIMITED | ST. MARTIN'S STREET, LONDON | 1935

Collation: vol. 1. A–X in 8s; [2],xiii,[xiv],315,[316–320].
           vol.2. A in 4s, B–Y in 8s; vii,[viii],333, [334–336]p. 220 × 146mm.

Contents: vol.1. p.[1–2] blank [i] ht. [ii] Macmillan addresses [iii] tp. [iv] "COPYRIGHT | PRINTED IN GREAT BRITAIN | BY R.&R. CLARK, LIMITED, EDINBURGH" v "NOTE ON THE TITLE [11 lines] | E.J.H." [vi] blank vii–ix "AUTHOR'S NOTE" [x] blank xi–xii contents xiii list of illustrations and maps [xiv] blank [1] "VOLUME I" [2] quotation from Horace Odes . . . 3–315 text, on p.315 "END OF VOLUME ONE | *Printed in Great Britain by* R.&R. CLARK, LIMITED, *Edinburgh*." [316] blank [317–320] Macmillan list: 16 titles.

Note on illustrations: frontispiece, 11 plates, 2 maps.

Contents: vol.2. p.[i] ht. [ii] Macmillan addresses [iii] tp. [iv] as vol.1 v–vi contents vii list of illustrations and maps [viii] blank [1] "VOLUME II" [2] quotation, Churchill 3–333 text [334] "*Printed in Great Britain by* R.&R. CLARK, LIMITED, *Edinburgh*" [335–336] blank.

Note on illustrations: frontispiece, 11 plates, 3 maps.

Binding case: deep/pink cloth (3), gold-lettered on spine, "WHITE MAN'S | COUNTRY | *Lord Delamere* | *and the* | *Making of Kenya* | E.HUXLEY [at foot:] VOLUME I [II] | 1870–1914 [1914–1931] | MACMILLAN".

Dust-jacket: black, white and green design of head and shoulders of a white man with a black man and spear over an outline of Africa; on spine, outline of Africa with Kenya in green, lettered "LORD DELAMERE AND THE MAKING OF KENYA [in green] | WHITE MAN'S | COUNTRY [in white] | ELSPETH | HUXLEY [in black]"; on spine, "WHITE | MAN'S | COUNTRY [white] | MACMILLAN [white]"; UC, signed "K"; LC, Macmillan list: 10 titles; UF, blurb, 2 vols. 25/-, net.

Paper: Novel antique wove.

Copies seen: EH, BL

Notes: Published 7 May 1935 in an edition of 2,000 copies (2,100 maps and jackets) at 25s. Lady Delamere commissioned EH to write her husband's life in 1932 when she was only 24, an indication of her respect for EH's writing which had started when she was only 14, see Section C. Harold Macmillan agreed in 1932 to publish it. On publication in 1935, the *Kenya Weekly News* urged its readers to buy the book 'even though it costs the equivalent of 8 sacks of maize'. The title was an expression of Lord Delamere's vision for Kenya, not EH's.

On 17 August 1949 EH wrote to Dan Macmillan, Harold's brother, asking if he would reprint the book in an abridged one volume with a new final chapter summarising the main events since 1931. EH was invited to meet HM who suggested that she rewrite the book as a short history, for which he offered her a contract. EH decided not to sign the contract – though asking for a higher royalty – 'in view of a lot of other commitments': HM suggested leaving 'the whole question of a contract and the terms till the MS is ready'. On 20 May 1952 EH wrote to HM asking if he was still interested in a reissue and if so whether someone else could do the abridgement: on 26 May, Thomas Mark replied that HM was now in Government but that Macmillans were not interested in an abridgement by another author. On 27 October it was agreed that the rights would revert to EH and the blocks of the illustrations were given to EH who then offered the book to Harold Raymond of Chatto & Windus.

Reviews: Evening Standard, 9 May 1935
Scotsman, 23 May 1935
Manchester Guardian, 29 May 1935
East African Standard, 31 May 1935
Field, 1 June 1935
Time and Tide, 1 June 1935
Observer, 2 June 1935
TLS, 13 June 1935
Times, 4 June 1935
Listener, 12 June 1935
Illustrated London News, 22 June 1935
New Statesman, 20 July 1935
Africa (a monthly periodical) July 1936
Nature, 3 August 1935

(b) First American issue (1935) as per 1(a)

Notes: Published in 1935 by Macmillan of New York (then controlled by Macmillan & Co., UK) at $10: the number they imported is not known.

Reviews: New York Times, 7th July 1935
Christian Science Monitor, 17th July 1935

(c) Chatto and Windus first issue (1953)

Titles: as in 1935 edition save: "VOLUME | ONE [TWO]" and at foot: "CHATTO AND WINDUS | [rule] | LONDON" (imprint omitted in vol.2).

Collation: vol.1. A in 6s, B–L in 16s; xv,[xvi],315,[316]
vol.2. A in 12s B–L in 16s; vii,[viii],333,[334–336]p. 215 × 139mm.

Contents: vol.1. p.(i) ht. (ii) " "*By the same Author*": 4 titles (iii) tp. (iv) "PUBLISHED BY | Chatto and Windus | LONDON | * | Clarke, Irwin & Co. Ltd. | TORONTO | [at foot:] First published 1935 | New Edition 1953 | PRINTED IN GREAT BRITAIN | BY LOWE AND BRYDONE (PRINTERS) LTD. | LONDON, N.W.10 | All rights reserved" v–ix "PREFACE | *To the Second Edition*" x–xii author's note xiii contents, vol.1 xiv blank xv list of illustrations and maps [xvi] blank [1] VOLUME I" [2] quotation from Horace 3–315 text [316] blank.

Note on illustrations: frontispiece, 10 plates, 2 maps: see *Notes.*

Contents: vol.2. p.[i–iv] as vol.1 v contents, vol.II [vi] blank vii list of illustrations and maps [viii] blank [1] "VOLUME II" [2] quotation, Churchill 3–333 text [334–336] blank.

Note on illustrations: frontispiece, 10 plates, 3 maps: see *Notes.*

Binding case: blue/green cloth (159), gold-lettered down spine, "WHITE | MAN'S | COUNTRY| *Lord Delamere* | *and the* | *Making of* | *Kenya* | * | ELSPETH | HUXLEY | VOL.I[II] | 1870–1914 [1914–1932] | [at foot:] CHATTO | & WINDUS".

Dust-jacket: buff with blue/grey design of cattle and foliage, etc.; lettered in red; UF and LF, blurb; UF, 36s.net; LC, reviews of 3 titles (2 by EH).

Paper: Universal antique wove.

Copies seen: Hants CL, EH

Notes: Published 27 July 1953 at 36s the set in 'edition' of 2,243 (including 35 paper covered proofs) of v.1 and 2,237 (no proofs) of v.2. These copies were printed offset, with certain changes to the prelims and illustrations, from Macmillan's first edition; hence it is described here as an issue not, as C & W called it, a new edition. Reprinted January 1956 (1,300).

The following changes were made in the 1953 issue from the Macmillan edition:

Volume one:

Prelims: 'Note on the title' was *omitted.* 'Preface by EH to the second Edition' was *inserted* v–ix. 'Author's Note' was *moved* from vii–ix to x–xii

Illustrations:
'Cedar Forest near Njoro' *moved from* facing page 136 to p. 244
'A Turkana Herdsman' *moved from* p. 244 to p. 136
'The Kenya Highlands' *moved to* Volume 2.
Thus the number of plates was *reduced* by one.

Volume two:

Illustrations:
'Masai Country: The Rift Valley' *moved from* facing p.16 to p.174 and called 'The Rift Valley'
'A Masai Herdsman' remained facing p.44. The caption *changed from* 'Head of a Masai' to 'A Masai Herdsman', as the Macmillan caption was incorrect.
'Lake Naitasha' was *omitted.*
'Lake Elmenteita' *moved from* p.198 to p.16.

4   A   Books and pamphlets

The total number of plates was reduced by one.
The two maps in v.1 and three in v.2 remained the same.

Reprinted in 1956 (1,292 of v.1 and 1,242 of v.2) at 42s, increased to 50s in 1958.

Review: BBC Third Programme 18th May 1954

(d) Chatto and Windus second issue (1968)

Titles: as in 1953 issue

Collation: vol.1. A–U in 8s; xv,[xvi],315,[316]p.
   vol.2. as in 1953, 215 × 135mm.

Contents: p.(i) ht. [ii] blank [iii] tp. [iv] "PUBLISHED BY | Chatto and Windus Ltd | 42 WILLIAM IV STREET | LONDON WC2 | * | Clarke, Irwin & Co Ltd | TORONTO | © Elspeth Huxley 1935 | Preface © Elspeth Huxley 1968 | First published 1935 | New Edition 1953 | Reprinted 1956 | Reprinted with a new preface 1968 | [at foot:] William Lewis (Printers) Ltd | Cardiff" v–xi preface, dated July 1967 xii–xiv author's note xv contents [xvi] blank [vol.1.ht.] [2] quotation from Horace 3–315 text [316] blank.

Note on illustrations: See *Notes* below.

Binding case: v.1,v.2 as in 1953 issue.

Dust-jacket: buff with blue/grey design of cattle and foliage; lettered in red; UF and LF, blurb and note on the author; at foot of UF, 2 volumes. Third impression. 75s net.; on LC, other books by EH: 13 titles.

Paper: Antique wove.

Copies seen: EH

Notes: Reprinted with New Preface by EH in 1968 at 75s in edition of 1,176 (v.1) and 1,213 (v.2) of which 520|500 were sold to Praeger (A.1d). The following changes were made:

Volume One: New Preface replaces that of 1953 and occupies v–xi. Contents has added before Maps 'Frontispiece – Lord Delamere 1923' but there is no list of illustrations and none is included, except for frontispiece.

Volume Two (1968) is identical to that of 1953 including all the illustrations (EH is mystified as to why they were omitted in v.1).

Reprinted 1969 (1,000), 1974 (1,000). For the paperback issue, see A.1(f)

(e) Second American issue (1968)

Titles: as in 1953 Chatto & Windus issue save: "[at foot: Praeger device] | PRAEGER PUBLISHERS | New York. Washington

Collation: as in 1953 Chatto & Windus issue save for differences indicated below.

Contents: as A.1(*d*), save: vol.1. p.[iv] "BOOKS THAT MATTER | Published in the United States of America | in 1968 by Praeger Publishers, Inc. | 111 Fourth Avenue, New York, N.Y. 10003 | The original edition of the book was published in the | United States of America in 1935 by The Macmillan | Company. A new edition was prepared in 1953 and is now published by Praeger Publishers, Inc., with a | new preface, written in 1967 | Second printing 1969 | © 1935, 1953, 1967 by Elspeth Huxley in London, England | ALL RIGHTS RESERVED" | Library of Congress no. | "Printed in Great Britain."

Binding case: green cloth (141).

Dust-jacket: design as A.1(*d*), adding on UC, "WITH A NEW PREFACE" and on UF, LF and spine, Praeger imprints; on UF, 2 vols: $16.00.

Paper: Universal antique wove.

Copies seen: Tiptree

Notes: Published in 1968 at $16 in edition of 500 copies of each volume, bought from C&W as 520/500 bound and jacketed books with cancel title with Praeger imprint. On the reverse of the title page it states that the original edition was published by Macmillan of New York and that the second printing was 1969. In 1970 Praeger imported 486 more copies of each vol, of which C&W bought back 100 copies in 1972. Rights reverted to C&W in 1975.
   Released by Books on Tape Inc. March 1990 at $144.

(f) First English paperback issue (1980)

Titles: as in 1968 impression.

Collation and Contents: as in 1968 impression save: p.[iv] "First issued in this paperback edition 1980" | ISBN no. | "PRINTED AND BOUND IN GREAT BRITAIN BY | REDWOOD BURN LIMITED | TROWBRIDGE AND ESHER".

Note on illustrations: all omitted but maps included.

Wrappers: cut flush, 215 × 135mm; each vol. carries a different photograph of Mt. Kenya; lettered on a green background, "WHITE MAN'S | COUNTRY [in white] | *Lord Delamere and the Making of Kenya* [in black] | ELSPETH HUXLEY [in white] | VOLUME ONE [TWO]: 1870–1914 [1914–1931] [in black]; vol.1, LC, publishers note and extracts from reviews; £12.50 the set | net in UK only; vol.2, UC, photograph by Sybil Sassoon, reproduced by courtesy of the Robert Harding Picture Library; LC, five extracts from reviews.

Copies seen: EH

Notes: Published in 1980 at £12.50 the set in edition of 3,000 of which 2,000 were sold to Sayed Mohammed of Westlands Sundries, Nairobi; of the remaining 1,000 copies, 701 were damaged at binders and were never for sale. Reprinted on 25 November 1985 (2,000).

6   A   Books and pamphlets

A.2   MURDER AT GOVERNMENT HOUSE

(a) First edition (1937)

Murder at | GOVERNMENT | HOUSE | *by* | ELSPETH HUXLEY | [Methuen device] | METHUEN & CO. LTD. LONDON| 36 ESSEX STREET

Collation: 1–18 in 8s; viii,277,[278–280]p. 185 × 123mm.

Contents: [i] ht. [ii] publishers blurb [iii] tp. [iv] "First published in 1937 | PRINTED IN GREAT BRITAIN" [v] "To. H.H. | [swelled rule] | What the doctor ordered" [vi] blank vii *"AUTHOR'S NOTE"* [viii] "GROUND FLOOR PLAN OF | GOVERNMENT HOUSE, MARULA" 1–277,[278] text [279–280] blank.

Binding case: grey/blue cloth (186).

Dust-jacket: design of a 2-seater plane over forest and smoke from a crashed plane, lettered in brown, "MURDER AT | GOVERNMENT | HOUSE | [in yellow:] ELSPETH | HUXLEY"; on spine, "MURDER | AT | GOVERNMENT HOUSE | ELSPETH | HUXLEY | METHUEN"; on LC, extract from book; on LF, publishers blurb . . . 7s.6d net.

Copies seen: EH

Notes: Published 22 April 1937 at 7s.6d in edition of 2,000 copies (with 2,400 d.js.). There is a record of a cancel title being printed in 1938 (350 copies) which evidently relates to what the Cumulative Index 1938–42 described as a 'cheaper edition at 3s.6d in 1938': this has not been seen. Type was distributed August 1937 and jacket blocks destroyed by enemy action, probably in 1942. The book went out of print in February 1954.

Reviews   TLS, 24 April 1937
    Times, 27 April 1937
    Manchester Guardian, 14 May 1937
    New Statesman, 15 May, 1937
    Spectator, 18 June, 1937

(b) First American edition (1937)

Murder at | GOVERNMENT | HOUSE| *By* ELSPETH HUXLEY | [device] | [short rule] | HARPER & BROTHERS PUBLISHERS | NEW YORK AND LONDON | 1937

Collation: signatures not established; ix,[x],282,[283–286]p. 190 × 130mm.

Contents: [i] ht. [ii] synopsis [iii] tp. [iv] "MURDER AT | GOVERNMENT HOUSE | Copyright, 1937, by Harper & Brothers, 49 East 33rd Street, | New York, N.Y. | 6|7| FIRST EDITION | F–M" [v] dedication [vi] blank [vii] author's note [viii] blank [ix] 2nd ht. [x] blank 1–282 text [283–286] blank.

IV. *Dust-jacket of the first edition of EH's first crime novel* Murder at Government House *published by Methuen & Co. in 1937.*

V. The cloth binding of the first US edition of Murder at Government House published by Harper and Brothers in 1937.

Binding case: black cloth; UC lettered in black on reddish|orange panels, "MURDER AT | GOVERNMENT HOUSE| ELSPETH HUXLEY"; lettered on spine in panels, "M A | G H | E H | [in silver] ∗ | HARPERS".

Dust-jacket: not seen.

Copies seen: photocopies and information by letter.

Notes: Published in 1937 at $2, no print quantity available.

Released by Books on Tape Inc. in October 1989 at $44.

Reviews: Saturday Review, 14 August, 1937
New York Times, 15 August, 1937
New York Herald Tribune, 22 August, 1937

(c) *First paperback edition (1987)*

[White letters in black panel:] MASTERCRIME | ELSPETH HUXLEY | Murder at | Government House | [at foot:] J.M.Dent & Sons Ltd | London Melbourne

Collation: no signature marks; [6],231,[232–234]p. 198 × 128mm.

Contents: p.[1] publishers blurb [2] "CRIME NOVELS BY ELSPETH HUXLEY", 2 titles [3] tp. [4] imprint information; "First published . . . 1937. This paperback edition first published by J.M.Dent & Sons Ltd, 1987 . . . This book is set in 11/12½ Garamond by Gee Graphics. Printed in Great Britain by Cox & Wyman Ltd, Reading | for J.M.Dent & Sons Ltd. | Aldine House, 33 Welbeck Street, London W1M 8LX"; British Library CIP data, ISBN [5] dedication [6] plan 1–231 text [223–234] list of Mastercrime titles and order form.

Wrappers: cover illustration by Edward Briant; on LC photograph of EH by Tara Heinemann, publishers blurb; quote from *Women's Review*; Everyman Paperbacks, Net UK £3.95; ISBN.

Copies seen: EH

Notes: Published 15 October 1987 at £3.95 in Mastercrime series of Everyman Paperbacks.

(d) *Second American issue (1988)*

[In a frame ending each side of 'HOUSE'] MURDER AT | GOVERNMENT | HOUSE | ELSPETH HUXLEY | [device] | VIKING

Collation: as in Dent edition 1987, save for differences indicated below; 209 × 127mm.

Contents: as in Dent 1987 edition save: p.[1] ht., at foot, "A VIKING NOVEL OF | MYSTERY | AND | SUSPENSE"; and on p.[4] "Published in 1988 by Viking Penguin Inc." | Copyright, Library of Congress CIP data | "Printed in the United States of America by | Arcata Graphics, Fairfield, Pennsylvania | set in Garamond".

10   A   Books and pamphlets

Binding case: Quarter black cloth on black paper boards lettered in silver down spine, "MURDER AT GOVERNMENT HOUSE ELSPETH HUXLEY | [across foot: rule] | VIKING | [rule]".

Dust-jacket: black with coloured design by Neil Stuart, illustration by Malcolm Farley; lettered on UC in white; on UF, FPTS $16.95, blurb; LF, photo of EH by Evelyn Hofer.

Copies seen: R. Smyer

Notes: Published 29 September 1988 at $16.95 in edition of 8,000 copies: none was bought by Penguin UK as their policy was not to buy hardbacks after paperback editions had been available in the UK market.

This book was offset from the Dent paperback edition A.2(c)

(e)   First American paperback issue (1989)

[In a frame ending each side of "HOUSE"] MURDER AT | GOVERN-MENT | HOUSE | ELSPETH HUXLEY| [at foot: Penguin device] | PENGUIN BOOKS

Collation: no signature marks; [8],231,[232]p. 175 × 105mm.

Contents: p.[1] ht. "PENGUIN CRIME FICTION | MURDER AT GOVERNMENT HOUSE" | note on author, 3 lines [2] blank [3] tp. [4] Penguin addresses: "Published in the United States of America by Viking Penguin, | a division of Penguin Books USA Inc. 1988 | Published in Penguin Books 1989 | 1 3 5 7 9 10 8 6 4 2" | copyright, Library of Congress CIP data | "Printed in the United States of America | set in Garamond" . . . [5] dedication [6] blank [7] 2nd ht. [8] plan 1–231 text [232] Penguin addresses

Wrappers: cover design by Neil Stuart, cover illustration by Neil Farley; on LC, blurb and extract from TLS review.

Copies seen: EH

Notes: Published 7 December 1989 at $3.95 in edition of 19,000 copies for USA and 1,000 for Penguin UK. Reprinted 25 April 1991 at $4.50 (4,000). By June 1993, 14,766 copies had been sold.

(f)   Second English paperback issue (1989)

Notes: Published in 1989 at £2.99 with 1,000 copies imported from Viking Penguin. these copies were identical to the Viking Penguin issue with the prices on back cover $4.95 CAN, $3.95 USA, but no UK price.

(g)   Large Print edition (1990)

Murder at | Government | House | ELSPETH HUXLEY | ISIS | LARGE PRINT | [2 short rules] | Oxford, England | Santa Barbara, California

Collation: no signature marks; [6],362p. 209 × 128mm.

Contents: p.[1] ht. [2] blank [3] tp. [4] "Copyright © Elspeth Huxley 1937 | First published in Great Britain 1937 | by Methuen & Co. Ltd | Published in Large Print 1990 by Clio Press, | 55 St Thomas' Street, Oxford, OX1 1JG, | by arrangement with | Heather Jeeves Publishing Consultant | All rights reserved" | British Library CIP data | "Printed and bound by Redwood Press Ltd., | Melksham, Wiltshire. | Cover designed by CGS Studios, Cheltenham." [5] dedication [6] plan 1–360 text [361–362] ISIS adverts. and list of books.

Binding case: black imitation cloth, no lettering.

Dust-jacket: UC, picture of a man slumped over desk, telephone off hook; lettered, "ISIS [in white] MURDER | at | Government House [in yellow] ELSPETH HUXLEY [in red].

Copies seen: Hants CL

Notes: Published in June 1990 by Clio Press for UK and USA markets in edition of 1,000 copies at £14.25 in UK and $21.95 in USA. The text was reset.

Released by Isis in complete unabridged readings by Jill Tanner on 8 cassettes (9 hours) in July 1990 at £35.50 +VAT.

A.3 MURDER ON SAFARI

(a) First edition (1938)

MURDER ON SAFARI | by | ELSPETH HUXLEY | [Methuen device] | [swelled rule] | METHUEN & CO. LTD. LONDON | 36 ESSEX STREET

Collation: 1–18 in 8s; [8],276,[277–280]p. 186 × 120mm.

Contents: p.[1] ht. [2] "*By the Same Author* | MURDER AT GOVERNMENT HOUSES [3] tp. [4] "*First published in 1938* | PRINTED IN GREAT BRITAIN" [5] "TO | J.C.G." [6] blank [7] 2nd ht. [8] blank 1–276,[277] text [278] "J. AND J. GRAY, | PRINTERS, | EDINBURGH" [279–280] blank.

Binding case: orange/brown cloth (72); lettered in dark blue.

Dust-jacket: a map with elephants, etc., in red, blue and green on white, "A.E.T.37" on UC and spine, and in red with blue shading, "Murder | on | Safari | [in red] ELSPETH | HUXLEY [and on spine]; on LC and LF, 9 extracts from reviews; on UF, publishers blurb, 7s 6d net.

Copies seen: EH

Notes: Published 24 February 1938 at 7s. 6d. in edition of 2,000 copies (2,600 d.js. and 2,020 endpapers). Type distributed August 1938, jacket and endpaper blocks destroyed by enemy action on 21 July 1942. Reported out of print 3 May 1939. EH dedicated this edition to her father JCG.

Methuen declined to exploit paperback rights which reverted to EH on 15 March 1954.

12   A   Books and pamphlets

Reviews: TLS, 26 February 1938
             Times, 1 March 1938
             Observer, 13 March 1938
             Manchester Guardian, 25 March 1938

Translations: French. *Safari sans retour* tr. Jacques Satori (Paris) – Librairie des Champs-Elysées, 1984 (paperback)
German. *Die Stunde des Leoparden* tr. F. A. Hofschuster – Bastei-Lubbe (paperback) 1989

(b)   First American edition (1938)

MURDER | ON SAFARI| [orn.] | ELSPETH HUXLEY | *Author of* | MURDER AT GOVERNMENT HOUSE | [at foot: device] | HARPER & BROTHERS PUBLISHERS | NEW YORK AND LONDON

Collation: no signature marks; [8],289,[290]p. 190 × 132mm.

Contents: p.[1] ht. [2] *"By the same author"*: 2 titles [3] tp. [4] *"Copyright, 1938, by Harper & Brothers | Printed in the United States of America* . . . FIRST EDITION" [5] "TO | ALICE AND BILL – | *fellow disciples of crime and croquet.* | NEW YORK NEW CANAAN" [6] blank [7] 2nd ht. [8] blank 1–289 text [290] blank.

Note on illustrations: the endpapers contain a double-page sketch map of camp and surroundings, signed, "A.E.T.37".

Binding case: orange (54) and blue (186) cloth; lettered in alternate colours on each.

Dust-jacket: not seen.

Copies seen: EH

Notes: Published in 1938 at $2. Print quantity not known. This edition has a different dedication to A.3(*a*): 'to Alice and Bill (Esty)', friends of EH and of Gervas in America.

Released by Books on Tape Inc. in September 1989 at $44.

Reviews: *New York Herald Tribune*, 25 May 1938
             New Yorker, 28 May 1938
             Saturday Review, 28 May 1938
             New York Times, 29 May 1938

(c)   First American paperback edition (1944) – not seen

Notes: Published by Crestwood Publishing Inc. in 1944. Not seen and no records found.

(d)   First English paperback edition (1957)

ELSPETH HUXLEY | MURDER ON SAFARI | [at foot:] PENGUIN BOOKS

Collation: no signature marks; 202,[03–208]p. 180 × 110mm.

Contents: p.[1] ht. [2] blank [3] tp. [4] Penguin imprints; "First published by Methuen in 1938 | Published in Penguin Books 1957 | Made and printed in Great Britain | by Hunt, Barnard & Co., Ltd, | Aylesbury" [5] dedication [6] "Sketch Map | of Camp and Surroundings" 7–202,[203] text [204–205] blank [206–208] descriptions of other Penguin crime novels (continued on inner LC).

Wrappers: green Penguin covers with title on UC in white band and "COMPLETE UNABRIDGED"; on LC, a photograph of EH and a brief biography.

Copies seen: EH

Notes: Published 18 April 1957 at 2s 6d in edition of 40–45,000 copies. EH was offered 7.5% royalty or 1.8d per copy with advance of £200; Canada was included in the territory. Reprinted in 1958 when there was a joint imprint implying Group terms. (see A.24(c) for details)

(e) Second American paperback issue (1982)

MURDER | ON SAFARI | [orn.] | ELSPETH HUXLEY| [at foot: orn.] | PERENNIAL LIBRARY | Harper & Row, Publishers | New York, Cambridge, Philadelphia, San Francisco | London, Mexico City, Sao Paulo, Sydney

Collation: p.[1] ht. and 3 quotes from reviews [2] blank [3] Perennial Library advert. [4] blank [5] tp. [6] imprint information; "Copyright 1938 by Harper and Brothers ... PERENNIAL LIBRARY edition published 1982" [7] dedication [8] blank [9] 2nd ht. and orn. [10–11] sketch map [12] blank 1–289 text [290] blank [291–302] list of Perennial Library titles and order page [303–306] blank.

Wrappers: pictorial, on UC, P587 Perennial Library $2.95; on LC, extracts from reviews, cover design by Myers & Noftsinger.

Copies seen: EH

Notes: Published in 1982 at $2.95 in Harper and Row's Perennial Library. It was offset from Harper's original edition A.3(b).

(f) Second English paperback edition (1988)

[White on black:] MASTERCRIME | ELSPETH HUXLEY | Murder on Safari | [at foot:] J.M.Dent & Sons Ltd | London Melbourne

Collation: no signature marks; 202,[203–204]p. 198 × 127mm.

Contents: p.[1] brief biography of EH [2] crime novels by EH [3] tp. [4] "This paperback edition first published by J.M.Dent & Sons Ltd 1988"; copyright; "Printed in Great Britain by Guernsey Press Co. Ltd., Guernsey, C.I., for J.M.Dent & Sons Ltd"; CIP data [5] dedication [6] map 7–202,[202–203] text [204] blank.

Wrappers: on UW, photograph by Oliver Hatch; on LW photograph of EH by Tara Heinemann; Everyman Paperbacks.

14   A Books and pamphlets

Copies seen: RC

Notes: Published in 1988 at £3.95, print quantity not known. Dent Everyman included this in their Mastercrime series and reset the text.

(g) Large Print edition (1988)

MURDER ON | SAFARI | Elspeth Huxley | ISIS | LARGE PRINT | [rule] | MAINSTREAM SERIES| [rule] | Oxford, England | Santa Barbara, California

Collation: no signature markes, sewing visible, [1–9 in 16s, 10 in 8s, 11 in 16s]; [6],328,[329–330]p. 214 × 135mm.

Contents: p.[1] ht. [2] blank [3] tp. [4] "Published in Large Print 1988 by | Clio Press, 55 St. Thomas' Street, Oxford OX1 1JG, | by arrangement with Elspeth Huxley. | All rights reserved" | British Library CIP data | ISBN | "Printed and bound by Redwood Burn Ltd. | Trowbridge, Wiltshire | Cover designed by CGS Studios, Cheltenham" [5] dedication [6] blank 1–328 text [329–330] list and addresses of ISIS large-print books.

Binding case: pictorial glazed covers; title lettered in white on red.

Dust-jacket: none.

Copies seen: EH, RC

Notes: Published in Isis Large Print Mainstream series in November 1988 at £8.95 in edition of 1,000 copies for the UK and USA markets: ABC-Clio, the then owner of Isis, sold the book at $18.95 in USA. The text was reset.

Released by Isis in complete unabridged readings by Janet Porter in 7 cassettes (8 hrs, 15 mins) in March 1990 at £31.95 + VAT.

(h) Second American issue (1989)

Notes: Published 26 January 1989 at $16.95 in edition of 9,000 copies by Viking Penguin. None was sold to Penguin UK. This book was offset from Dent Everyman's edition.

(i) Third American paperback issue (1990)

[In a frame ending each side of "SAFARI"] MURDER ON | SAFARI | ELSPETH HUXLEY | [at foot: Penguin device] | PENGUIN BOOKS

Collation: no signature marks; 202,[203–208]p. 175 × 105mm.

Contents: p.[1] ht. "PENGUIN CRIME FICTION | MURDER ON SAFARI" | note on author, 5 lines [2] blank [3] tp. [4] Penguin addresses; "First published in Great Britain by Methuen & Co. Ltd 1938 | First published in the United States of America by Viking Penguin, a division of | Penguin Books USA Inc. 1989 | Published in Penguin Books 1990 | 10 8 7 6 5 4 3 2 1 | Copyright Elspeth Huxley, 1938 | Copyright renewed Elspeth Huxley, 1966 . . . | Printed in the United States of America . . ." [5] dedication [6] sketch map [vertical] 7–202,[203] text [204] blank [205–208] list of Penguin Crime titles.

Wrappers: cover design by Neil Stuart; cover illustration by Malcolm Farley; on LC, blurb and extract from TLS review.

Copies seen: EH

Notes: Published by Viking Penguin 26 July 1990 at $3.95 in edition of 25,000. By June 1993, 11,820 had been sold. This was offset from Viking Penguin's hardback printing, A.3(g)

(j) Third English paperback issue (1990)

Notes: Published July 1990 at £3.50: 1,000 copies were imported from Viking Penguin, New York, with no change to the cover or title page. Presumably the UK price was stickered on back cover, as the printed price remained unchanged.

A.4 RED STRANGERS   1939

(a) First edition (1939)

Elspeth Huxley | [swelled rule] | RED STRANGERS | [swelled rule] | *A Novel* | [illustration of an African head with headband and ear decorations] | 1939 | CHATTO & WINDUS | LONDON

Collation: [A in 4s], B–CC in 8s, DD in 4s; viii,1–405,[406–408]p. 208 × 137mm.

Contents: p.[i] ht. [ii] "TO MY MOTHER| who first suggested this book, | and helped to bring it into being." [iii] tp. [iv] "PUBLISHED BY | *Chatto & Windus* | LONDON | . | *The Macmillan Company* | *of Canada, Limited* | TORONTO | PRINTED IN GREAT BRITAIN | ALL RIGHTS RESERVED" v–vi foreword [1]–405,[406] text [407] "PRINTED IN GREAT BRITAIN | BY RICHARD CLAY AND COMPANY, LTD., | BUNGAY, SUFFOLK." [408] blank.

Note on illustrations: There are 16 unnumbered pages on artpaper with 18 illustrations and on first page it states that all photographs are by the author: these 8 leaves are inserted p. 406 and are followed by pp. 406 and 408 as above.

Binding case: orange|yellow cloth (71), gold-lettered in red cloth panels with gold flames below and above "RED STRANGERS | A NOVEL BY | Elspeth Huxley | CHATTO AND WINDUS".

Dust-jacket: not seen.

Paper: Ivory shade antique wove.

Copies seen: EH

16   A   Books and pamphlets

Notes: Published 1 June 1939 in edition of 2,110 copies at 8s 6d. Reprinted 13 June 1939 (1,520); 3 August 1939 (900). In January 1944, 3,110 copies were reprinted at 12s 6d despite strict paper rationing, due to Margery Perham's recommendation 'in her position in the Institute of Colonial Studies' that paper be granted. The 1939 edition had 16 pages of illustrations at the back of the book on art paper, these were dropped by 1944, so no reference in prelims as in 1939 edition p.vi. Reprinted 10 June 1948 (3,040) bound in red cloth blocked in imitation gold; reprinted in 1952 (1,979); reprinted in 1955 (2,673) when the dust-jacket and the title page were altered to include a subtitle, 'A Story of Kenya', under the title in each case, and 'A Novel by' was printed above the author's name at the foot of the jacket. Reprinted in 1964 (2,673) at 21s when the following alterations were made to the prelims: verso of half title changed from Dedication to a list of 9 non-fiction titles and 8 fiction (not all C&W) by the same author; verso of title page changed from 'Published by C&W and Macmillan Company of Canada' (see above) to 'First published June 1939'. The title page and dust-jacket had been changed in 1955 reprint to 'A Story of Kenya' introduced under the title; in addition the d.j. had a quote from Field-Marshal Smuts on the front flap and Julian Huxley's quote on the back panel preceding the blurb in the 1944 reprint, whereas in the 1964 reprint both those quotes were on the back flap. The head of the African taken from a drawing of a sculpture by Dora Clark, remains on the front panel of the d.j. and the title page. These reprints were from existing negatives.

This book, EH's fourth novel, was originally offered to Macmillan & Co. as they were EH's publishers at the time. HM wanted considerable cuts including all the section on female circumcision, commenting in his letter 'the whole idea is unfamiliar and abhorrent to European readers'. EH replied to this sharply: 'the whole of native life is unfamiliar to European readers and it is the purpose of this book to make them a little more familiar with it than they are at present. To do this is, in my opinion, utterly impossible merely to present those aspects of native life which are pleasant and acceptable to the European mind and to omit those which do not commend themselves to Europeans. This destroys the whole basis of the book which is to present it as it is, not as certain people in this country would like to think it is, whether some aspects are abhorrent or not is beside the point'. As a result of this 4-page letter to HM, of which this is an extract, Macmillan & Co. declined to publish the book.

EH then offered the novel to Harold Raymond of Chatto & Windus, thus beginning the fruitful relationship between author and publisher for 46 years, which was a model of its kind (their correspondence between 1938 to 1980 is in the Reading University Archive). EH wrote to HM finally on 31 January 1939 telling him that C&W had taken it 'at once'. The Macmillan Company of Canada had Canadian rights as C&W's agent and distributed the book there as their parent company encouraged them to build up agency systems, distributing any agency book they wished. EH had described her book to HR as 'a novel and it is not a sort of anthropological or African work', though she did see it as presenting the other side of the coin to *White Man's Country*. C&W asked for cuts up to 40,000 words, which EH carried out with the swiftness and efficiency which became typical of her: the 40,452 words cut were indicated by her, page by page. On the subject of female circumcision EH wrote to HR: 'I should say that people find it more puzzling than abhorrent and their usual comment is: "but what exactly do they do?", so I thought it better not to leave them guessing.' HR agreed to its inclusion ending with a publisher's caution 'we will see how the passage looks in cold print'. The original MS was pulped with EH's permission in 1941.

HR offered EH 10% royalty on first 1,000, 15% on next 4,000 and 20% thereafter, with a colonial royalty of 10% of price received. By 17 February 1954, 13,000 copies had been sold.

While writing *Red Strangers* EH attended a course on anthropology at the London School of Economics under Malinowski, see p.60 *The Sorcerer's Apprentice,* so that she could check the accuracy of what she was writing. Kenyatta was on the same course and when she delivered her lecture 'The Influence of Environment on Land Tenure, Kinship Grouping with Special Reference to the Kikuyu' (see Appendix), she described in a letter to RC, 12.3.94 'This reminded me of the Seminar when I had to read the paper: most alarming, not so much because of Malinowski and Firth but because there was Jomo Kenyatta – ridiculous for *me* to read a paper about *his* land tenure and kinship system: I was naturally terrified of his response. He spared me: he adopted an aloof, paternalistic, benign approach, wrapping up his few remarks in a swaddle of words with little bearing on the subject, like the skilful politician that he was'.

EH wrote 'for many Africans white men are still Red Strangers' in the *Times* 30 June 1960 (C.489).

Reviews: Manchester Guardian, 2 June 1939
Times, 2 June 1939
Times Literary Supplement, 3 June 1939
New Statesman, 3 June 1939
Sunday Times, 11 June 1939
Spectator, 16 June 1939

(b) First American issue (1939)

Title: as in first UK edition save: [device, replacing illustration] | HARPER & BROTHERS PUBLISHERS | NEW YORK and LONDON | 1939

Collation: as in A.4(a) 204 × 132mm.

Contents: p.[i] ht. [ii] dedication [iii] tp. [iv] publication data v–vi contents vii–viii foreword [1] Book I tp [2] blank 3–171 text [172] blank [173] Book II tp. [174] blank 175–286 text [287] Book III tp. [288] blank 289–[406] text [407] British printers' imprint [408] blank.

Note on illustrations: see A.4(a).

Binding case: dark red cloth (16) with reddish orange panel (35) lettered in white, "RED | STRANGERS | ELSPETH HUXLEY"; spine has a medallion in same colour as front panel lettering also in white, "RED STRANGERS | [orn.] | ELSPETH HUXLEY | HARPERS [at foot, in white]".

Dust-jacket: pinkish brown with 2 quotations by General Smuts, 1 by Julian Huxley, and a short blurb; on UF, price $2.50, blurb, no.4087; on LF, notice of *American Nabob* by Holmer Alexande, no.4060; quotations from 10 British journals.

Copies seen: photocopies and descriptions by letter.

VI. *The dust-jacket of the first US edition of* Red Strangers *published by Harper and Brothers in 1939.*

Notes: Published by Harper & Brothers, New York, in 1939 at $2.50 who bought 780/750 folded and collated sheets with the Harper imprint from C&W on 15 April: they reordered 270 f. and c. sheets with 2 pp. cancel title on 3 August 1939.

Reviews: Christian Science Monitor, 8 July 1939
New Yorker, 9 September 1939
New York Times, 10 September 1939
Time, 25 September 1939

(c) Queen's Classics edition (1965)

RED | STRANGERS | A Story of Kenya | *by* | Elspeth Huxley | *Edited and abridged* | *by Ingaret Giffard* | ["Q.C." device] | Chatto & Windus | LONDON

Collation: [A], B–G in 16s; 199,[200]p. 183 × 122mm.

Contents: p.[1] "THE QUEENS' CLASSICS" [details of book] [2] "THE QUEEN'S CLASSICS" | General Editor: Denys Thompson, M.A. list of titles [3] tp. [4] "Published by | Chatto and Windus (Educational) Ltd | 42 William IV Street | London WC2 | * | Clarke, Irwin and Company Ltd | Toronto . . . Queen's Classics | Abridged edition © Elspeth Huxley 1965 | Printed in Great Britain by | Butler & Tanner Ltd, Frome and London" [5] contents [6] dedication [7] foreword [8] blank [9]–199 text [200] blank.

Binding case: blue cloth (182); UC gold lettered, "*Red Strangers* | * | ELSPETH HUXLEY | Q.C.[device]"; spine, "Q.C." [device] | [on red cloth shield] "*Red Strangers* | [scroll] | ELSPETH HUXLEY".

Dust-jacket: none.

Copies seen: EH

Notes: Published in 1965 in C&W's educational series at 8s. This was edited by Ingaret Giffard (wife of Laurens van der Post) who was asked by NS to abridge the original text and reduce to 60–65,000 words. Her revision cut out all reference to female circumcision but EH refused to agree to this, saying in her letter of 26 September 1964 to NS 'it is quite amazing that 27 years later the same question should arise'. The Editor of the series finally agreed to the reference being restored.

A.5 DEATH OF AN ARYAN 1939

(a) First edition (1939)

DEATH OF AN ARYAN | BY | ELSPETH HUXLEY | [Methuen device] | METHUEN & CO. LTD. LONDON | 36 *Essex Street Strand W.C.2*

Collation: [1]in 4s, 1–16 in 8s, 17 in 4s; [8],261,[262–264]p. 185 × 125 mm.

20　A　Books and pamphlets

Contents: p.[1–2] blank [3] ht. [4] "Also by Elspeth Huxley | MURDER ON SAFARI | MURDER AT GOVERNMENT HOUSE" [5] tp. [6] "*First published in 1939* | PRINTED IN GREAT BRITAIN" [7] "DEATH OF AN ARYAN" [8] blank 1–261, [262] text, at foot, "*Jarrold & Sons, Limited, The Empire Press, Norwich*" [263–264] extracts from reviews of two earlier detective novels.

Binding case: black cloth, lettered on spine in red, "DEATH | OF AN | ARYAN | ELSPETH HUXLEY | METHUEN".

Dust-jacket: not seen.

Copies seen: EH

Notes: Published 19 October 1939 at 8s in edition of 3,000 copies (with 3,800 d.j.s). Type was distributed in January 1940 and jacket blocks destroyed by enemy action on 12 July 1942. The book was reported out of print on 9 February 1954.

When published by Harper and Brothers in USA in 1940, the title was changed to *The African Poison Murders*, which was eventually to be adopted in the UK. A.5(g)

Reviews:　TLS, 28 October 1939
　　　　　　Times, 14 November 1939
　　　　　　Manchester Guardian, 1 December 1939

(b)　First American edition (1939)

THE AFRICAN | POISON MURERS | [orn.] | ELSPETH HUXLEY | *Author of* | *MURDER AT GOVERNMENT HOUSE* | *MURDER ON SAFARI, etc.* | *19* [device] *40* | HARPER & BROTHERS PUBLISHERS | NEW YORK AND LONDON

Collation: signatures not established; v,[vi],279,[280–283]p. 188 × 130mm.

Contents: p.[i] ht. [ii] blank [iii] tp. [iv] "THE AFRICAN POISON MURDERS | Copyright, 1939, by Harper & Brothers | Printed in the United States of America | All rights in this book are reserved [7 lines] | Harper & | Brothers, 49 East 333rd Street, New York | N.Y. | I–O | FIRST EDITION | L–O | *This story is published in England* | *under the title of* | DEATH OF AN ARYAN" [v] 2nd ht. [vi] blank 1–279 text [280–283] blank.

Binding case: light green cloth (144), lettered in mid-red brown (43); on UC, "THE AFRICAN | POISON | MURDERS" with publishers device, and on spine, "THE | AFRICAN | POISON | MURDERS | [rule] | Elspeth | Huxley | HARPERS".

Dust-jacket: pictorial, a red feathered, black arrow pointing to a brown pot over a fire across a yellow spiral background, lettered in red, "THE | AFRICAN | POISON MURDERS"; spine title lettered in black edged with white, author in white, Harpers in red; on LC, other Harper titles including novel by Zane Grey; on UF, blurb, no.4200, price $2.00; on LF, blurb for novel by John Dickson Carr, no.4157.

Copies seen: photocopies and information by letter.

Notes: Published by Harper and Brothers at $2.00 under the title of *The African Poison Murders*: the year of publication is printed as 1940 on the title page and yet

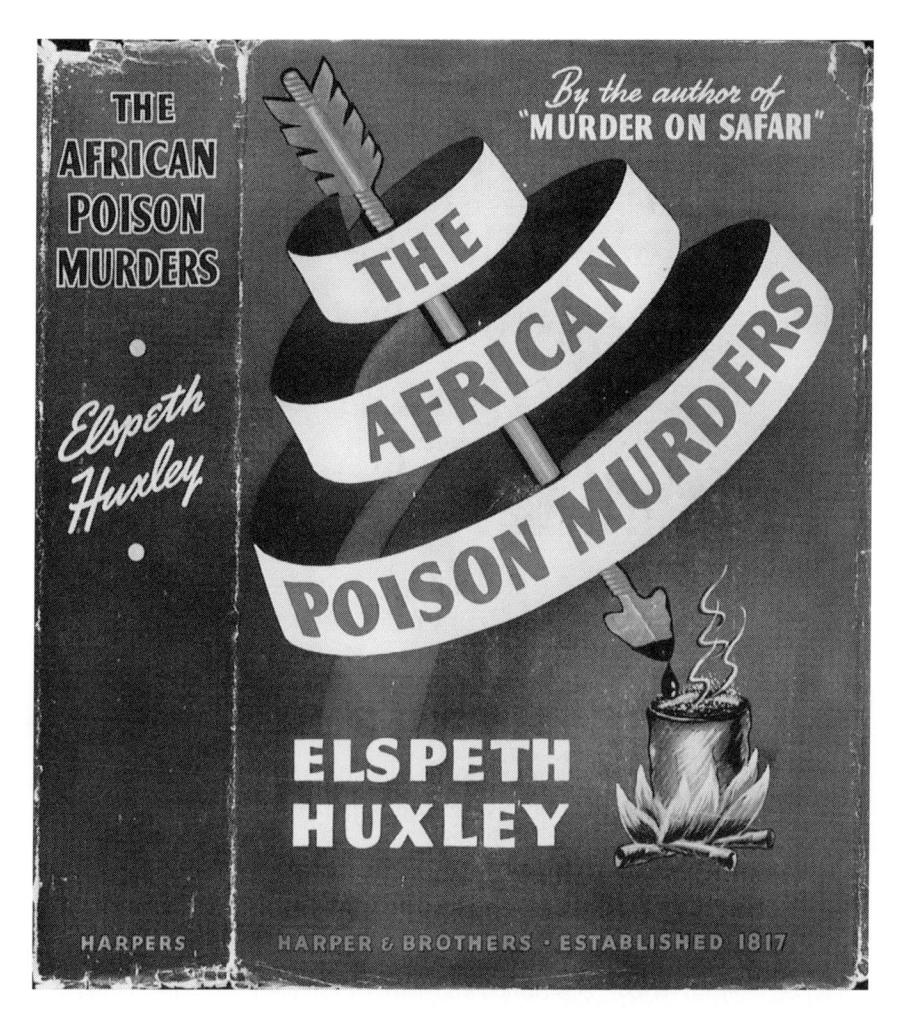

VII. *The dust-jacket of the first US edition of* The African Poison Murders *(UK title:* Death of an Aryan) *published by Harper and Brothers in 1940.*

22   A   Books and pamphlets

the copyright line reads Copyright, 1939, by Harper and Brothers: the early dates of the reviews suggest that it may have been published late 1939.

Subsequently published in paperback in Harper and Row's Perennial Library at $2.25 in 1981. A.5(*f*)

Released by Books on Tape Inc. at $48.00 in January 1988.

Reviews: Saturday Review, 6 January 1940
New Yorker, 6 January 1940
New York Herald Tribune, 6 January 1940
New York Times, 7 January 1940

(c) First paperback edition (1947) – not seen

Notes: Published by Popular Library in 1947, as *The African Poison Murders*.

(d) First English paperback edition (1957) – not seen

Notes: Published 18 April 1957 at 2s 6d. In 1955, EH, who had recovered the volume rights from Methuen, was offered by Penguin 7.5% royalty or 1.8d per copy on print-run of 40–50,000 copies.

(e) Second American issue (1976)

THE AFRICAN | POISON MURDERS | Elspeth Huxley | *Garland Publishing, Inc., New York & London* | [oval device] | *1976*

Collation: no signature marks; [6],279,[280–282]p. 214 × 136mm.

Contents: p.[1] "*A Garland Series* | [thick above thin short rules] | FIFTY | CLASSICS | OF | CRIME | FICTION | 1900–1950 | [thin above thick short rules] | *Edited with* | *prefaces by* | Jacques Barzun | and | Wendell Hertig Taylor" [2] blank [3] tp. [4] Note on series, "This edition published by arrangement | with Harper and Row, Publishers, Inc. | Copyright © 1939 by | Harper & Brothers. | Introduction Copyright © 1976 by | Jacques Barzun and Wendell H. Taylor. | All rights reserved" | Library of Congress CIP data | "Printed in the United States of America" [5–6] preface, biography of EH 1–279 text [280–281] list of series: 50 titles [282] blank.

Binding case: reddish orange cloth (35), lettered in blue down spine, "[double horizontal rule] Huxley The African Poison Murders | GP [monogram] | Garland | [double horizontal rule]".

Dust-jacket: none.

Copies seen: BL

Notes: Published by Garland in 1976 as *The African Poison Murders* in their '50 Classics of Crime Fiction 1950–75', with a Preface, described as an Introduction in the copyright line, by Jacques Barzun and Wendell H. Taylor. Offset from A.5(*b*).

(f) Second American paperback issue (1981)

Notes: Published in Harpers' paperback series Perennial Library in 1981 at $2.25; offset from A.5(*b*). For style, see A.3(*e*).

(g) Second English paperback edition (1986)

[White letters in black panel] MASTERCRIME | ELSPETH HUXLEY | The African Poison Murders | [at foot:] J.M. Dent & Sons Ltd | London Melbourne

Collation: no signature marks; [4],214,[215–218]p. 198 × 128mm.

Contents: p.[1] publishers blurb [2] "CRIME NOVELS BY ELSPETH HUXLEY": 2 titled [3] tp. [4] imprint information; "First published... by Methuen Ltd 1939 | under the title *DEATH OF AN ARYAN* | This paperback edition first published by J.M. Dent & Sons Ltd 1986 | ...This book is set in 11|12½ Linitron 202 Garamond | by Inforum Ltd, Portsmouth | Printed in Great Britain by | The Guernsey Press Co. Ltd, Guernsey C.I., for | J.M. Dent & Sons Ltd | Aldine House, 33 Welbeck Street, London W1M 8LX"; British Library CIP data, ISBN 1–214 text [215–217] Mastercrime list [218] blank.

Wrappers: pictorial, UW illustration by Liz Dalton; on LW a photograph of EH, publishers blurb, Everyman Paperbacks, GB £3.75NET +003,95; ISBN.

Copies seen: EH

Notes: Published for the first time in the UK under the title of *The African Poison Murders* in Dent's Mastercrime series at £3.75. Reset.

Review: TLS, 18 July 1986

(h) Large Print edition (1988)

THE AFRICAN | POISON MURDERS | ELSPETH HUXLEY | ISIS | LARGE PRINT| [short rule] | MAIN STREAM SERIES | [short rule] | Oxford, England | Santa Barbara, California

Collation: no signature marks, sewing visible, [1–10, in 16s]; [4],313,[314–316]p. 216 × 138mm.

Contents: p.[1] ht. [2] blank [3] tp. [4] "Copyright © 1939 Elspeth Huxley | First published in Great Britain 1939 by | Methuen Ltd. under the title *Death of an Aryan* | First published in the U.S.A. 1940 by Harper & Row Publishers Inc. | Published in Large Print 1988 by Clio Press, | 55 St Thomas' Street, Oxford OX1 1JG, | by arrangement with | Elspeth Huxley | All rights reserved" | British Library CIP data, ISBN | "Phototypeset, printed and bound by | Unwin Brothers Limited, Old Woking, Surrey. | Cover designed by CGS Studios, Cheltenham." 1–313 text [314–316] ISIS addresses and lists.

24   A   Books and pamphlets

Binding case: glazed paper boards, pictorial UC, two spears behind a lion's head above a stretched skin on a red background (14); on UC titles lettered in pink and author in yellow, and down spine.

Dust-jacket: none.

Copies seen: RC

Notes: Published in January 1988 in Isis Large Print Mainstream series in edition of 1,250 copies at £9.25 in UK and $18.95 in USA (ABC Clio) under the title of *The African Poison Murders*.

The text was reset.

(i) Third American issue (1988)

THE | AFRICAN | POISON | MURDERS | [dec. scroll] | ELSPETH | HUXLEY | [device] | VIKING

Collation: no signature marks; [6],214p. 209 × 130mm.

Contents: p.[1] ht. and "A VIKING NOVEL OF | MYSTERY | AND | SUSPENSE" [2] "Also by Elspeth Huxley": 3 titles [3] tp. [4] Viking|Penguin addresses, "Published in 1988 by Viking Penguin Inc. | Copyright Elspeth Huxley, 1939 | Copyright renewed Elspeth Huxley, 1967 | All rights reserved | First published in Great Britain under the title *Death of an Aryan*" | Library of Congress CIP data | Printed in the United States of America by | Arcata Graphics, Fairfield, Pennsylvania | Set in Garamond" [5] 2nd ht. [6] blank 1–214 text.

Binding case: yellowish pink paper boards (29), quarter bound in pink cloth (15), lettered in gold down spine, "THE AFRICAN POISON MURDERS ELSPETH HUXLEY", with rule beneath; at foot between rules, "VIKING".

Dust-jacket: pictorial, design by Neil Stuart, jacket illustration by Malcolm Farley; on UF, blurb and FPT $16.95; on LF, photograph of EH and publishers imprint.

Copies seen: EH

Notes: Published in hardback as *The African Poison Murders* on 26 May 1988 at $16.95 in edition of 10,000 copies. This was offset from the Dent edition. None was sold to Penguin UK.

(j) Third American paperback issue (1989)

THE | AFRICAN | POISON | MURDERS | [3-line scroll | ELSPETH | HUXLEY| [at foot: Penguin device] | PENGUIN | BOOKS

Collation: no signature marks; [6], 214, [215–218]p. 174 × 105mm.

Contents: p.[1] ht. "PENGUIN CRIME FICTION | THE AFRICAN POISON MURDERS" | note on author, 3 lines [2] blank [3] tp. [4] Penguin addresses: "Published in the United States of America by | Viking Penguin Inc. 1988 | Published in Penguin Books 1989 | 1 3 5 7 9 10 8 6 4 2" | © 1939, renewed 1967 . . . "Printed in the United States of America | Set in Garamond" . . . [5] 2nd ht. [6] blank 1–214 text [215–218] list of Penguin addresses and Penguin Crime titles.

Wrappers: cover design by Neil Stuart; cover illustration by Malcolm Farley; on LC, blurb.

Copies seen: EH

Notes: Published by Viking Penguin in November 1989 at $3.95 in edition of 25,000 including 1,000 copies for the UK. This was offset from Dent edition. Reprinted in January 1990 (4,500).

(k) Third English paperback issue (1989)

Notes: Published in November 1989 at £3.50 in edition of 1,000 copies imported from Viking Penguin. No changes were made to the American copies for the UK market.

A.6 EAST AFRICA 1941

(a) First edition (1941)

EAST AFRICA | ELSPETH HUXLEY| With | *twelve plates in colour* | *and seventeen illustrations in* | *black and white* | [at foot: vignette of classical facade] | *Published for* | PENNS IN THE ROCK PRESS | *by* | WILLIAM COLLINS OF LONDON | 1941

Collation: no signature marks; [1–6],7–47,[48]p. 222 × 161mm.

Contents: [1] "THE BRITISH COMMONWEALTH IN PICTURES | EAST AFRICA" [2] Acknowledgements of Editorial Committee [3] tp. [4] at foot, "PRODUCED BY ADPRINT LONDON | PRINTED IN GREAT BRITAIN" [5–6] list of illustrations 7–47 text.

Binding case: cream paper boards with all-over design of red and brown, Catherine wheels, lettered in red and brown.

Dust-jacket: same design as on boards on UC; on UF, blurb headed by The British Commonwealth in Pictures; on LC, note on Britain in Pictures series; LF, list of titles in 3 series.

Paper: Double Crown 50lb. woodfree offset.

Copies seen: RC

Notes: Published in March 1941 at 3s 6d in edition of 14,273 copies of which 13,474 are known to have been sold. EH received an outright sum of £50 for all rights.

This was one of 7 titles, all unnumbered by the publisher, in the British Commonwealth in Pictures series, which itself was Series II in the overall project known as 'Britain in Pictures' running to 113 volumes. This was the brainchild of Hilda

26   A   Books and pamphlets

Matheson, the first Director of the Joint Broadcasting Committee, for whom EH worked at the start of the war – part of the newly formed Ministry of Information whose object was to put out propaganda by radio to all parts of the world especially USA, Latin America and the Commonwealth. Hilda Matheson conceived the idea of 'Britain in Pictures' in order to provide accurate information about Britain in 1940 when the country was at a low ebb and when 'Hitler had destroyed the centre of the British book world' (*Observer*, 23 March 1941) in the air raids on London.

In this endeavour Hilda Matheson, who died before the first book was published, was supported by two editors, Walter Turner, and Dorothy Wellesley, who supplied the imprint 'Penns in the Rocks Press' being the name of her house in Withyham and with the logo from the temple built there in memory of W. B. Yeats. She turned to Adprint for the design and manufacture of the books which was run by Wolfgang Foges and Walter Neurath, two brilliant innovators in the design of illustrated books, who had come from Vienna in the late 1930s. The books, subsidised by the Ministry of Information, were then bought and published by William Collins who were fortunate to have enough paper at a time of tight rationing: they remained the publishers of all 139 volumes produced in this manner. This book was available from Hastings House, New York at $1.25.

Reviews: *Listener,* 20 March 1941 (on launch of series)
   Observer, 23 March 1941
   TLS, 5 April 1941

(b) Second English issue (1943)

THE | BRITISH COMMONWEALTH | AND EMPIRE | Edited and with an introduction | by | W.J.TURNER | *With* | *48 plates in colour* | *and* | *173 illustrations in* | *black and white* | [orn,: front of colonnaded building] | WILLIAM COLLINS OF LONDON | MCMXXXXIII

Collation: no signature marks; 311,[312]p. 220 × 160mm.

Contents: p. [1] ht. "BRITAIN IN PICTURES | THE BRITISH COMMON-WEALTH | AND EMPIRE" [2] list of section titles [3] tp. [4] "PRODUCED BY | ADPRINT LIMITED LONDON | . . . THE PAPER AND BINDING OF THIS BOOK | CONFORM TO THE AUTHORISED ECONOMY STANDARD | COPYRIGHT: ALL RIGHTS RESERVED | PRINTED IN GREAT BRITAIN BY | CLARKE & SHERWELL LTD., NORTHAMPTON | ON MELLOTEX BOOK PAPER | MADE BY TULLIS RUSSELL & CO. LTD. | MARKINCH FIFE"; editors' acknowledgements [5 lines] 5–13 list of illustrations 13–14 brief historical chronologies 15–[20] introduction [21]–[312] text.

p. 229–[270] "EAST AFRICA | ELSPETH HUXLEY" [in 4 chapters, with 6 colour illustrations on 3 plates, 1 map and 16 black-and-white illustrations in the text].

Binding case: red cloth (16) gold-lettered across spine, THE | BRITISH | COMMON | WEALTH | AND | EMPIRE | [stamp of lion] | COLLINS".

Dust-jacket: probably none.

Copies seen: RUL

Notes: East Africa was included in the Omnibus volume of the series *"British Commonwealth and Empire"*, edited with an Introduction by W. J. Turner: William Collins published it in 1943 at £1. 1s, no print quantity is known. Reprinted Spring 1949. It was produced by Adprint and printed by Clarke and Sherwell Ltd of Northampton. The same text was included except for the 4th and 5th paragraphs in chapter one which was reduced in length, with all the black and white illustrations, but those in colour were reduced from 12 to 6 and their sequence altered. On the half-title the name of the series was confusedly described as 'Britain in Pictures', although this title was subsequently used for the whole series.

There were 7 Omnibus volumes, all edited by W J Turner who died before the last 3 were published: *The British Commonwealth and Empire* (1943), *Impressions of English Literature* (1945), *The Englishman's Country* (1945), *Nature in Britain* (1946), *British Adventure,* (1947), *Aspects of British Art* (1947), *British Craftsmanship* (1948).

A.7 THE STORY OF FIVE ENGLISH FARMERS 1941

First edition (1941)

THE STORY OF | FIVE ENGLISH FARMERS| by | ELSPETH HUXLEY | *Author of "White Man's Country" and* | *"Red Strangers"* | LONDON | THE SHELDON PRESS | NORTHUMBERLAND AVENUE, W.C.2

Collation: 1–4 in 8s; [i–iv],v,[vi],7–64p. 183 × 123mm.

Contents: p.[i] ht. [ii] blank [iii] tp. [iv] "*First published* 1941 | MADE IN GREAT BRITAIN" v contents [vi] blank 7–64 text; at foot of p.64, "*Printed in Great Britain by* | *Billing and Sons Ltd., Guildford and Esher*".

Note on illustrations: line drawings on p.10, 16, 20, 23, 43, 48.

Wrappers: mottled grey; on UW in dark blue, "THE STORY | OF FIVE | ENGLISH | FARMERS | ELSPETH | HUXLEY"; on LW, 9d.

Copies seen: RH

Notes: Published in August 1941 at 9d. Print quantity not known by SPCK who are the owners of Sheldon Press: the latter was founded in 1720 by the Rev. Thomas Bray, Rector of Sheldon. This book was commissioned by the Foreign Literature Committee of the Sheldon Press for use in East African schools when teaching materials were very scarce during the War. It is interesting that African children were to be taught about farming in England with the advice that African farmers should follow the English practice of conserving fertility. This was EH's belief which has hardly been followed here since the War.

A.8 ATLANTIC ORDEAL 1941

(a) First edition (1941)

28   A   Books and pamphlets

ELSPETH HUXLEY | [swelled rule] | ATLANTIC ORDEAL | *The Story of Mary Cornish* | [swelled rule] | 1941 | CHATTO AND WINDUS | LONDON

Collation: [A]–F in 8s; [8],86,[87–88]p. 185 × 122mm.

Contents: [1] ht. [2] blank [3] tp. [4] "PUBLISHED BY | Chatto & Windus | LONDON | * | The Macmillan Company | of Canada, Lmited | TORONTO | PRINTED IN GREAT BRITAIN | ALL RIGHTS RESERVED" [5] note on royalties [6] blank [7] list of illustrations [8] blank 1–86 text [88] "PRINTED IN GREAT BRITAIN | BY R. & R. CLARK, LIMITED | EDINBURGH".

Note on illustrations: 4 plates of photographs.

Binding case: blue cloth (186), lettered in silver across the spine, "Elspeth | Huxley | * "; down spine, "ATLANTIC ORDEAL | [wavy rule] | *The Story of Mary Cornish*".

Dust-jacket: white with a monochrome photograph on UC lettered in white, "*Atlantic | Ordeal* | THE STORY OF | MARY CORNISH | Elspeth Huxley"; down spine in black, "ATLANTIC ORDEAL | *[rule]* | E. HUXLEY"; on LC, blurb; on UF, 4s. NET.

Copies seen: EH

Notes: Published 15 December 1941 in total edition of 10,000 copies at 4s net, of which 6,000 were printed on 13 October and 4,000 on 22 October. Macmillan Company of Canada was the Canadian distributor. In 1962, 2,000 copies were pulped.

On 12 November 1985 in a BBC Blue Peter programme on the City of Benares incident (subject of the book) a copy of *Atlantic Ordeal* was shown.

Reviews: TLS, 20 December 1941
           New Statesman, 3 January 1942

(b)   First American issue (1942)

ATLANTIC | ORDEAL | *The Story of Mary Cornish* | *By* | Elspeth Huxley | [Harper device] | PUBLISHERS | *HARPER & BROTHERS* | *NEW YORK LONDON*

Collation: no signature marks; [8],102p. 205 × 138mm.

Contents: [1] ht. [2] "*Books by the Same Author*": 4 titles [3] tp. [4] copyright notice: "*Copyright 1941, 1942, by Elspeth Huxley | Printed in the United States of America.* FIRST EDITION | A.R." [8] blank 1–102 text.

Note on illustrations: 4 plates of photographs.

Binding case: grey imitation cloth (266); Harper device blocked in silver bottom R of UC; lettered down spine on black strip in silver, "ATLANTIC ORDEAL: *The Story of Mary Cornish Elspeth Huxley Harper*".

Dust-jacket: on UC, a photograph (same as that facing p. 30); on LC, piece on Harper's One hundred twenty-fifth anniversary year; on UF, blurb, price $1.00; on LF, reviews of *Inside Latin America* by John Gunther.

Copies seen: EH

Notes: Published in 1942 at $1.00, offset from C&W edition with requisite changes to the prelims. *Harpers Magazine* serialised the book, reducing it by half, in January 1942 (C.249). In 1960 Franklin Publications Inc. included a selection of passages entitled 'The only woman in the Lifeboat' in their book *Gentlemen, Scholars and Scoundrels* by Horace Knowles: this was translated into Arabic, Persian, Urdu, Bengali and Indonesian Malay.

Reviews: New Yorker, 7 March 1942
New York Times, 8 March 1942

A.9 ENGLISH WOMEN 1942

(a) First edition (1942)

ENGLISH WOMEN | by | ELSPETH HUXLEY | *Author of "White Man's Country" and* | *"Red Strangers"* | LONDON | THE SHELDON PRESS | NORTHUMBERLAND AVENUE, W.C.2 | DAR-ES-SALAAM: JOHANNESBURG: SALISBURY

Collation: 1–3 in 8s, 4 in 6s; [i–iv],v,[vi]; 7–60p. 182 × 123mm.

Contents: p.[i] ht.[ii] *"By the same Author* | THE STORY OF FIVE ENGLISH FARMERS | Sheldon Press. 9d." [iii] tp. [iv] *"First published* 1942 | MADE IN GREAT BRITAIN" [v] contents [vi] blank 7–60 text, at foot of p.60, "Printed in Great Britain by | *Billing and Sons Ltd., Guildford and Esher".*

Wrappers: mottled grey, on UW in dark blue, "ENGLISH | WOMEN | ELSPETH | HUXLEY"; on LW, The Sheldon Press 9d.

Copies seen: RH, SPCK Archive file copy

Notes: Published between January and June 1942 at 9d. Like A.7, EH was asked to write this booklet for use in African schools by the Foreign Literature Committee of the SPCK and Sheldon Press. Reprinted in 1953 at 1s.

It is interesting to note that EH recommended in 1942 that African girls should follow English ones by seeking a profession: once again EH is describing typical English women in their own country and not in Africa.

(b) First edition in Swahili (1953)

WANAWAKE WA | UINGEREZA | KIMETUNGWA NA | ELSPETH HUXLEY | KIMEFASIRIWA NA | ROBERT R.K. MZIRAI | SHELDON PRESS, LONDON | * * * | MACMILLAN AND CO. LIMITED | ST. MARTIN'S STREET, LONDON | 1953

Collation: no signature marks; vi,[viii],56p. 183 × 132mm.

30   A   Books and pamphlets

Contents: p.[i] ht. [ii] "*The translation was obtained through the East African | Literature Bureau from the English edition first published | in 1942.* | The Swahili in which this book is written has been | approved by the Inter-Territorial Language (Swahili) Committee for the East African Dependencies. | JOHN WILLIAMSON | Secretary, I.L.C. | 17.3.1950 | *The photographs are reproduced by | courtesy of the British Council*" [iii] tp. [iv] copyright details; "PRINTED BY CAHILL AND CO. LTD. | PARKGATE PRINTING WORKS, DUBLIN, IRELAND" v–vi Utangulizi [signed Mzirai, May, 1949] vii Yaliyomo [viii] blank 1–56 text.

Wrappers: red, with cream centre band, lettered in white on red, red on cream.

Copies seen: BL, SPCK Archive file copy.

Notes: Published under the title of *Wanawake wa Uingereza* in 1953 by the Sheldon Press and Macmillan and Co. Ltd. at 1s 6d, through the offices of the East African Literature Bureau, which EH had helped to form. The translator was Robert R. K. Mzirai whose translation was approved by the Inter-territorial Language (Swahili) Committee for the East African Dependencies. The photographs were supplied by the British Council, being newly introduced into the book.

See Appendix: Section 4.

A.10   BRAVE DEEDS OF THE WAR   1943

First edition (1943)

BRAVE DEEDS OF | THE WAR | BY | ELSPETH HUXLEY | CONTENTS [6 lines] | LONDON | THE SHELDON PRESS | NORTHUMBERLAND AVENUE, W.C.2

Collation: no signature marks; two centre staples, [1] in 8s; 1–15,[16]p. 163 × 104mm.

Contents: p.[1] tp 2–15,[16] text; on p.[16], "*These talks were prepared for broadcasting to | Africa from local stations, and are published by | courtesy of the London Transcription Service of | the British Broadcasting Corporation*"; at foot, "*Printed in Great Britain by | Billing and Sons Ltd., Guildford and Esher*".

Wrappers: mottled grey, on UW, "BRAVE DEEDS OF | THE WAR | By | ELSPETH HUXLEY" in black; on LW, "AFRICAN HOME LIBRARY | (Each 1d.)"; list of 34 titles, Brave Deeds is no.34 | "LONDON | THE SHELDON PRESS | NORTH-UMBERLAND AVENUE W.C.2" in black.

Copies seen: SPCK Archive file copy.

Notes: Published in 1943 at 1d as No.34 in the African Home Library. This series was produced by the Foreign Literature Committee of the SPCK and Sheldon Press, finally numbering 42 titles; some were aimed at a specifically female readership in Africa.

EH was at the time working for the BBC on broadcasts aimed at increasing the orale in the British Empire and Commonwealth. This pamphlet was derived from some of the stories of heroism in the war, such as Douglas Bader. As EH was in the employ of the BBC, the copyright in her works remained that of her employer, as was the case with George Orwell who was also employed by the BBC with his attention directed to the Far East.

The two succeeding pamphlets were No.35, *Birds, Flowers and Insects: A Story about African Wildlife* and No.36 *English Etiquette and Custom.*

A.11 RACE AND POLITICS IN KENYA   1944

(a) First edition (1944)

RACE AND POLITICS | IN KENYA | *a correspondence between* | ELSPETH HUXLEY | *and* | MARGERY PERHAM | *with an introduction by* | LORD LUGARD | [at foot] FABER AND FABER LTD | 24 *Russell Square* | *London*

Collation: A–P in 8s, Q in 4s; 247,[248]p. 218 × 135mm.

Contents: p.[1] ht. [2] *"by Elspeth Huxley"*: 3 titles; *"by Margery Perham"*: 5 titles [3] tp. [4] *"First published in Mcmxliv | by Faber and Faber Limited | 24 Russell Square London W.C.1 | Printed in Great Britain by | Latimer Trend & Co Ltd Plymouth | All rights reserved . . . This book is produced in complete conformity | with the authorized economy standards"* 5 contents 6 list of maps 7–13 introduction [14] blank 15–247 text [248] blank.

Note on illustrations: 3 folded maps of Kenya by Stanford, London.

Binding case: grey cloth (20), gold-tooled down spine, "RACE AND POLITICS IN KENYA | Elspeth Huxley and Margery Perham FABER | & Faber".

Dust-jacket: red and black lettering on creamy white paper; on UF, blurb, 12s 6d net; on LC, reviews of *African discovery,* by Perham and Simmons.

Copies seen: EH

Notes: Published 5 May 1944 at 12s 6d in edition of 2,250 copies. (An erratum slip was included in 1945 but there seems to be no record of what it contained). Second edition revised see A.11*(b).* EH read an extract from the book on Home Service 19 April 1955 (D.168).

The following is a recent extract from what EH described as her motive in her correspondence with Margery Perham: 'I tried to defend the unpopular cause of the white settlers, largely because I thought that they had so much bad publicity: almost the whole of the British press was very much against them, perhaps rightly in some respects, but it was overdone. Things were said that were not true and nobody was trying to answer back, and there are always two sides to every case.'

(b) Second English edition (1956)

Title: as in 1944 edition save, between Lugard and Faber: "NEW AND REVISED EDITION"

32   A   Books and pamphlets

Collation: [A],B–T in 8s; 302,[303–304]p. 217 × 138mm.

Contents: p.[1–2] blank [3] ht. [4] "*by Elspeth Huxley*" [5 titles] "*by Margery Perham*" [6 titles] [5] tp [6] "*First published in mcmxliv | by Faber and Faber Limited | 24 Russell Square London WC1 | Second revised edition mcmlvi | Printed in Great Britain by | Latimer Trend & Co Ltd Plymouth | All rights reserved*" 7–9 contents, list of maps [10] blank 11–14 chronology 15–21 introduction 22–302 text [303–304] blank.

A note on illustrations: as in 1944.

Binding case: green cloth (145), gold-tooled on spine, "RACE AND | POLITICS | IN | KENYA | [2 short rules] | Elspeth | Huxley | and | Margery | Perham | Faber".

Dust-jacket: yellow (86) lettered in black with red rules, "RACE AND | POLITICS | IN KENYA | Elspeth Huxley & | Margery Perham | with an introduction by Lord Lugard | [in red] *NEW AND REVISED | EDITION*"; LC & LF, books by Faber; UF, blurb, 25s net.

Copies seen: EH

Notes: Published 10 February 1956 as a revised edition at 25s in edition of 1,850. An Introduction by Lord Lugard was included. The blurb was written by Margery Perham. This edition included an extra Part 5: Reassessment by EH and MP each writing without seeing the other's script: 'not continuation of correspondence but two independent statements about the present situation'.

(c) First American issue (1975)

Title: as in 1956 edition save imprint: "[GP Greenwood Press monogram] | GREENWOOD PRESS, PUBLISHERS | WESTPORT, CONNECTICUT"

Collation: as in 1956 edition save size: 215 × 138mm.

Contents: as in 1956 edition save: p[1] ht. [2] blank [3]tp. [4] Library of Congress CIP data; quote from Faber on large no. of printer's errors in 1944 edition. All rights reserved . . . "Reprinted in 1975 by Greenwood Press, a division of Williamhouse-Regency Inc. Library of Congress Catalog card Number . . . ISBN. . . . Printed in the United States of America" 7 to end, as in 1956 edition.

Binding case: green cloth, gold-lettered on spine, "HUXLEY | . | [down spine] RACE AND POLITICS IN KENYA [at foot, GP Greenwood Press monogram]".

Dust-jacket: None.

Copies seen: EH

Notes: Published by Greenwood Press, Westport, Connecticut, on 1 August 1975; it was offset from the Faber second edition, A.11(*b*).

A.12   COLONIES: A READER'S GUIDE   1947

First edition (1947)

A Reader's Guide
COLONIES
by
ELSPETH HUXLEY

ONE SHILLING NET

THE READER'S GUIDES

C. Day Lewis — ENJOYING POETRY
Michael Sadleir — BOOK COLLECTING
Hubert Foss — BOOKS ABOUT MUSIC
G. M. Trevelyan — BIOGRAPHY
Arnold L. Haskell — BALLET
W. P. Matthew — HOME HANDYMAN
F. J. Osborn — TOWN AND COUNTRY PLANNING
Elspeth Huxley — COLONIES
Roger Manvell — FILM

To be published during 1948

A. G. Street — FARMING
R. St. Barbe Baker — TREES
Alan Dent — THEATRE-GOING
F. Seymour Smith — PAMPHLET BIBLIOGRAPHIES
John Moore — FISHING
R. W. Symonds — ENGLISH FURNITURE

Each 1s. net

NATIONAL BOOK LEAGUE
CAMBRIDGE UNIVERSITY PRESS

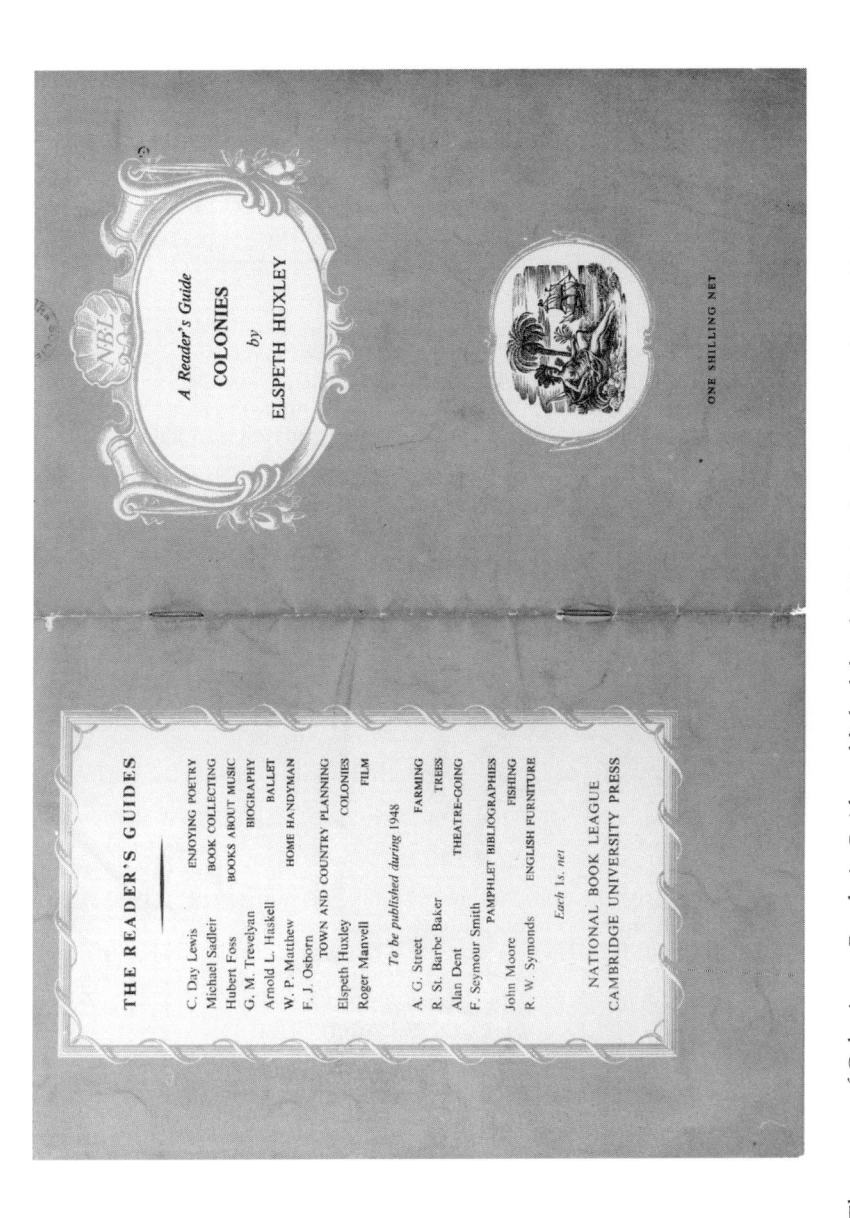

VIII. *The covers of* Colonies: a Reader's Guide *published for the National Book League by Cambridge University Press in 1947.*

34   A Books and pamphlets

[Within a triple frame of thick rule, thin rule and round brackets] COLONIES | [swelled rule] | *A Reader's Guide by* | ELSPETH HUXLEY | [illustration of books standing flat and open] | 1947 | PUBLISHED FOR | THE NATIONAL BOOK LEAGUE | BY THE CAMBRIDGE UNIVERSITY PRESS

Collation: no signature marks; 2 staples in centre of section. [1] in 8s; 16p. 135 × 215mm.

Contents: p.[1] tp. [2] National Book League advert., and "*The wood-engravings are by Joan Hassall* | *First Published 1947* | *Cambridge University Press* | *London: Bentley House* | *Toronto: Bombay: Calcutta* | *Madras: Macmillan* | *All Rights Reserved*" 3–16 text.

Wrappers: brown and orange; within a dec. oval cartouche at head, "N.B.L. *A Reader's Guide* | COLONIES | *by* | ELSPETH HUXLEY | [within an oval: a woman on a desert island, sailing ship] | ONE SHILLING NET"; on LW, within a dec. frame, 'THE READER'S GUIDES | [9 titles, and 6 to be published in 1948] | *Each 1s net* | NATIONAL BOOK LEAGUE | CAMBRIDGE UNIVERSITY PRESS".

Copies seen: RC

Notes: Published December 1947 at 1s. No other records exist.

Review: West Africa, 15 January 1949

A.13   THE WALLED CITY   1948

(a) First edition (1948)

The | Walled City | A Novel by | Elspeth Huxley | 1948 | Chatto and Windus | London

Collation: 1–21 in 8s; xvi,319,[320]p. 206 × 136mm.

Contents: [i] ht. [ii] "By the same Author": 2 titles [iii] tp. [iv] "PUBLISHED BY | Chatto & Windus | London | * | Oxford University Press | Toronto | THIS BOOK IS PRODUCED IN COMPLETE | CONFORMITY WITH THE AUTHORIZED | ECONOMY STANDARDS | ALL RIGHTS RESERVED" v–xvi prologue 1–319 text [320] "PRINTED IN GREAT BRITAIN | BY EBENEZER BAYLIS AND SON, LTD., THE | TRINITY PRESS, WORCESTER, AND LONDON".

Binding case: pink cloth (16), lettered in light blue on spine, "THE | WALLED | CITY | * | Elspeth | Huxley | CHATTO | & WINDUS".

Dust-jacket: pictorial in brown, purple and blue, signed E.C.; on UF, designed by Edward Bawden; 10s 6d net, Book Society Choice; on LF, blurb, Book Society Choice.

Copies seen: EH

Notes: Published 22 March 1948 at 10s 6d in edition of 25,000 copies of which 14,500 were for the Book Society Choice with joint imprint of C&W and Book

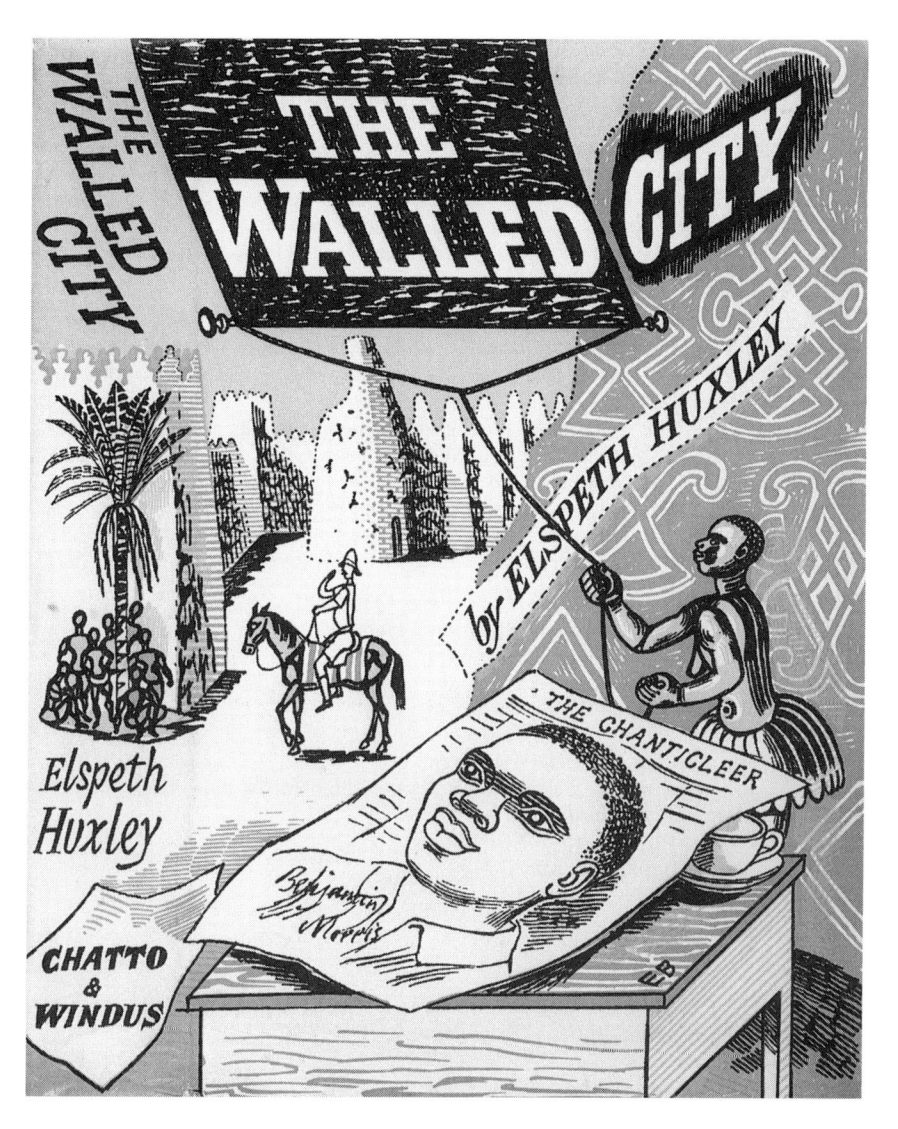

IX. *The dust-jacket of the first edition of* The Walled City *published by Chatto & Windus in 1948: the designer was Edward Bawden.*

36   A   Books and pamphlets

Society on title page. Reprinted in May 1973 (1,507) at £2.50, with President changed to Resident on 1.20 p.277: in June 1978, 500 quires were destroyed by fire at Redwood Burn, Esher, so evidently only 1,007 had been bound of the reprint.

NS described it as 'a very remarkable first novel' [incorrect] but suggested some cutting after a report from their reader, C. Day Lewis: EH completed these with her usual celerity. Terms offered were an improvement on those for *Red Strangers* (which NS evidently regarded as non-fiction) being: 15% on first 1,000 copies and 20% thereafter, thus indicating C&W's enthusiasm for EH as a writer. The advance however was a modest £150.

The Book Society was to supply paper for their printing which was undertaken by C&W but the dimensions were wrong and so C&W paper was used: this was replaced by the Book Society later from their quota – paper rationing still being in existence. They asked EH to sign 200 copies offering to pay £5 to any charity she named and EH wrote that she was 'delighted to deface copies of *The Walled City* with my atrocious signature'. This book with *Four Guineas*, (A.18), is studied, together with relevant works by Graham Greene and V. S. and Shiva Naipaul, concerning the relationship between Europe and Tropical Africa over 50 years demonstrating the growing empathy of these authors for the African people. (Dr. S. T. Harrington. *British Writers in Tropical Africa*, University Microfims 1995.)

Reviews: Daily Mail, 20, March 1948 (Peter Quennell)
Observer, 21 March 1948 (Lionel Hale)
Daily Telegraph, 25 March 1948
Scotsman, 25 March 1948
TLS, 27 March 1948
Sunday Times, 28 March 1948
Spectator, 2 April 1948 (Robert Kee)
John o' London, 2 April 1948 (Pamela Hansford Johnson)
Manchester Guardian, 8 April 1948
Punch, 14 April 1948
New Statesman, 8 May 1948

(b)   First American edition (1949)

THE | WALLED | CITY | By ELSPETH HUXLEY | 1949 | J.B. LIPPIN-COTT COMPANY | PHILADELPHIA AND NEW YORK

Collation: no signature marks; 350p. 200 × 140mm.

Contents: (1) ht. (2) blank (3) tp (4) "COPYRIGHT 1948, BY ELSPETH HUXLEY | FIRST EDITION | PRINTED IN THE UNITED STATES OF AMERICA" (5) 2nd ht. (6) blank 7–350 text.

Binding case: smooth black cloth (267), lettered in silver on UC, "THE | Walled | City", and on spine, "ELSPETH | HUXLEY | THE | Walled City | LIPPINCOTT".

Dust-jacket: yellowish|pink (30) streaked with white, lettered in black within a white panel bordered with a black machiolated frame, "THE | [dec.] Walled | City | BY | ELSPETH HUXLEY"; below, blurb; down spine in black: "THE [dec.] Walled City ELSPETH | HUXLEY | [horizontal] LIPPINCOTT"; UF, blurb, 4 paragraphs, and *"This novel was a Book Society choice in England; | it has not been serialized in America.* | WC | $3.00"; portrait of EH and biography, 3 paragraphs; LF, blurb for *Beau Geste* by P.C. Wren.

Copies seen: Tiptree

Notes: Published 5 January 1949 at $3.00. No records available since Lippincott were taken over by Harper Collins. President was corrected to Resident on p.307. This edition was reset in USA.

Reviews: New York Times, 7 January 1949 (Orville Prescott)
Saturday Review, 8 January 1949
New York Herald Tribune, 9 January 1949
New Yorker, 22 January 1949
Christian Science Monitor, 27 January 1949

A.14   SETTLERS OF KENYA   1948

First edition (1948)

SETTLERS OF KENYA | *By* | ELSPETH HUXLEY | HIGHWAY PRESS, NAIROBI | LONGMANS, GREEN AND CO. | LONDON [orn.] NEW YORK [orn.] TORONTO

Collation: [A],B|B*–E.E* in 12s; [i–iv],v,[vi],vii–viii, 1–126,[127–128]p. 184 × 125mm.

Contents: [i] ht. [ii] blank [iii] tp. [iv] Longmans addresses; "First published 1948 | PRINTED IN GREAT BRITAIN | BY WESTERN PRINTING SERVICES LTD., BRISTOL" v contents [vi] blank vii–viii introduction 1–126 text [127–128] blank.

Note on illustrations: map of Kenya, p.117.

Wrappers: mottled light-brown, with blank endpapers; UW in brown within a dec. border, "Settlers of Kenya | by | ELSPETH HUXLEY | LONGMANS"; LW, in brown Longmans device.

Copies seen: RH, EH

Notes: Published 3 May 1948 at 3s in edition of 5,000. A booklet in the series 'The People of Kenya', it was commissioned by the East African Literature Bureau which EH had helped found.

Longmans used the Highway Press as their distributor in Nairobi.

Published in USA by Greenwood Press on 6 August 1975 (not seen).

A.15   AFRICAN DILEMMAS   1948

First edition (1948)

AFRICAN | DILEMMAS | *by* | ELSPETH HUXLEY | LONGMANS GREEN AND CO. | LONDON NEW YORK TORONTO

38   A Books and pamphlets

Collation: no signature marks; [1 in 12s]; [1–4],5–22,[23–24]p. 215 × 140mm.

Contents: p.[1] ht., at head, "BRITISH COMMONWEALTH AFFAIRS – No.4" [2] "THIS series is published under the auspices of the | Royal Empire Society in order to provide a forum | for the discussion of current questions relating to | the British Commonwealth and Empire. The views | expressed are those of the respective authors, and not | necessarily those of the Society." [3] tp. [4] Longmans addresses, and, *"First Published 1948 | Made and printed in Great Britain by | Cheltenham Press Ltd, Cheltenham"* 5–22 text [23–24] blank.

Note on illustrations: map of West Africa, p.15.

Wrappers: orange/brown wrappers, with two staples in centre of section; on UW a design of a map of Africa with two heads of Africans a spear between in black and orange, lettered, "BRITISH COMMONWEALTH AFFAIRS No.4 | AFRICAN DILEMMAS | by Elspeth Huxley | LONGMANS *Price One Shilling Nett.*" inside UW, publishers blurb, 19 lines; on LW, a list of 4 nos. in series, at foot, *"Price 1/- Each | NET"*.

Copies seen: RH

Notes: Published 1st November 1948 in edition of approximately 4,500 at 1s, as No 4 in the British Commonwealth Affairs series, under the auspices of the Royal Empire Society and its Imperial Studies Committee. The Society contributed £150 and the Rhodes Trustees £500 towards the cost of the first 4 pamphlets, and Longmans sold *African Dilemmas* on commission; this pamphlet was also available through Longmans Green's New York office.

Longmans withdrew from selling this pamphlet in January 1956 and the remaining stock was distributed free to libraries and at conferences. The Minutes of the Committee are in the Royal Commonwealth Collection in the Cambridge University Library.

Review: West Africa, 6 November 1948

A16   THE SORCERER'S APPRENTICE   1948

First edition (1948)

THE | SORCERER'S | APPRENTICE | A Journey through East Africa | by | ELSPETH HUXLEY | [illus. of seated African playing instrument by drum, signed, J.K.] | 1948 | CHATTO AND WINDUS | LONDON

Collation: A–AA in 8s; xviii,365,[366]p. 218 × 138mm.

Contents: p.[i] ht. [ii] "By the same Author": 3 titles [iii] tp [iv] "PUBLISHED BY | Chatto & Windus | LONDON | * | Clarke, Irwin & Company Ltd | TORONTO | THIS BOOK IS PRODUCED IN COMPLETE | CONFORMITY WITH THE AUTHORIZED | ECONOMY STANDARDS | ALL RIGHTS RESERVED" [v] quotation from Boulton's A compleat history of magick, 1715 [vi] blank vii–xiii contents [xiv] blank [xv–xvi] list of illustrations xvii–xviii introduction 1–365,[366] text, on last page, "MADE AND PRINTED IN GREAT BRITAIN | BY EBENEZER

BAYLIS AND SON, LTD., THE | TRINITY PRESS, WORCESTER, AND LONDON".

Note on illustrations: plates containing 36 photographs, mainly by EH; folded map.

Binding case: orange/brown cloth (54), gold-lettered on spine, "THE | SORCERER'S | APPRENTICE | [dec.scroll] | Elspeth | Huxley | CHATTO | & WINDUS".

Dust-jacket: enlarged version of tp. illustration in orange, lettered in black, signed, "Kinsey"; on UF, publishers blurb, 18s net.

Paper: Antique Wove

Copies seen: EH

Notes: Published on 4 November 1948 at 18s in edition of 5,735 copies: reprinted June 1949 (3,288), May 1951 at 21s (2,470) and October 1956 (1,631). Sales between November 1948 and February 1956 were 10,875.

After publication EH spotted an error, making a nonsense of the meaning, on p.268 l.4f which was correct in page proofs: 'to hold to this idea through many difficulties and against the scepticism of them the view of life which she believed them to possess and to show Mrs Trowell fortunately has more than her fair share of these' was changed in second impression to 'to hold to this idea through many difficulties and against the scepticism of most of her colleagues has taken much faith, energy and humour. Mrs Trowell fortunately has more than her fair share of these'.

HR received a letter from Kilindini Harbour Wharf and Estate Company dated 24 January 1949 complaining about the following passage on p.127 penultimate paragraph: 'It is a curious commentary on human nature that Torr's, Nairobi's largest hotel, is Indian owned and most of the others belong to Indians or Jews'. They stated 'In so far as Torr's Hotel is concerned this statement is libellous and immediate steps must be taken to correct same. . . the Hotel is and always has been owned by the above Company the whole of whose shareholders are and always have been British born Europeans'. HR refers in a letter dated 28 January 1949 to an erratum slip having been inserted with the necessary correction and to a change being made in the next reprint. The offending sentence was in fact removed in the third impression. In addition Mrs. Rydon objected to the last sentence on p.100 l.2 'The Millenium starts in nineteen fifty three': this was deleted in the third impression.

EH marked up her copy of the first edition with the following corrections which were not incorporated:
pp.17 & 20 Wito *should* be Witu
p.40 l.3f. *should* be 6,000
p.73 l.10f 7 *should* be 15
p.174 facing: caption of upper illustration *should* be Lion on the Serengeti Plains
p.203 l.16f. Irundi *should* be Urundi
p.216 l.7 *should* be nearly a thousand species
p.226 hookworm *should* be roundworm (Ascaris)
p.237 l.15 forks *should* be ground
p.259 l.2f. *should* be tall bands of buff and black
p.282 l.14 Buganda *should* be Baganda
p.289 Ramogi *should* be Gamboze
p.325 *should* be Cupressus benthami
p.365 l.12f. *should* be Pancrates

40 A Books and pamphlets

Reviews: Evening Standard, 9 November 1948 (George Malcolm Thomson)
Sunday Times, 28 November 1948
Spectator, 3 December 1948
Times, 11 December 1948
Time and Tide, 11 December 1948
TLS, 5 February 1949
Observer, 7 March 1949
Tablet, 12 March 1949

(b) First American issue (1975)

Title: as in 1948 edition save for imprint: "[at foot: GP monogram] | GREENWOOD PRESS, PUBLISHERS | WESTPORT, CONNECTICUT"

Collation: as in 1948, save, lacking signature marks and size: 215 × 140mm.

Contents: [i] ht. [ii] blank [iii] tp. [iv] Library of Congress CIP data, "Reprinted in 1975 by Greenwood Press, | a division of Williamhouse-Regency Inc. | Printed in the United States of America." p.[v] to end, as in 1948 edition without printer's imprint on last page.

Note on illustrations: as in 1948.

Binding case: orange/brown cloth (43), lettered in black down spine, "HUXLEY | THE SORCERER'S APPRENTICE | [horizontal GP device]".

Dust-jacket: none.

Copies seen: EH, Tiptree

Notes: Published 2 June 1975, print number and price unknown. Greenwood Press Offset from C&W's first edition so none of the corrections was incorporated. Released by Books on Tape Inc. October 1988 at $104.

A.17   I DON'T MIND IF I DO   1950

(a) First edition (1950)

I DON'T MIND | IF I DO | [dec. rule] | Elspeth Huxley | [at foot:] 1950 | Chatto and Windus | LONDON

Collation: 1–16 in 8s; 256p. 197 × 128mm.

Contents: p[1] ht. [2] "*By the same Author*": 4 titles [3] tp [4] "Published by | CHATTO & WINDUS | LONDON | * | CLARKE, IRWIN & CO. LTD. | TORONTO | [at foot] COPYRIGHT BY | ELSPETH HUXLEY 1950 PRINTED IN GREAT BRITAIN | BY EBENEZER BAYLIS AND SON, LTD., THE TRINITY PRESS, | WORCESTER AND LONDON" 5–256 text.

Binding case: olive yellow cloth (107), lettered in gold in a brown dec. panel on spine, "I DON'T | MIND | IF I DO | [dec. flourish] | ELSPETH | HUXLEY".

Dust-jacket: design over white ground on UC and spine initialled: C.H.; lettered in brown; on UF, blurb, Recommended by the Book Society, 9s.6d. NET; on LC, new novels, Chatto and Windus: 4 titles; on LF, Chatto address.

Paper: Antique laid.

Copies seen: RC

Notes: Published 25 September 1950 at 9s 6d in edition of 8,019 copies. Reprinted October 1950 (4,018). Price reduced to 4s 6d on 2 November 1953, increased to 6s on 1 January 1958.

Sales from September 1950 to February 1956 were 11,448.

EH received same royalties as for *The Walled City.*

(b) First paperback edition (1993)

I DON'T MIND | IF I DO | [swelled rule] | Elspeth Huxley | [at foot:] mulberry books | 62 bis rue de Vic 62100 CALAIS

Collation: as in 1950 edition; 214 × 139mm.

Contents: p.[1] ht. [2] blank [3] tp. 4 "Published by Mulberry Books, 62 bis rue de Vic, 62100 Calais, in 1993. | © Elspeth Huxley. | All rights reserved." 5–256 text, as in 1950 edition, with blank leaves before and after.

Wrapper: green (162), pictorial UW; on LW, publishers blurb, RRP UK £8.50, US $14.50, 68.00 French francs.

Copies seen: EH

Notes: In 1993 Mulberry Books of Calais published a sewn paperback at £8.50, Fr.68, US $14.50. This book is a facsimile of the C&W edition and in the words of the publisher 'We do not have such a thing as a print quality, which is obsolescent. We make as many copies as we can sell, continuously as orders come in, for the life of the copyright.'

A.18   FOUR GUINEAS   1954

(a) First edition (1954)

FOUR | GUINEAS | A Journey through | West Africa | *By* | ELSPETH HUXLEY | [orn.tree with feathery leaves] | 1954 | CHATTO AND WINDUS | LONDON

Collation: A–T in 8s, U in 6s; xi,[xii],303,[304]p. 216 × 140mm.

Contents: p.[i] ht. [ii] "*By the same Author*": 6 titles [iii] tp [iv] "PUBLISHED BY CHATTO AND WINDUS LTD | LONDON | * | CLARKE, IRWIN AND CO LTD | TORONTO | PRINTED IN GREAT BRITAIN | ALL RIGHTS RESERVED" v–vi

42 A Books and pamphlets

author's note vii contents viii maps in text ix–xi list of plates [xii] map of West Africa 1–303 text [304] "*Printed in Great Britain | by Richard Clay and Company, Limited | Bungay, Suffolk*".

Note on illustrations: 59 plates of photographs "by the author unless otherwise stated"; 5 maps.

Binding case: orange brown cloth (74), gold-lettered on spine in blue cloth oval, "*Four | Guineas | [scroll] |* ELSPETH | HUXLEY | CHATTO & | WINDUS".

Dust-jacket: pictorial in black, white, blue and brown showing 7 African fishermen pulling on a rope; on UF, publishers blurb, Recommended by the Book Society, 21s.net; on LF, also by Elspeth Huxley: 3 titles.

Paper: Wireless wove.

Copies seen: EH

Notes: Published 11 February 1954 at 21s in edition of 5,131 copies. Reprinted in March and September 1954 (2,538 and 3,116 copies). Reprinted in 1957 (1,848 copies). Prices increased to 22s 6d on 1 January 1956 and to 25s in July 1957.

Sales between 11 February 1954 and 20 February 1956, 9,149 copies. A Book Society Recommendation.

NS asked for some cuts and additions on 10 June 1953 and all revisions were completed by EH by 3 July, despite her farming responsibilities: a good example of her professionalism as a writer.

For the first time EH consulted the Society of Authors about the C&W agreement and, with her resulting comments, she added 'Please don't think that I suggest it because the worm of distrust is gnawing at my vitals'. NS doubted the need for an index 'I am not sure it adds a great deal': an interesting comment on publishing 40 years ago.

After publication the following mistakes were drawn to C&W's attention and were corrected in the third impression:
pp.v, 98 and index: Sir George and Lady Lillie Costello *changed* to Major Lillie Costello
pp. 122, 125, 127, 147 and index: Bowditch *changed* to Bowdich.

Trouble then brewed with Dr J. B. Danquah, barrister-at-law and solicitor in Ghana who objected to remarks on p.92 and 93 (first edition) as being libellous; he wrote to the printer, Richard Clay, the publisher and booksellers in Ghana threatening proceedings. C&W chose to ignore the warning due to their legal advice that Dr. Danquah had misunderstood EH's use of pot calling kettle black. When the Reprint Society edition was due to be published (A.18(*b*)) NS thought it wise to pacify Dr. Danquah in view of the large edition, and EH made quite substantial changes.

Uncorrected passages:
p.92 l.4 'Danquah – a relative of several of the murderers – and other lawyers for the defence, then proceeded to conduct an elaborate game of cat and mouse.'
p.93 l.6–7 '... lived to see the fat chicken he was stalking fall to a hunter even cleverer than he.'
p.93 l.20 'It is said that Dr. Danquah has never forgiven the British for the execution of his three kinsmen. However that may be ... (of its 84 members only 6 are Europeans) ...'

p.93 l.15–29 'Over tea and cakes in a well, but stiffly furnished upstairs parlour, decorated in old gold, the reputation of pots were heavily blackened by kettle [unfortunately Dr. Danquah took this metaphor as an insult relating to the state of his kitchen pots.] Tales of bribes, extortion, threats and thuggery were told which, whether true or exaggerated, do not make the sort of battlecry likely to gather popular support for such an old hand at the political game as Dr. Danquah. He opposes also the C.P.P.'s attack on chieftainship. Here perhaps his voice is more beguiling. The C.P.P. has put through a measure which takes from the Stools their land and their revenues and vests both in District Councils which are mainly elected and which the Party naturally hopes to control. This will at one stroke cripple the chiefs, and entrenching the C.P.P. so firmly that only a disintegration of the Party could dislodge it. . . . This is indeed to emasculate them.'

In subsequent impressions before the Reprint Society edition, Dr. Danquah's name became Danv. Dquah (page 94) as if to disguise his name by the misprint.

Corrected passages in Reprint Society edition:
p.104 l.22 l.20 'The lawyers for the defence then proceeded to conduct an elaborate game of cat and mouse.'
p.105 l.20 'As for Dr. Danquah, the closing of the case did not quench his belief that his relatives and the other convicted men were victims of a plot to discredit his distinguished family which has produced many leaders in public life – and the Gold Coast's first woman doctor. Nor did he abandon politics.'
p.105 l.6f 'One of the measures he has attacked with fire and eloquence – but without effect, so tiny is the opposition – is a CPP Bill to take the land and revenues attached to the Stools away, and put them under District Councils. Two thirds of the members of these Councils are elected; thus the CPP expects to bring them all into its fold. . . . This will indeed be to emasculate them.'
p.106 l.19 '. . . lived to see younger hands snatch from his the standard of freedom and the trumpet of fame, just as the walls of the beleaguered city started to crumble.'

Similarly the Asantehene protested about two passages in the C&W edition, which C&W decided to change in the Reprint Society edition.

Uncorrected passages:
p.127 l.8f 'You wait in a dead room. The bungalow itself is solitary, there is no sound.'
p.128 l.9 'Bitterest, perhaps, of all, he sees the British officials whose word he trusted revoke their promises to acknowledge the Asantehene as the ruler of the Ashanti nation and to recognise the traditional forms of Ashanti Government.'

Corrected passages:
p.141 l.14 'The bungalow seems to hold itself aloof from those soft, warm, human noises which accompany the flow of life in an ordinary village at home.'
p.141 l.3 'Now he must watch, in dignity and silence, a *volte face* of British policy, formerly based (it seemed securely) on the recognition of chiefs and their traditional councils as the lynch-pins of administration.'

Strangely enough these corrections were not made in the 1957 C&W reprint.

Reviews: *Times,* 13 February 1954
Time and Tide, ndk
John O'London, ndk (C.V. Wedgwood)
Economist, ndk.

44   A   Books and pamphlets

(b) Reprint Society edition (1955)

[In an oval arch of foliage:] FOUR | GUINEAS | A Journey through | West Africa | by | ELSPETH | HUXLEY | [at foot] R.S. | THE REPRINT SOCIETY | LONDON

Collation: A–K in 16s; 320p. 183 × 119mm.

Contents: p.[1] ht [2] "*By the same Author*": 6 titles [3] tp [4] "FIRST PUBLISHED 1954 | THIS EDITION PUBLISHED BY THE REPRINT SOCIETY LTD. | BY ARRANGEMENT WITH CHATTO AND WINDUS LTD 1955 | . . . PRINTED IN GREAT BRITAIN BY RICHARD CLAY AND COMPANY LTD. | BUNGAY, SUFFOLK" 5 contents 6–7 list of plates [8] map [9] 2nd ht. "GAMBIA" 10–11 "A NOTE ON | GAMBIA" 13–320 text.

Note on illustrations: 28p. of photographs, 5 maps.

Binding case: black imitation cloth, lettered in gold in red cloth lettering-piece with gold borders, "FOUR | GUINEAS | ELSPETH | HUXLEY".

Dust-jacket: all-over design of repeated animals and figures and 'R.S.' in blue on purple ground; lettered in blue; UF, blurb; LC, Looking ahead: 6 titles; LF, photograph of EH and brief list of likes and dislikes supplied by her. (Variant dj: UC and spine, squares of mottled yellow, blue lines, mottled blue and yellow, yellow); foot of UF, THIS IS A BOOK CLUB EDITION OF A BOOK ORIGINALLY PUBLISHED AT 21/-.

Copies seen: RC

Notes: Published in 1955 as their July choice in edition of 225,000 copies. The Society provided their own paper and specified printing and binding. Corrections were made to standing type to incorporate all the changes listed in A.18(*a*) but, in the process, Asantehene was omitted from the index. The following additional changes were made to the prelims: 'Maps in text' were combined with 'Contents' p.5: Author's Note was deleted: 3 illustrations were deleted and some rearranged as set out in List of Plates on p.6.

(c) First American impression (1974)

Title: as in 1954 edition save: "[at foot:GP monogram] | GREENWOOD PRESS, PUBLISHERS | WESTPORT, CONNECTICUT"

Collation: as in 1954 edition.

Contents: as in 1954 edition, save, on p.[iv] "Reprinted from an original copy in the | collections of the University of Illinois Library | Reprinted in 1974 by Greenwood Press, | a division of Williamhouse-Regency Inc. | . . . Printed in the United States of America".

Binding case: orange cloth, lettered in black down spine, "HUXLEY | FOUR GUINEAS | [horizontal] GP".

Dust-jacket: none.

Copies seen: EH

Notes: Published in 1974. This was photographed from a C&W copy in the collection of the University of Illinois Library, so none of the Reprint Society corrections was incorporated.

Released by Books on Tape Inc. in March 1991 at $72.

A.19 A THING TO LOVE   1954

First edition (1954)

A | thing to Love | *A Novel by* | ELSPETH HUXLEY | *And death and hate and hell declare* | *That men have found a thing to love.* | G.K. CHESTERTON | 1954 | CHATTO & WINDUS | LONDON

Collation: A–R in 8s (Q omitted); 255,[256]p. 198 × 128mm.

Contents: p.[1–3] blank [4] ht. [5] tp. [6] "PUBLISHED BY | CHATTO AND WINDUS LTD | LONDON | * | CLARKE, IRWIN AND CO LTD | TORONTO | [at foot] PRINTED IN GREAT BRITAIN BY | EBENEZER BAYLIS AND SON LTD., WORCESTER | ALL RIGHTS RESERVED" [7] "*To Cleggy* | *whose labours so greatly* | *lighten mine*" [8] blank 9–255,[256] text.

Binding case: Red/pink cloth (15), gold-lettered on spine, "A THING | TO LOVE | [orn. flourish] | ELSPETH | HUXLEY | CHATTO | & WINDUS".

Dust-jacket: pictorial on black, signed, "BIRO"; lettered in gold and white; on UF, blurb, Book Society Recommendation, 12s.6d.net; LC, Also by Elspeth Huxley: 6 titles; LF, Chatto address.

Paper: Antique wove.

Copies seen: RC

Notes: Published 11 October 1954 at 12s 6d in edition of 9,122 copies of which 120 were paper covered (probably for sales purposes) and 253/250 were sold to Blunt (library suppliers) as folded and collated sheets including dust-jackets. Reprinted in October 1954 (6,845 copies).

'Arse' on p.122 worried NS in case it affected sales to Boots libraries: EH agreed and referred to the change as the 'arse into bottom transmutation'.

The book was a Book Society Recommendation (printed on front flap of d.j.). *John Bull* serialised it in six instalments from 14 August to 18 September 1954 (C.376).

An analysis of this book with many quotes was made by Michael Harris in *Outsiders and Insiders,* Vol.1 in 'Studies of World Literature in English' edited by Norman Cary, published by Peter Lang Publishing Inc. New York in 1962. The chapter concerned, entitled 'The Struggle for Independence' pp.111 to 142, compared EH's books on Africa to those of Kipling's on India.

Reviewed by Negley Farson 1954 ndopk
              John Connell 1954 ndopk

46   A   Books and pamphlets

A.20   KENYA TODAY   1954

First edition (1954)

KENYA TODAY | *by* | ELSPETH HUXLEY | author of | *White Man's Country; Lord Delamere* | *and the Making of Kenya* | *Race and Politics in Kenya* | with Margery Perham | etc. | [device of Lutterworth Press] | LUTTERWORTH PRESS | LONDON

Collation: no signature marks; two metal staples in centre, [1] in 18s; [1–3],4–36p. 198 × 132mm.

Contents: p.[1] tp [2] "ALL RIGHTS RESERVED | *First published* 1954 | *Also in the "Today" series* | SOUTH AFRICA TODAY, *by Alan Paton* | SUDAN TODAY, *by John Hyslop* | The cover picture, which is used by courtesy of | the Kenya Public Relations Office, shows schoolboys | of Kenya's three races at an Inter-Racial Course on | Mt. Kilimanjaro. | Printed in Great Britain by | Page Bros. (Norwich) Ltd." [3]–36 text.

Note on illustrations: map of Kenya and surrounding countries, p.18–19.

Wrappers: pale green; on UW, picture (as in contents) in red, and, "KENYA TODAY | BY ELSPETH HUXLEY"; LW, in red within double rules, "KENYA TODAY | *Elspeth Huxley* | The author writes . . . [24 lines.] at foot Lutterworth Press device] | *LUTTERWORTH PRESS*".

Copies seen: RH, EH

Notes: Published on 30 November 1954 at 2s. 6d.

Copyright was bought for £20. Lutterworth Press has no record of the print number.

A.21   WHAT ARE TRUSTEE NATIONS?   1955

First edition (1955)

WHAT ARE | TRUSTEE NATIONS? | [swelled rule] | by | ELSPETH HUXLEY | [at foot] LONDON | THE BATCHWORTH PRESS

Collation: no signature marks: two metal staples in centre, [1] in 12s; [1–4],5-22, [23–24]p. 184 × 123mm.

Contents: p.[1] ht. [2] "THE AUTHOR": 13 lines [3] tp. [4] "*Published in 1955 by* | *Batchworth Press Ltd* | *54 Bloomsbury Street, London, W.C.1* | *Catalogue No.Z/4241* | *Printed in Great Britain by* | *Clarke, Doble & Brendon Ltd* | *Oakfield Press, Cattedown, Plymouth*" 5–22 text [23–24] two maps.

Note on illustrations: the maps are of Equatorial Africa, and the Western Pacific.

Wrappers: orange; on UW, a white question mark and in black, "WHAT ARE | TRUSTEE | NATIONS | *by* | *Elspeth Huxley* | A BACKGROUND BOOK *One Shilling*"; inside UW, within a triple rule, "BACKGROUND BOOKS | EDITOR :

BACKGROUND SPECIALS

THE PEOPLE'S HEALTH
A Study of the Development of Public Health
by Professor Fraser Brockington   2s 6d

EDUCATION AND SOCIETY
Five Essays
with an Introduction by Sir John Sargent   5s

WHAT HAPPENED IN KOREA?
A Study of Collective Security
by Guy Wint
'*Valuable—timely—enthralling*'—Lord Salter in the
MANCHESTER GUARDIAN   5s

THE SPY WEB
A Study of Communist Espionage
by Francis Noel-Baker
'*A useful and exciting book*'—TIMES LIT. SUPP.   10s 6d

HOW RUSSIA IS RULED
by Walter Kolarz   7s 6d

HOW DID THE SATELLITES HAPPEN?
with a Preface by the Rt. Hon. Hector McNeil, P.C., M.P.   10s 6d

Background Books list inside cover
The Batchworth Press
54 BLOOMSBURY STREET, LONDON, WC1

WHAT ARE TRUSTEE NATIONS

by *Elspeth Huxley*

A BACKGROUND BOOK   One Shilling

X.   *The covers of* What are Trustee Nations? *published by The Batchworth Press in 'Background Specials' in 1955.*

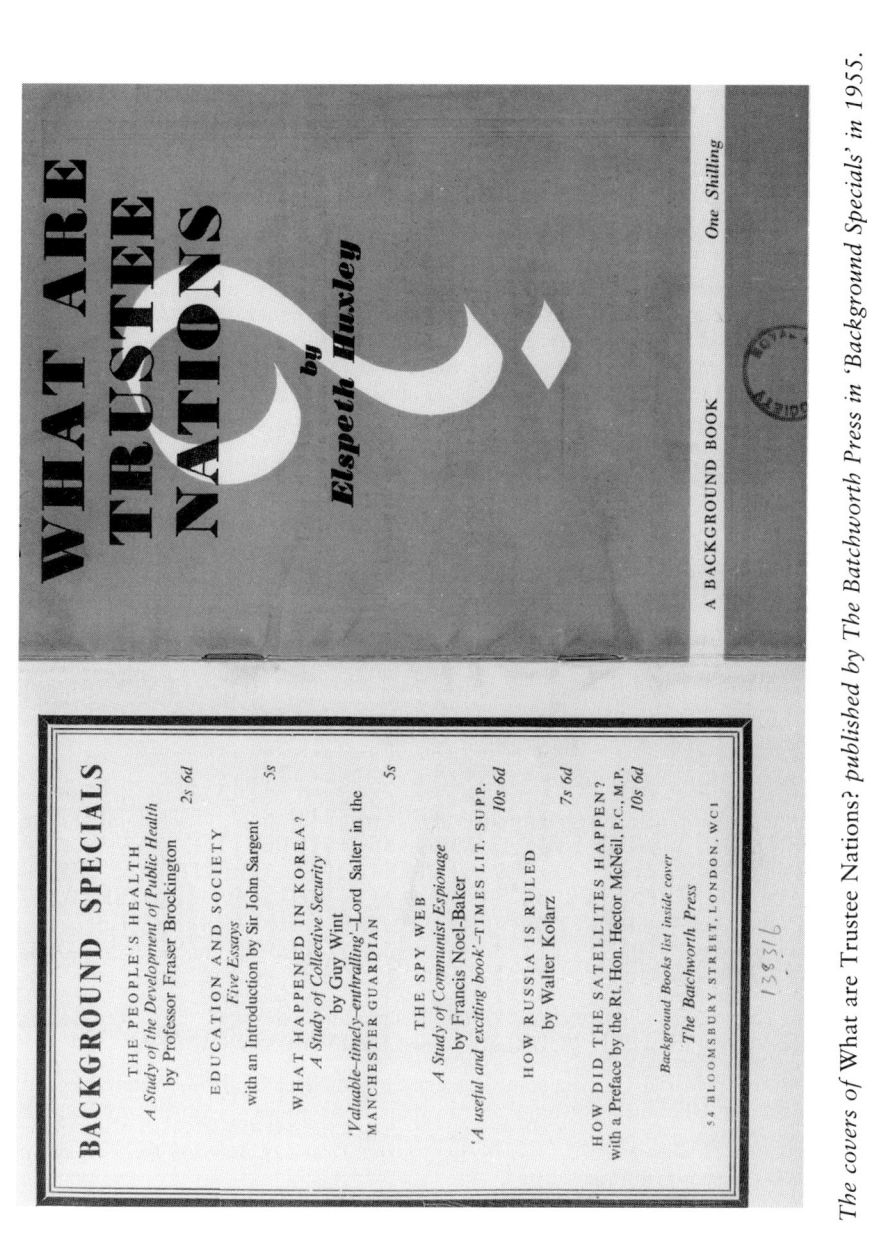

48 A Books and pamphlets

STEPHEN WATTS": 15 lines of information; inside LW, within a triple rule, "BACKGROUND BOOKS | THE CURRENT AFFAIRS SERIES": list of titles; on LW, within a triple rule, "BACKGROUND SPECIALS": list of titles.

Copies seen: RH

Notes: Published in 1955 at 1s as part of the Background Books Series, edited by Stephen Watts. Batchworth Press went into liquidation in the mid-50's and this series was taken over by Phoenix House, a subsidiary of Dent, who may have reprinted this pamphlet though no records exist to substantiate this. In 1960 Bodley Head took over the series.

The Background Books Series was sponsored by the Foreign Office's Information Research Department (IRD): the editor had been involved in propaganda work during the Second World War, and was director in the 1950s of Ampersand, a company closely associated with IRD. Although the series was published by commercial companies, the choice of topic and of the authors was decided by Stephen Watts in consultation with IRD. It appears that there was a subsidy in the form of a bulk purchase by Ampersand for distribution overseas.

EH's target audience was probably English-speaking students of the Third World.

A.22   THE RED ROCK WILDERNESS   1957

(a) First edition (1957)

The Red Rock | Wilderness | *A Novel by* | ELSPETH HUXLEY | [at foot] 1957 | CHATTO & WINDUS | LONDON

Collation: A–R in 8s (Q omitted); 255,[256]p. 196 × 125mm.

Contents: p.[1] ht. [2] "*By the same Author*": 8 titles [3] tp. [4] "PUBLISHED BY | CHATTO AND WINDUS LTD | 42 WILLIAM IV STREET | LONDON WC2 | * | CLARKE, IRWIN AND CO LTD | TORONTO | . . . PRINTED IN GREAT BRITAIN BY | EBENEZER BAYLIS AND SON LTD. | WORCESTER, AND LONDON | ALL RIGHTS RESERVED" [5] "*The red rock wilderness | Shall be my dwelling place . . .* | SIDNEY KEYES" [6] blank [7] contents [8] blank 9–255,[256] text.

Binding case: reddish brown cloth (43); gold-lettered down spine, "The | Red Rock | Wilderness | * | ELSPETH | HUXLEY | . . . CHATTO | & WINDUS".

Dust-jacket: pictorial UC and spine designed by Michael Charlton; lettered in red and black; on UF, blurb, Recommended by the Book Society; LC, Also by Elspeth Huxley: reviews of 4 books; on LF, Chatto address.

Paper: Ivory shade antique wove.

Copies seen: RC

Notes: Published 16 May 1957 at 15s in edition of 12,097 copies of which 10,597 were bound (60 paperbound for sales purposes and 48 as early copies of which 13 were bound in 'dark cloth' [not seen]) and 1,500 were kept as quires which were sold

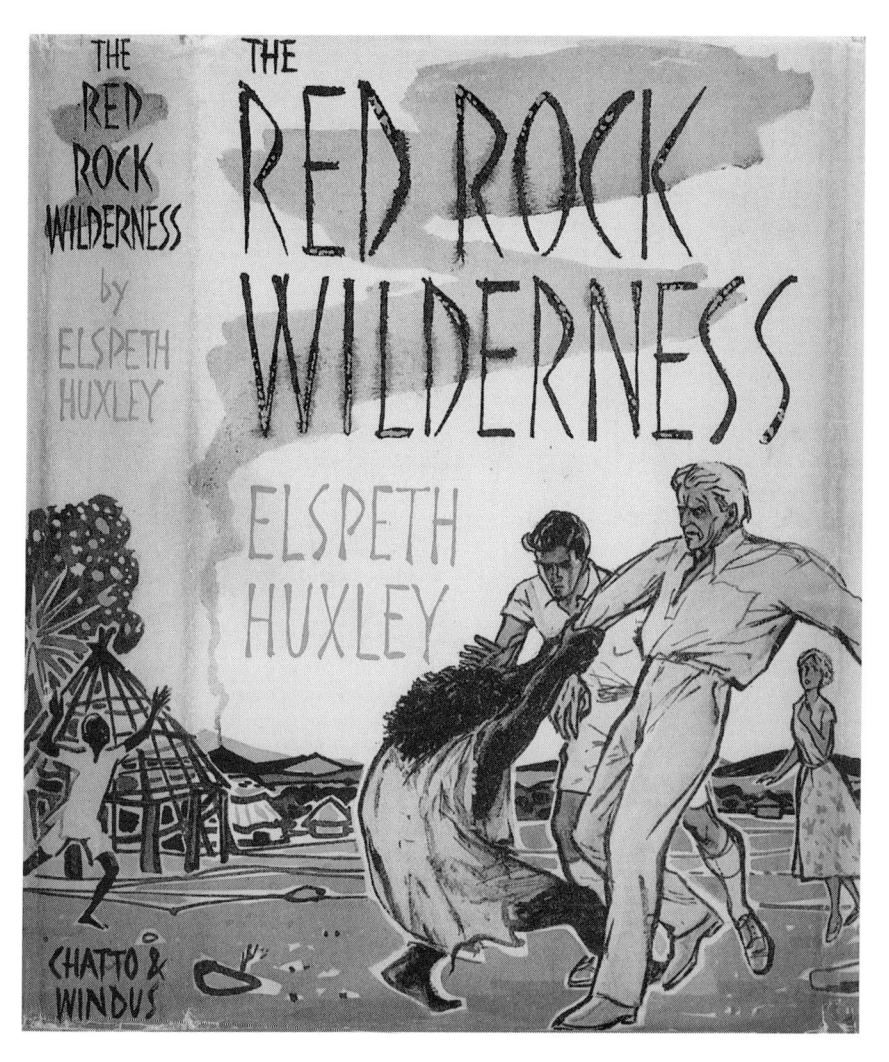

XI. *The dust-jacket of the first edition of* The Red Rock Wilderness *published by Chatto & Windus in 1957.*

50   A   Books and pamphlets

in 1960 to Books for Pleasure as remainders. By 29 May 1957, 8,044 had been sold. The book was a Book Society Recommendation and the cover was banded as such. In July 1958 Odhams published it in their Condensed Book series No.16 in edition of 10,000 copies at 7s 6d: the text was reduced to one third of its original length by Odhams' editorial staff and included in an Omnibus with three other titles.

NS had asked for considerable cuts which EH did expeditiously: she also pressed for the villain to be finished off at the end in true 'John Buchan style', rather than the local district officer reporting on how he had escaped. EH acceded to this but see below for her views today.

EH was offered 15% royalty on first 4,000, 17.5% on next 4,000 and 20% thereafter. When the book was at corrected page proof stage, Morrow's editor (A.22*b*) sent in a list of 35 queries which NS considered apposite and recalled the proofs from the printers. Why the following were not changed is difficult to understand:

p.84 l.7f. esperiments *not changed* to experiments 33b
p.127 l.11f. took over it *not changed* to took it over
p.231 l.21 *should be* Brazzaville not Stanleyville
p.232 l.11 & 14 *should be* Brazzaville
p.243 l.17–18 *should be* Brazzaville and French authorities
See A.22(*b*) for further textual changes.

EH's letter of 21 April 1995 to RC throws interesting light on the ending and the Brazzaville question: 'I remember that I did set the scene in French Territory – the character of Clauser was of course roughly derived from Schweitzer – so should have called the capital Brazzaville from the start, and not brought in Stanleyville and the Belgians. Norah suggested quite a lot of changes to the book, including the end: in my original version, the villain, Roland, wasn't killed by a rhino, he escaped and vanished into the depths of central Africa. Norah said this was all wrong, and the villain must be finished off in any respectable thriller, so I brought in the rhino and several reviewers picked on this as a false note, a *deus ex machina* brought in to round off the story. I still think my ending was better if less dramatic, but expect she was right'.

Reviews: Listener, 16 May 1957
   New Statesman, 18 May 1957
   Manchester Guardian, 21 May 1957
   TLS, 31 May 1957

Translation: German, *Der Felsen von Bamili*, Tr. Friedrich A. Hofschuster. Bastei-Lubbe, 1989 (paperback)

(b)   First American edition (1957)

THE | *Red Rock Wilderness* | [2 type orns. facing] | By Elspeth Huxley | The red rock wilderness | shall be my dwelling place... | Sidney Keyes | WILLIAM MORROW & COMPANY | New York. 1957

Collation: signatures not established; 288p. 200 × 135mm.

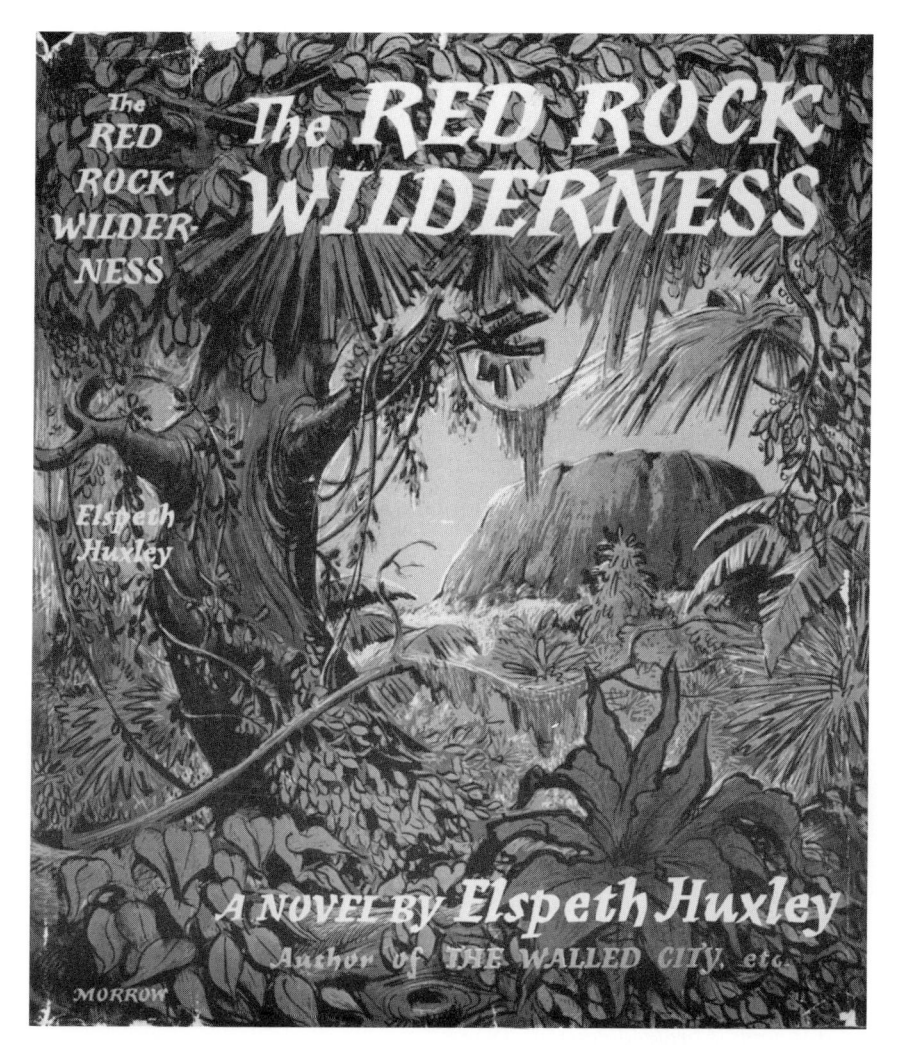

XII. *The dust-jacket of the first US edition of* The Red Rock Wilderness *published by William Morrow & Company in 1957.*

52   A   Books and pamphlets

Contents: p.[1] ht. [2] blank [3] tp. [4] "© 1957 by Elspeth Huxley. | [acknowledgement to Routledge Kegan Paul] | All rights reserved. | Printed in the United States of America" [5] contents [6] blank 7–8 introduction 9–193 text [194] blank 195–231 text [232 blank 233–288 postscript.

Binding case: moderate yellow|green cloth (120); spine in dark red cloth (16), lettered in silver, "THE | Red Rock | Wilderness | [2 orns.] | Elspeth | Huxley | MORROW".

Dust-jacket: pictorial over UC and spine, large rock in background, large tree in foreground, lettered in white; on UF, $3.75, jacket by Charles Geer; LC, 4 paragraphs from introduction to book.

Copies seen: photocopies and information by letter.

Notes: Published 12 June 1957 at $3.75.

John G. Willey (President of Morrow) decided on different d.j. so that title could be better explained to American readers: this was designed by Charles Geer. In his letter to NS he pointed out that if C&W's edition came out before Morrow's he would have to take out *ad interim* copyright in USA, which in effect gave the book 5 years copyright protection in USA.

Morrow's editor who had shown greater skills than had C&W's in spotting inconsistencies and mistakes, and in putting them right, did not follow in this edition her own advice on the following: 'We'd like to change Stanleyville (p.231 l.21) to Brazzaville here, as author has done on p.233 l.7f. It is the French authorities they are worried about throughout, not the Belgian, and we feel it would be clearer if the choice all through here was between Juba and Brazzaville'.

All references to Belgian authorities were changed to French but references to place were altered to Stanleyville which should have been Brazzaville: pp.261 l.2, p.262 l.16, p.263 l.4–13f., p.274 l.15.

Reviews: *New York Herald Tribune,* 23 June 1957
Time, 24 June 1957
New York Times, 28 June 1957 (Orville Prescott)
Boston Globe, 30 June 1957
New Yorker, 13 July 1957

(c)   Odhams Abridged edition (1958)

ODHAMS | CONDENSED BOOKS | [short swelled rule] SIXTEENTH SERIES [short swelled rule] | The Red Rock Wilderness | ELSPETH HUXLEY | [orn.] | The Tichborne Claimant | DOUGLAS WOODRUFF | [orn.] | Hurrah! the Flag | PHILIP MACKIE | [orn.] | Inside the C.I.D. | EX-CHIEF SUPERINTENDENT BEVERIDGE | [device] | ODHAMS PRESS LIMITED | LONG ACRE, LONDON

Collation: A–M in 16s; 384p. 182 × 120mm.

Contents: p.[1] ht. [2] blank [3] tp. [4] "*The condensations in this volume | appear by special arrangement with | the holders of the copyrights concerned | and may not*

be reproduced either whole | or in part . . . "MADE AND PRINTED IN GREAT BRITAIN | AT THE VILLAFIELD PRESS, BISHOPBRIGGS, GLASGOW" [5] contents [6] blank [7] section title, "THE RED ROCK WILDERNESS" [8] biography of EH [9] introduction, signed, Duncan Colquhoun [10] blank 11–98 text 99–384 text of other works in vol.

Binding case: bluish green imitation cloth (164); on UC, blind-stamped device as on tp.; spine lettered in gold, ODHAMS | CONDENSED | BOOKS", 4 titles in cut-out dark green panels, at foot "16TH [device] SERIES".

Dust-jacket: not seen.

Copies seen: BL

Notes: for details see A.22(*a*)

(d) First paperback issue (1969)

THE RED ROCK | WILDERNESS | ELSPETH HUXLEY | [at foot: device] | HODDER PAPERBACKS

Collation: no signature marks; 254,[255–256]p. 178 × 112mm.

Contents: as in 1957 edition save, on p.[4] "HODDER PAPERBACK EDITION 1969 | Made and printed in Great Britain | for Hodder Paperbacks Ltd., | St. Paul's House, Warwick Lane, London, E.C.4, | by Richard Clay (The Chaucer Press), Ltd, | Bungay, Suffolk".

Wrappers: pictorial; spine no.4350; on LW, publishers' blurb; quotes from 4 reviews, United Kingdom: 6/-.

Copies seen: EH

Notes: Published 16 June 1969 at 6s. Print quantity between 10–15,000 but exact number not known. The setting was taken from A.22(*a*).

A.23 NO EASY WAY   1957

First edition (1957)

NO EASY WAY | By | ELSPETH HUXLEY | A HISTORY OF THE | KENYA FARMERS' ASSOCIATON | AND | UNGA LIMITED

Collation: no signature marks; xi, [xii–xiv],225,[226]p. 223 × 135mm.

Contents: p.[i] ht. [ii] *By the same Author*: 14 titles [iii] tp. [iv] at foot: "PRINTED IN KENYA BY EAST AFRICAN STANDARD LTD NAIROBI" v foreword, signed: Michael Blundell [vi] blank vii–x author's note xi contents [xii] blank [xiii] list of illustrations [xiv] blank [1]–225 text [226] blank.

Note on illustrations: identical end-paper maps, black with white on green background; portraits and illustrations on inserted plates.

54   A   Books and pamphlets

Binding case: yellow/brown cloth (87), lettered in blue on UC, "NO EASY | WAY | By ELSPETH HUXLEY", and on spine in blue, "NO | EASY | WAY".

Dust-jacket: pictorial, black with white on green background, lettered in white over both covers and spine; on UF, Shs.21/-.

Copies seen: RC

Notes: Published in June 1957 by the East African Standard at 21 shillings. It was to have been in association with Oliver and Boyd in the UK but this was thought to infringe EH's option agreement with C&W who at a later stage, decided against their own involvement in the book. It was therefore distributed in the UK by the London office of the East African Standard to whom were sent 200 copies: the total print quantity is not known. Index was done by Terence H. O'Brien.

This book was commissioned by the Kenya Farmers' Association: the title was the winning entry from 600 sent in.

A.24   THE FLAME TREES OF THIKA   1959

(a) First edition (1959)

THE | FLAME TREES | OF THIKA | *Memories of an African Childhood* | Elspeth Huxley | [at foot] 1959 | CHATTO & WINDUS | LONDON

Collation: 1–9 in 16s; 288p. 215 × 132mm.

Contents: p.[1] "*By the same Author*": 16 titles [2] frontispiece [3] tp. [4] PUBLISHED BY | CHATTO AND | WINDUS LTD | 42 WILLIAM IV STREET | LONDON WC2 | * | CLARKE, IRWIN & CO LTD | TORONTO | *To the images | of whom Robin and Tilly are reflections, | and the ghosts who sleep at Thika*" | at foot: "© ELSPETH HUXLEY 1959 | PRINTED IN GREAT BRITAIN BY | EBENEZER BAYLIS AND SON LTD | WORCESTER AND LONDON 5–288 text.

Note on illustrations: frontispiece signed: Kinsey.

Binding case: olive green Linson (126), gold-lettered on spine, "*The | Flame | Trees | of Thika* | [dec.rule] | ELSPETH HUXLEY | [at foot] CHATTO | & | WINDUS".

Dust-jacket: design over UC and spine of flowers and foliage in red, green and yellow on a pink ground by Rosemary Seligman; lettered in olive green; on UF, Book Society Choice, blurb, 16s net.; on LC, Also by Elspeth Huxley: 5 titles; on LF, Chatto address.

Paper: Antique wove.

Copies seen: EH

Notes: Published 2 March 1959 at 16s jointly with the Book Society in edition of 23,351 copies of which 10,050 had joint imprints on title page: of the remaining 13,301, 2,650/2,500 were sold to Morrow as f. and c. sheets with endpapers (A.24b) and 10,651 had C&W imprint only: Boots bought 1,000 in glazed dark blue linson binding and Blunt 252/250 f. and c. sheets. 8,750 copies were banded in black on vivid yellow 'Book Society Choice'. Second impression 5 June 1959 (6,133); third impression 11 October 1959 (3,009) when prelims were corrected: fourth impression 24 November 1959 (2,996 copies of which 1,497 were bound in December 1959, 990 March 1960 and 509 December 1961): fifth impression printed at 18s. in 1962 with new d.j. by John Woodcock (3,275): sixth impression July 1980 (1,049): seventh impression July 1982 (1,611 copies of which 602 went to Readers Union / Nationwide Book Club as their August 1982 and Spring 1983 Choices priced at £6.90 for members).

In second quarter of 1960 the Reprint Society took 78,000 as the World Book Choice for the month, and by August, 69,157 copies had been sold.

From the start there was some ambiguity about the classification of the book: a subtitle was introduced as 'A Fictional Autobiography' and finally became 'Memories of an African Childhood.' EH was against illustrations as suggesting non-fiction but finally agreed to a frontispiece by Joan Fryer (spelt in their correspondence as Friar). EH informed Morrow (A.24b) that book is 'classified under General Books, though not wholly non-fiction'. White Lion Publishers offset an edition in the region of 11,000 in 1977 for their readers. BBC Woman's Hour serialised the book in the Light Programme read by Fay Compton, from 4 to 8 May 1959 (D.212). EH interviewed on Schools Programme on Radio 4 regarding Christian Focus 14 June 1968 (D.287). From 27 February to 10 March 1978, BBC Radio 4 serialised it again, abridged by P. M. Wilson on Story Time in ten solo voice recordings by Virginia McKenna of 25 minutes each (D.296). In Autumn 1981 Thames TV produced seven one-hour instalments from a film scripted by John Hawkesworth (of Euston Films, the originator of the *Upstairs Downstairs* series) directed by Chris Neame, starring Hayley Mills as Tilly, Holly Aird as EH and David Robb as Robin (D.303). The great success of this film in UK was followed by its appearance in Mobil Masterpiece Theater, introduced by Alistair Cooke (A.22(*b*)), and subsequently in many other countries (D.310).

The success of the film on all sides revitalised the book, resulting in many paperback impressions A.24(*c*) and (*d*).

F.A. Thorpe published a Large Print edition in June 1983 at £6.95 in edition of 2,750 copies. The Australian Library for the Blind were given recording rights in 1982, read by Barbara Huxtable. Reader's Digest published a condensed version, illustrated by Ted Lewin, in April 1985 A.24(*g*).

Reviews: *Times,* 5 March 1959 (Laurens van der Post)
Listener, 12 March 1959 (Philip Mason)
TLS, 13 March 1959
New Statesman, 21 March 1959
Manchester Guardian, 3 April 1959
Sunday Times, 19 April 1959
Observer, ndk (William Plomer)
Illustrated London News, ndk (Sir Charles Petrie)

Translations: Danish, *Flammetræerne I Thika* tr. Annelise Schønnemann (Copenhagen), Lindhardt og Ringhof, 1983
Finnish, *Liekkipuiden Varjossa,* tr. by Kylliki Villa, (Helsinki), Otava, 1982
French: *Les pionniers du Kenya* tr. Geneviève de la Gorce (Paris): Mercure de France, 1965

German, *Die Flammenbäume von Thika* tr. F. A. Hofschuster, Bastei-Lubbe 1988
Norwegian, *Flammetræerne I Thika* tr. Arne Hem (Oslo), Cesam Media 1990

(b) First American issue (1959)

Title: as in UK edition save, "[at foot] WILLIAM MORROW AND COMPANY | NEW YORK"

Collation: as in UK edition save signature marks omitted. 212 × 142mm.

Contents: as in UK edition save, on p.4 Chatto and Baylis omitted and replaced by, "© ELSPETH HUXLEY 1959 | ALL RIGHTS RESERVED | Printed in the United States of America".

Binding case: reddish-orange cloth (37). white-tooled spine, "Elspeth | Huxley | [dec. rule] | THE | FLAME | TREES | OF | THIKA | [dec. rule] | MORROW".

Dust-jacket: red, white and green lettering on black ground, a red and white flower and green leaves; on UF, jacket by H. Lawrence Hoffman, blurb; on LF, English reviews by Laurens van der Post, John Godden, William Plomer, Philip Mason.

Copies seen: Tiptree, HRHRC. Although the copy described was C&W's file copy, it is not certain that this is the first American issue as the book is described as being printed in the USA, not in the UK: the copy in the HRHRC Library also has 'Printed in the USA'.

Notes: Published on 26 August 1959 at $4.00 in printing of 2,500 copies imported from C&W as 2,750 f. and c. sheets and bound in USA with new d.j. by H. Lawrence Hoffman; this small order reflected JGW's initial lack of enthusiasm. By 6 August Morrow had reprinted 3,000 copies having photographed C&W's edition for £52 (20% of original setting cost): in September 1959, further 4,000 were printed making 9,750 copies – US Army Libraries took 800. JGW reported excellent reviews particularly a long lead-review in *New Yorker*.

Christian Herald made it their March 1960 selection for Family Bookshelf, for which they guaranteed a payment of $3,000 or 20,000 copies at 15c: Doubleday bought it for September 1961 Selection in their Reviewers' Choice Book Club, at advance of $1,800 against royalties of 12c per copy. Both companies asked for Canadian market which was agreed by C&W's agent, Clarke Irwin: up until then that market had been tightly held by British publishers as part of their traditional territory and was therefore highly prized by American publishers.

John Hawkesworth's film was shown on Public Broadcasting System in Mobil Masterpiece Theater from 3 January to 14 February 1982 in seven episodes D.310; repeated 14 August to 25 September 1983 and episode 3 only, 20 January 1991. This success, followed by many showings in other US TV networks prompted renewed interest and Literary Guild of America, a Doubleday company, bought exclusive book club rights for 5 years in USA and non-exclusive in Canada, as their Alternative joint-Selections for August 1982 (this included *The Mottled Lizard* A.26). Both books were reproduced from C&W's film and manufactured in USA (plus Thames TV stills and C&W's jacket) for members and as advertised in their Bulletin

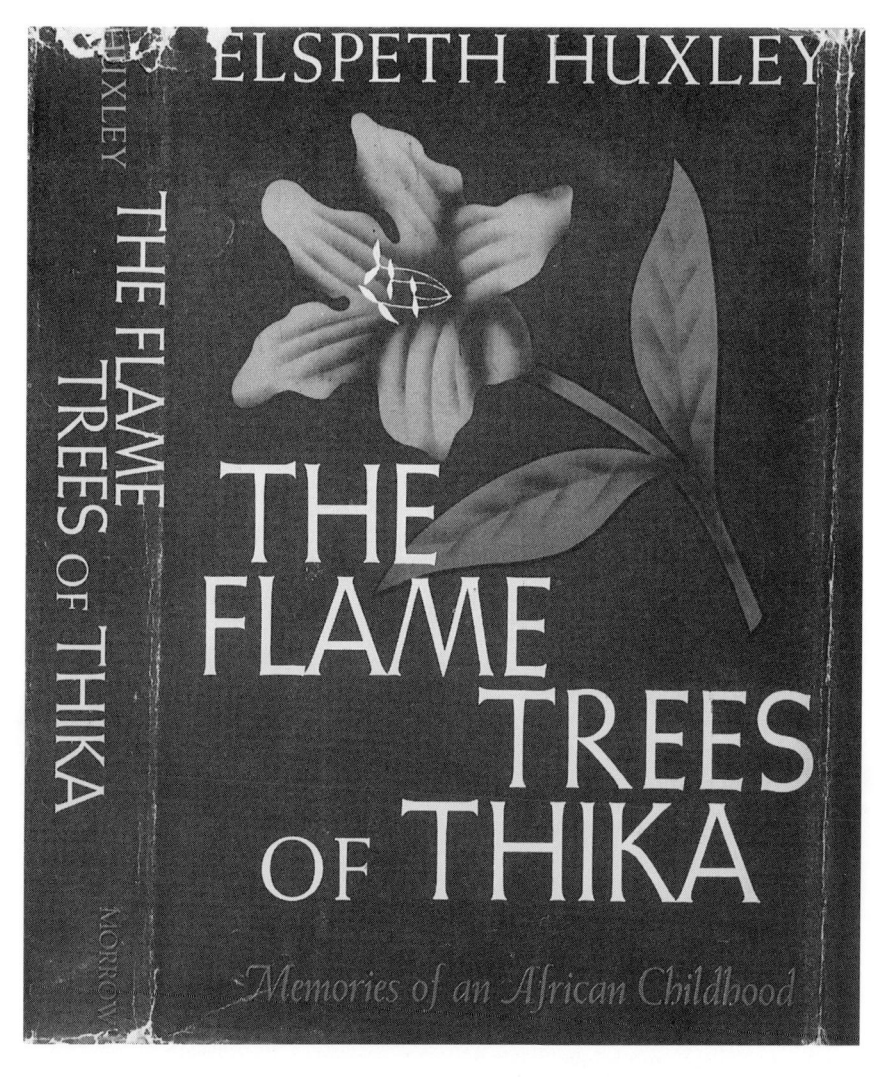

XIII. *The dust-jacket of the first US edition of* The Flame Trees of Thika *reset and published by William Morrow & Company in their Apollo series.*

58   A   Books and pamphlets

$33.90 for non-members (this price must have been incorrect): 2,689 were remaindered in 1984.

Rights reverted from Morrow on 26 June 1978 and C&W used Merrimack Book Service (USA), who took copies on consignment and published at $19.95 in 1982.

Released by Books on Tape Inc. in January 1984 at $48.

Reviews: New York Times, 13 September 1959 (Nadine Gordimer)
Christian Science Monitor, 22 September 1959
Saturday Review, 26 September 1959 (Mary Renault)
New Yorker, 3 October 1959
Boston Globe, 11 October 1959
New York Herald Tribune, 19 December 1959 (Naomi Bliven)
Atlantic Monthly, ndk (Charles Rolo)

(c)   First English paperback edition (1962)

Elspeth Huxley | THE FLAME TREES | OF THIKA | Memories of an African Childhood | [at foot, Penguin device] PENGUIN BOOKS | IN ASSOCIATION WITH | CHATTO & WINDUS

Collation: no signature marks; 280,[281–282]p. 196 × 127mm.

Contents: p.[1] brief biography of EH [2] blank [3] tp. [4] Penguin Books addresses; "Published in Penguin Books 1962 | 20 . . . Printed in England by Clay Ltd, St Ives plc, set in Monotype Plantin . . ." [5] dedication [6] blank 7–280,[281] text [282] blank, followed by 6pp of Penguin adverts.

Wrappers: illustration by Francesca Pelizzoli.

Copies seen: EH

Notes: Published in April 1962 at 5s in association with Chatto & Windus who offered 7.5% royalty on 3s 6d (became 5s) for a five year licence with advance of £400, NS explaining to EH in letter of 18 November 1959 that 'as Chatto is a member of the Penguin Publication Group we publish jointly with Allen Lane and take a publishing profit, so we offer you 7.5% intact.'

This Group Scheme started in 1948 and then consisted of C&W, Faber, Hamish Hamilton, Heinemann and Michael Joseph; it allowed Penguin early access to important authors and books.

Penguin asked if they could sell their paperbacks to library suppliers – to be rebound in hardback – and NS not surprisingly refused. Canada was not included until 1967.

Penguin reprinted 1962, 1963 at 5s, 1967, 28 February 1974 at 40p with African child on cover (15,000 Australia taking 1,500), 31 March 1977 at 80p (11,000), June 1980 at £1.25 (7,500), August 1981 with Hayley Mills and Holly Aird on Thames TV cover (40,000, Australia taking 600) September 1981 (15,000, Canada taking 2,500, New Zealand 1,500), February 1982 at £1.50 (40,000 of which 30,000 were exported to Viking Penguin A.24(f). In April 1982 (8,000 printed in Australia at $4.95) October 1982 (7,000 printed in Australia) May 1983 at £1.95 (10,000), November 1983 at £2.25 (10,000), December 1983 (5,000 printed in

Australia), July 1985 at £2.95 (10,000), August 1988 at £3.99 (14,000, of which Viking took 5,000 and South Africa 500), March 1989 at £4.50 (10,000, of which Viking took 3,000), March 1990 at £4.95 (10,000, Viking taking 2,000), June 1991 (10,000, Viking taking 1,024), March 1993 at £5.99 (5,000, Viking 1,500), January 1994 at £6.99 (6,000, Viking 1,500), May 1995 (4,000, Viking 1,500)

In 1986 Penguin UK had renewed their 5 year licence with advance of £10,000 against flat 10% royalty.

(d) First American edition (1964)

Title: as in 1st American issue

Collation: no signature marks; 264p. 208 × 137mm.

Contents: p.[1] blank [2] frontispiece [3] tp. [4] dedication; at foot "© ELSPETH HUXLEY 1959 | ALL RIGHTS RESERVED | Printed in the United States of America | [4 full points]" [5]–264 text.

Binding case: pinkish-red balacron (15), quarter bound in grey imitation cloth; spine lettering as in 1st American issue but in red.

Dust-jacket: as in 1st American issue but spine lettering colour and reviews on flaps changed: UF, Orville Prescott, *New York Times*; LF, Naomi Bliven, *The New Yorker*; Stuart Cloete.

Copies seen: RC

Notes: Published in March 1964 at $1.95. Their market included Canada. Morrow offered 5% of retail to 15,000 and 6% thereafter for rights to publish in their Apollo series. This edition contains no reference to the year of publication nor to having been included in the Apollo series, and no Library of Congress Catalog Card number is quoted. This edition was reset.

(e) First American paperback edition (1966)

THE FLAME TREES | OF THIKA | Memories of an African Childhood | ELSPETH HUXLEY | [at foot] PYRAMID BOOKS [device] NEW YORK

Collation: no signature marks; 318,[319–320]p. 180 × 112mm.

Contents: p.[1] extracts from 3 American reviews [2] "*Pyramid | Worlds of Discovery | Books*": 5 titles [3] tp. [4] dedication; "A Pyramid Book | Published by arrangement with William Morrow & Co. Inc. | Morrow & Company edition published August, 1959 | Pyramid edition published August, 1966 | . . . Printed in the United States of America | Pyramid Books . . . | 444 Madison Avenue, New York, New York 10022, U.S.A." 5–318 text [319–320] Pyramid adverts. and order page.

Wrappers: pictorial by J. Schoenherr; UW, Pyramid T-1481; 75c.; LW, blurb and brief biography (variant: on UW, quote from *The Atlantic*; on LW, different quotes).

60   A   Books and pamphlets

Copies seen: EH, Tiptree

Notes: Published August 1966 in Pyramid Books at 75c per copy: advance of $1,250 was paid. Reprinted April 1973 at 95c with change to cover.

(f)   Second American paperback issue (1982)

Elspeth Huxley | THE FLAME TREES | OF THIKA| Memories of an African Childhood | [at foot: Penguin device] | PENGUIN BOOKS

Collation: no signature marks; 280,[281–287]p. 180 × 110mm.

Contents: p.[1] "PENGUIN BOOKS | THE FLAME TREES OF THIKA" | [note on author, 18 lines] [2] blank [3] tp. [4] Penguin addresses ... Published in Penguin Books 1961 | Reprinted 1963, 1967, 1974, 1977, 1980, 1981 (twice), | 1982 | Copyright © Elspeth Huxley 1959 | All rights reserved | Printed in the United States of America by | George Banta Co. Inc., Harrisonburg, Virginia | Set in Monotype Plantin | ..." [5] dedication [6] blank 7–280, [281] text [282] blank [283] Penguin addresses, United States, Canada, UK [284–287] blanks.

Wrappers: cover designed by Neil Stuart, cover painting by Richard Mantel | Push Pin; UC headed "NOW A MOBIL MASTERPIECE | THEATRE PRESENTATION"; on LC, blurb and note on Mobil Masterpiece Theatre drama of the book on PBS by WGBH-TV, Boston.

Copies seen: EH

Notes: Viking Penguin New York published in February 1982 at $3.95 importing 30,000 copies from Penguin UK to tie in with PBS screening of Hawkesworth film (D308): cover had at head 'Now a Mobil Masterpiece Theater Presentation' and at foot 'She left the misty shores of England for an Eden in Africa'. Reprinted February 1982 (10,000), December 1983 (7,500), October 1984 (8,000), May 1986 at $4.95 (7,000), November 1986 (7,500), March 1987 (8,000). For subsequent imports from UK see A.24 *(c)*.

Viking Penguin had offered $4,000 against royalties of 7.5% to 15,000 and 10% thereafter.

(g)   Large Print edition (1983)

ELSPETH HUXLEY | [swelled rule] | THE | FLAME TREES | OF THIKA | Memories of an African Childhood | *Complete and Unabridged* | [Castle device] | ULVERSCROFT | Leicester

Collation: FTT1–35 in 8s; [8],546,[547–552]p. 205 × 130mm.

Contents: p.[1] 8-line poem by Janice James [2] blank [3] blurb [4] frontispiece [5] tp [6] "First published 1959 by | Chatto and Windus Ltd. | London | First Large Print Edition | published June 1983 | by arrangement with | Chatto & Windus Ltd. | London | © Elspeth Huxley 1959 | All rights reserved" | British Library CIP data | "Published by | F.A. Thorpe (Publishing) Ltd. | Anstey, Leicestershire | Printed and bound in Great Britain by | T.J.Press (Padstow) Ltd., Padstow, Cornwall" [7] dedication [8] blank 1–[547] text [548–552] adverts. and lists of Ulverscroft books.

Binding case: green laminated boards (141) with white band; colour picture on UC of an African driving cattle, nests in trees in background.

Dust-jacket: none.

Copies seen: Hants CL

Note: Published in June 1983 at £6.95 in edition of 2,750 copies.

(h) Reader's Digest abridged edition (1985)

READER'S DIGEST | [swelled rule] | CONDENSED BOOKS | [three titles: Carter's Castle by Wilbur Wright ... The great husky race by José Giovanni, The red fox by Anthony Hyde, then:] THE FLAME TREES | OF THIKA | by Elspeth Huxley | PUBLISHED BY CHATTO & WINDUS, LONDON

Collation: (text of work by EH) p.[400]–509[510–512].

Contents: p.[400–401] double-page pictorial tp, on the R: "The Flame Trees | of Thika | A CONDENSATION OF THE BOOK BY | ELSPETH HUXLEY | ILLUSTRATED BY TED LEWIN" 402 publisher's summary 403–509,[510] text [511] brief biography and photograph of EH on set of Thames Television production on location with Holly Aird who played the part of the young Elspeth [512] Reader's Digest imprint and copyright information.

Copies seen: Hants CL

Notes: Published in November 1985 on pp.403–510 in edition of 100,000 for the UK market; separately published in Australia in September 1986. It was not published in USA. Illustrated by Ted Lewin.

(i) First English illustrated edition (1987)

THE FLAME TREES | OF THIKA | MEMORIES OF AN | AFRICAN CHILDHOOD | WITH A NEW INTRODUCTION BY THE AUTHOR | ELSPETH HUXLEY | ILLUSTRATED BY FRANCESCA PELIZZOLI | [putti device] | CHATTO & WINDUS | LONDON

Collation: no signature marks, 287,[288]p. 240 × 190mm.

Contents: p.[1] ht. and illustration [2] frontispiece [3] tp. [4] "This edition published in 1987 by | Chatto & Windus Limited | ... | Designed and produced by Shuckburgh Reynolds Limited | 289 Westbourne Grove, London W11 2QA"; copyrights, British Library CIP data | "Designer: David Fordham | Assistant designer: Carol McLeeve | Animal silhouettes by Philip Hood | Picture research by Jenny de Gex | Photographs kindly supplied by Elspeth Huxley ... | Typeset by SX Composing Ltd. | Colour separation by Aragon Reproductions Ltd., London |

Printed in Spain by Graficas Estella, Estella Navarra" [5] contents [6] map 7–9 introduction signed Elspeth Huxley 1987 [10] blank 11–287,[288] text.

Binding case: grey cloth (266), gold-lettered down spine, "THE FLAME TREES OF THIKA ELSPETH HUXLEY [orn.]".

Dust-jacket: design by David Fordham; painting by Francesca Pelizzoli; decorative illustration by Philip Hood.

Paper: Coated Cartridge

Copies seen: EH

Notes: Published 29 October 1987 at £14.95 in edition of 6,000 copies. This book was completely reset, with a new Introduction by EH who also wrote the captions for all the illustrations. It contained 63 colour illustrations by Francesca Pelizzoli and 84 black and white photographs, many taken by EH. The book was designed and produced by Shuckburgh Reynolds Ltd.

Reader's Digest had made Francesca Pelizzoli's illustrations one of their 1985 and 1986 Choices in their Art Competition for Young Illustrators in conjunction with the Association of Illustrators.

Readers Union took 100, Red House 500 and Doubleday 1,000 for Australia and New Zealand.

(j) First American illustrated issue (1987) – not seen

Notes: Published by Weidenfeld of New York in 1987 and produced by Shuckburgh Reynolds in edition of 7,500 plus 5,000 for the Book of the Month Club and 2,500 to Barnes and Noble. The d.j. was identical to A.24(*i*) except that the background colour is pale yellow as compared to grey; the binding is black in contrast to C&W's grey imitation cloth.

A.25 A NEW EARTH   1960

(a) First edition (1960)

A | NEW EARTH | An Experiment in Colonialism | [swelled rule] | ELSPETH HUXLEY | [at foot] 1960 | CHATTO & WINDUS | LONDON

Collation: A–T in 8s [Q omitted]; 288p. 215 × 135mm.

Contents: p.[1] ht. [2] "*By the same author*": 16 titles [3] tp [4] "*Published by* | Chatto & Windus Ltd | ... | Clarke, Irwin & Co Ltd | Toronto | [at foot] "© ELSPETH HUXLEY 1960 | Printed in Great Britain by | Ebenezer Baylis & Son, Ltd. | The Trinity Press | Worcester and London" [5] contents [6–8] list of illustrations 9–288 text.

Note on illustrations: 32p. of plates; 3 maps (1 folded).

Binding case: bluish-green cloth (164); gold-lettered down spine, "A NEW | EARTH

| * | *An Experiment | in Colonialism* | * | ELSPETH | HUXLEY | [horizontal at foot] CHATTO | & WINDUS".

Dust-jacket: photograph of African boy and calf, design by Ralph Mabey; lettered in white and black on yellow, white and orange background; on UF, blurb, 30s NET; on LC, 5 extracts of reviews of *The Flame Trees of Thika*; LF, Chatto address.

Paper: Antique wove.

Copies seen: RC

Notes: Published 30 June 1960 at 30s net in edition of 9,936 copies of which there were 8 sets of unbound proofs, and 93 bound page proofs with illustrations for sales purposes. By 19 September 1960, 7,000 copies had been sold. The Government of Kenya bought 270 copies.

In April 1961 reprinted 3,500 copies of which 1,500 were kept as sheets which were pulped in 1966. Morrow ordered copies three times from C&W, see A25(*b*).

EH received 15% on first 4,000, 17.5% on next 4,000 and 20% thereafter, with an advance of £500.

The *Geographical Magazine* published a condensed version of one chapter in their August 1959 number, pp.170–5 entitled 'African Water Engineers' (C.482) According to the C&W files *The Reporter* in USA serialised a small extract in 1960 but it has not been possible to corroborate this.

Reviews: *Times*, 30 June 1960
              TLS, 15 July 1960
              Spectator, 15 July 1960
              Manchester Guardian, 5 August 1960
              New Statesman, 17 September 1960
              Observer, ndk (Margery Perham)

(b) First American issue (1960)

A | NEW EARTH | [short swelled rule] | ELSPETH HUXLEY | 1960 | WILLIAM MORROW & COMPANY, INC | NEW YORK

Collation, Contents, and Illustrations: as in UK edition including name of UK printer, with addition of Library of Congress Catalog Card Number.

Binding case: strong bluish-green cloth (160); spine gold-lettered, "A NEW | EARTH | [orn.] | ELSPETH HUXLEY | MORROW".

Dust-jacket: as in UK edition save that Morrow replaces Chatto & Windus on spine; "An experiment in colonialism" is omitted from UC; there are 5 American reviews and 1 UK review in place of 5 UK reviews of *The Flame Trees of Thika*; at foot is "WILLIAM MORROW AND COMPANY INC 425 Park Avenue South, New York, N.Y."; on UF, $6.00, title and author in orange, blurb in black; on LC, the blurb continued with biographical note on EH.

Copies seen: photocopies and information by correspondence.

64   A   Books and pamphlets

Notes: Published by William Morrow 21 September 1960 at $6.00, who bought 2,080/2,000 bound and jacketed copies from the first C&W printing: JGW asked for 'An Experiment in Colonialism' to be deleted from the dust-jacket and the title page of the American copies, as being 'most unselling to our readers', and this was duly done.

In October 1960 Morrow bought 550/500 bound and jacketed copies with cancel title: whether the C&W d.j. was used, history does not reveal. In 1961, 1,000 bound and jacketed copies were bought from C&W's 1961 reprint. Rights reverted to C&W on 7 July 1978.

Reviews: *New York Times,* 25 September 1960
  America, 8 October 1960
  New York Herald Tribune, 9 October 1960
  Library Journal, 1 November 1960
  Christian Science Monitor, 17 November 1961

(c) Second American issue (1973)

Title: as in 1960 American issue save, date omitted and imprint: "[GP monogram] | GREENWOOD PRESS, PUBLISHERS | WESTPORT, CONNECTICUT"

Collation: as in 1960 American issue; 215 × 138mm.

Contents: as in 1960 American issue save, on p.[4] "Originally published in 1960 | by William Morrow & Company, Inc., | New York | Reprinted with the permission | of William Morrow & Company Inc. | First Greenwood Reprinting 1973 | . . . Printed in the United States of America".

Binding case: darkish-green cloth (147), gold-tooled down spine, "HUXLEY | [horizontal rule] | A NEW EARTH | [at foot GP monogram horizontal]".

Dust-jacket: none.

Copies seen: RC

Notes: Greenwood Press published an issue on 25 June 1973 which was offset either from a Morrow or C&W copy.

A.26   THE MOTTLED LIZARD   1962

(a) First edition (1962)

THE | MOTTLED | LIZARD | *By* | Elspeth Huxley | [line drawing of lizard] | [at foot] 1962 | CHATTO & WINDUS | LONDON

Collation: 1–10 in 16s, 11 in 8s; 335,[336]p. 217 × 138mm.

Contents: p.[1] ht. [2] "*By the same author*": 17 titles [3] tp [4] "PUBLISHED BY | CHATTO AND WINDUS LTD ... CLARKE, IRWIN AND CO LTD ... © ELSPETH HUXLEY 1962 | PRINTED IN GREAT BRITAIN | BY EBENEZER BAYLIS AND SON LTD. . . . [5] "For V.G. | who remembers Robin" [6] "Put forth to watch, unschooled, alone, | 'Twixt hostile earth and sky – | The mottled lizard 'neath the stone | Is wiser here than I. | RUDYARD KIPLING" 7–335 text [336] blank.

Binding case: orange cloth (43), gold-tooled down spine, "*The | Mottled | Lizard |* [orn.] | ELSPETH | HUXLEY | [at foot] CHATTO | & | WINDUS" [1982 reprint had bluish-green cloth (164)].

Dust-jacket: on UC and spine, coloured picture of lizard, design by Rosemary Grimble; lettered in green and red on mottled brown background; on UF, blurb, 21s NET; LC, Some opinions of *The flame trees of Thika*, and *A new earth*; on LF, Also by Elspeth Huxley: 3 titles, Chatto address.

Paper: Antique wove

Copies seen: RC

Notes: Published 10 May 1962 at 21s in edition of 16,722 of which 152/150 were sold to Blunt as f. and c. sheets and the rest bound, plus 3,494 sets of sheets: these were considered too expensive to bind in light of demand and 2,500 were pulped in 1970, 344 sold off to BCN in 1973 and 650 were destroyed in a fire.

Reprint Society took 60,000 copies in 1964 which were printed from C&W stereos and sent to Society as folded sheets. Foyle's took 8,000 flat sheets for their Quality Book Club: paper supplied.

EH received from C&W advance of £1,000 against royalties of 15% to 3,000 and 17.5% thereafter (20% royalty had ceased by then). The Hawkesworth film demand necessitated second impression January 1982 at £9.95 (1,022) printed by Redwood Burn and third impression August 1982 (1,036) with new d.j. by Rosemary Grimble.

The two books, *The Flame Trees of Thika* and *The Mottled Lizard*, were originally written as one and submitted to C&W, but NS advised dividing the book in half. EH commented in retrospect that she was surprised that publication of the second half was delayed for three years with a different book (*A New Earth*) published in between, despite the success of *Flame Trees*.

BBC Woman's Hour serialised it in 5 episodes at one guinea per minute from 19 to 27 April 1962, read by Adrienne Corri, abridged by Ben Mason (D.256). John Hawkesworth had first option on film rights, as continuation of *Flame Trees*, but was unable to raise the money to have it filmed.

Reviews: *Times,* 10 May 1962
  Daily Mail, 10 May 1962
  Spectator, 11 May 1962
  Sunday Telegraph, 13 May 1962
  Listener, 17 May 1962 (Lucy Mair)
  Illustrated London News, 19 May 1962 (Sir Charles Petrie)
  New Statesman, 25 May 1962

66   A   Books and pamphlets

Translations: German, *Der Eidechsenfad,* tr. F. A. Hofschuster, Bastei-Lubbe 1988 (paperback)
Finnish, *Pilvien Varjot Akaasioissa,* tr. Kyllikki Villa (Helsinki), Otava, 1982.

(b)   First American edition (1962)

[Double-page spread] On the Edge of the Rift | [L. hand page] MEMORIES OF KENYA | [R. hand page] BY ELSPETH HUXLEY | [L. hand page] *William Morrow and Company* | [R hand page] *New York,* 1962

Collation: no signature marks; [6],409,[410]p. 209 × 138mm.

Contents: p.[1] ht. [2–3] double-page tp. and on p.[2] "*By the same author*": 3 titles [4] "Copyright © 1962 by Elspeth Huxley | Published in Great Britain under | the title, *The Mottled Lizard.*" | Library of Congress no. | "Manufactured in the United States of America | by H.Wolff, New York | designed by Leda Glassman" [5] ht. [6] blank 1–409 text [410] blank.

Binding case: half-bound black paper boards, half-bound reddish-orange cloth (43); lettered across spine in white, "HUXLEY", and in brown, "*On the | Edge | of the | Rift* | [in white] *MORROW*".

Dust-jacket: pictorial UC and spine; lettered in black and white; on UF, $5.95, blurb, jacket by Harvey Kidder; on LC and LF, blurbs.

Copies seen: Tiptree

Notes: Published with a different title *On the Edge of the Rift* on 26 September 1962 at $5.95: print quantity not known. Family Reading Club (affiliated to Literary Guild) made it their December 1962 selection; their entry into Canada was refused as Reprint Society already had rights. After the success of the *Flame Trees* TV film in USA, C&W sold to Literary Guild (a Doubleday company) exclusive book club rights in USA and with non-exclusive entry into Canada for 5 years, as their Alternative Joint Selection in August 1982: 15,000 copies were printed by the Club who photographed the C&W edition.

In 1982 after rights had reverted from Morrow, Merrimack Inc. became C&W's agent in USA for this book, taking copies from C&W's printing on consignment, selling at $19.95: they thereby introduced the original title into the US market.

Released by Books on Tape Inc. in March 1984 at $80 under the title of *The Mottled Lizard.*

Reviews: *Publishers Weekly,* 10 September 1962
Saturday Review, 29 September 1962
New York Times, 29 September 1962
Washington Post, 30 September 1962
New York Herald Tribune, 14 October 1962
Christian Science Monitor, 1 November 1962
Los Angeles Times, 4 November 1962
New Yorker, 8 December 1962

(c) First English paperback edition (1965)

The Mottled | Lizard | ELSPETH HUXLEY | [at foot: device] | A FOUR SQUARE BOOK

Collation: no signature marks; 316,[317–320]p. 180 × 112mm.

Contents: p.[1] ht. and quotes from 3 reviews [2] blank [3] tp. [4] dedication, imprint, "FIRST FOUR SQUARE EDITION 1965 | *Four Square Books are published by The New English Library Limited,* | *from Barnard's Inn, Holborn, London, E.C.1.* | *Made and printed Great Britain by C.Nicholls & Company Ltd.*" 5–316,[317] text [318–319] adverts for Four Square editions [320] blank.

Wrappers: green and brown; on UW, giraffes, 5/-; on spine, no.1262; on LW; blurb.

Copies seen: EH

Notes: New English Library published on 3 June 1965 in Four Square edition at 5s, paying advance of £500 for licence until 1970.

(d) Second English paperback edition (1981)

Elspeth Huxley | THE | MOTTLED LIZARD | [line drawing of lizard] | [at foot, Penguin device] | PENGUIN BOOKS

Collation: no signature marks (perfect binding): 334[335–336] 197 × 127mm.

Contents: p.[1] brief biography of EH [2] blank [3] tp. [4] Penguin addresses, "Published in Penguin Books 1981 | . . . Printed in England by Clays Ltd., St Ives plc. Set in Linotype Plantin . . ." [5] dedication [6] quotation 7–334 text [335–336] adverts for Penguin Books.

Wrappers: cover illustration £1.50 has view from Kilaguni Lodge in Tsavo National Park.

Copies seen: EH

Notes: Published 27 August 1981 at £1.50 in edition of 20,000 of which Penguin Australia took 800, reprinted October 1981 (10,000), November at £1.75, 22,5000 copies of which Canada took 5,000 and Australia 1,000 (see A.26(*e*) for copies to USA), Penguin Australia in February 1982 reprinted 4,000 for their market priced at A$4.95, January 1982, 10,000 see A.26(*e*), August 1982, 8,000 priced at £1.95, December 10,000 at £2.25, June 1983, 10,000 at £2.50, January 1985 at £3.95 8,000 of which Australia took 200, October 1985 8,000 see A.26(*e*) November 1986, 6,000 see A.26(*e*), May 1987, 10,000 see A.26(*e*), May 1988, 6,000 at £4.99, of which Canada took 300 and South Africa 200, March 1990, 5,000 see A.24(*e*) price £5.99, September 1992, 3,500 at £6.99, August 3,000. It seems that these reprints are not specifically referred to on the reverse title pages, see the 1992 reprint.

68   A   Books and pamphlets

(e) First American paperback issue (1982) – see A.26(d)

Notes: Viking Penguin published 14 January 1982 at $3.95 with initial import from Penguin UK of 10,000 copies. Paid to EH advance of $1,250 against royalties of 7.5%/6% to 60,000 and 10%/8% thereafter.

Further imports January, 5,000, February 1983, 3,000, March 1985, 3,000 at $4.95 October 1985, 3,000 at $5.95. November 1986, 3,500, May 1987, 4,000 at $6.95, March 1990, 2,000 at $7.95, since raised to $10.95.

(f) Large Print edition (1983)

ELSPETH HUXLEY | [swelled rule] | THE | MOTTLED LIZARD | *Complete and Unabridged* | [device] | ULVERSCROFT | *Leicester*

Collation: ML1–33 in 8s; [8],506,[507–520]p. 215 × 135mm.

Contents: p.[1] 8-line poem by Janie James [2] blank [3] brief biography of EH [4] "*Books by Elspeth Huxley in the* | *Ulverscroft Large Print Series*": 2 titles [5] tp. [6] "First Large Print Edition | published November 1983 | by arrangement with | Chatto and Windus Ltd., London" | British Library CIP data | "Published by | Thorpe (Publishing) Ltd. | Anstey, Leicestershire | Printed and Bound in Great Britain by | T.J. Press (Padstow) Ltd., Padstow, Cornwall" [7] dedication [8] quotation 1–506,[507] text [508–520] Ulverscroft lists."

Binding case: green laminated boards (141) with white band; coloured picture of lizard on UC.

Copies seen: EH

Notes: Published by F.A. Thorpe in November 1983 at £6.95 in edition of 2,500 copies.

A.27   THE MERRY HIPPO 1963

(a) First edition (1963)

THE | MERRY HIPPO | A Novel by | ELSPETH HUXLEY | [at foot] 1963 | CHATTO & WINDUS | LONDON

Collation: A–Q in 8s; 253,[254–256]p. 197 × 130mm.

Contents: p.[1] plot summary [2] "*By the same Author*": 17 titles [3] tp. [4] "Published by | Chatto & Windus Ltd | ... | Clarke, Irwin & Co Ltd | ... © ELSPETH HUXLEY 1963 | Printed in Great Britain | by Ebenezer Baylis & Son Ltd., ..." [5] author's note [6] blank [7] "The Connor Commission" [8] blank 9–253,[254] text [255–256] blank.

Binding case: bluish-green imitation cloth (164), gold-lettered down spine, THE | MERRY | HIPPO | [leaf orn.] | Elspeth | Huxley | [at foot] CHATTO | & WINDUS".

Dust-jacket: over UC and spine a design of branch, fruit, leaves in red, brown and green on a pale green ground by Rosemary Grimble; lettered in black and red; on UF, blurb, 18s net; LC, Some opinions of *The Flame Trees of Thika, The Mottled Lizard*; LF, Also by Elspeth Huxley: 18 titles, Chatto address.

Paper: Antique wove.

Copies seen: RC, EH

Notes: Published 4 April 1963 at 18s in edition of 7,621 copies of which 303/300 were sold to Blunt as f. and c. sheets, and 85 sets of page proofs were used for sales purposes. Reprinted April 1963 4,470 copies of which 2,470 were bound and 2,000 kept as sheets, pulped in 1966 (1.500) and 1972 (500).

The background to this book was EH's membership of the Monckton Commission on the Central African Federation, when they visited the three territories concerned, then Southern Rhodesia (Zimbabwe), Northern Rhodesia (Zambia) and Nyasaland (Malawi) hearing evidence for and against the Federation (mostly against, and it was subsequently dissolved). 'Most of the characters were invented but that of the Chairman, Lord Monckton, was rather thinly disguised. The book, a crime story set in central Africa, took a somewhat irreverent look at the work of official commissions.' (This is a quote from a letter from EH to RC.)

The title was originally to be 'Shooting Star' but the African agent pointed out that another book had had same title and been a flop.

Editorial cuts were proposed by C. Day Lewis and executed by EH in a week.

In discussion about the advance (final sum not known) EH commented ironically, 'I am amazed by your remarks. Surely you know by now that I have a mind far above money? The question has not polluted my thoughts. Now, however, you have introduced the pollution . . .'

Reviews: TLS, 5 April 1963
New Statesman, 3 May 1963

Translation: German: *Zwischen Magic und Macht* (Stuttgart), Kokhlhammen Verlag 1965 (with 20% cuts agreed by EH)

(b) First American edition (1964) – not seen.

Notes: Published on 8 January 1964 at $3.95 by William Morrow under the full title of *The Incident at the Merry Hippo*, print quantity not known. Rights reverted from Morrow 10 November 1978.

Reviews: New York Times, 12 January 1964
Saturday Review, 29 February 1964
Library Journal, 1 March 1964

(c) First paperback issue (1965)

The Merry Hippo | Elspeth Huxley | [at foot, Penguin device] | Penguin Books | in association with Chatto and Windus

70   A   Books and pamphlets

Collation: no signature marks; 255,[256]p. 180 × 110mm.

Contents: p.[1] "Penguin Book 2321", brief biography of EH [2] blank [3] tp. [4] Penguin addresses; "Published in Penguin Books 1965 ... Richard Clay (The Chaucer Press) Ltd., Bungay, Suffolk. Set in Linotype Baskerville" [5] note by author [6] blank [7] "The Connor Commission" [8] blank 9–255,[256] text.

Wrappers: cover design by John Sewell; on LW, blurb, photograph of EH; on UC, Penguin Crime, 4/-.

Copies seen: RC

Notes: Published 26 August 1965 at 4s. Penguin followed text of C&W's second impression. Advance £350 v. royalties of 7.5%, for period of 5 years from publication. Canadian market for paperback edition was excluded as already sold to Morrow, who do not appear to have utilised it.

A.28   FORKS AND HOPE: AN AFRICAN NOTEBOOK   1964

(a) First edition (1964)

FORKS | AND HOPE | [dec. rule] | AN AFRICAN NOTEBOOK | [dec. rule] | ELSPETH HUXLEY | *Illustrated by Jonathan Kingdon* | [at foot] 1964 | CHATTO & WINDUS | LONDON

Collation: A–I in 16s; xi,[xii],272,[273–276]p. 216 × 136mm.

Contents: p.[1] ht., and *"By Elspeth Huxley"*: 18 titles [2] frontispiece [3] tp. [4] "Published by | Chatto & Windus Ltd ... Clarke, Irwin & Co Ltd | Toronto | ... © ELSPETH HUXLEY 1964 | Printed in Great Britain | by Ebenezer Baylis & Son Ltd ..." v–[ix] contents [x] blank xi author's note [xii] map 1–272 text [273–276] blank.

Note on illustrations: 22 drawings by Jonathan Kingdon and two maps.

Binding case: purplish-blue cloth (197), lettered on spine in gold, "FORKS | AND HOPE | *An* | *African* | *Notebook* | * | ELSPETH HUXLEY | [at foot] CHATTO | & WINDUS".

Dust-jacket: UW and spine design in red and blue on a white ground by Jonathan Kingdon; lettered in white; UF, blurb, 30s net.; LC, Some opinions of *A new earth*: LF, Some opinions of *The flame trees of Thika, The mottled lizard*; Chatto address.

Paper: Esparto antique wove.

Copies seen: RC

Notes: Published 6 February 1964 at 30s in edition of 8,086 of which 140 were bound as page proofs for sales purposes, 151 sets of f. and c. sheets with endpapers sold to Dunn and Wilson, 303 f. and c. sheets to Blunt and 406 were bound in dark blue glazed Linson for Boots. Reprinted 6 February 1964 in 2,030 copies of which 1,104 were bound and 900 left as quires, subsequently remaindered.

C. Day Lewis made certain editorial suggestions which EH followed; jacket and 22 line drawings by Jonathan Kingdon, 2 maps by Denys Baker. EH accepted advance of £1,000 against 15% on first 3,000 and 17.5% thereafter.

NS asked if any material had been published before and EH referred to an article in *Encounter* (C.499) in 1961 and in *Blackwood* (C.536). *Sunday Telegraph* used 2,000–2,500 words in December 1963 and paid £750 for first serial rights (C.550); *Liverpool Daily Post* serialised 20,000 words starting 10 February 1964 and paid £200 for second serial rights (C.557); *Johannesburg Sunday Chronicle* serialised 12,500 words without illustrations in 1964 from 13 September to 4 October in four instalments (C.589). EH was interviewed on Tonight on 11 February 1964 (D.271), and on World of Books 22 February (D.272).

Reviews: *TLS*, 13 February 1964 (Thomas Hinde)
New Statesman, 14 February 1964 (Margery Perham)

(b) First American issue (1964) – not seen.

Notes: Published 24 June 1964 at $5.95 by William Morrow under title *With Forks and Hope*, print quantity not known. Offset from C&W edition except illustrations were originated in USA and d.j. was changed with new title.

According to Chatto correspondence *New York Times Magazine* published extract in 1964 of 2,500 to 3,000 words for $400 but there is no record in their file.

The Globe Book Company published adaptation of an extract in USA and Canada in 1974.

After rights had reverted from Morrow, Merrimack sold C&W stock on consignment with original d.j. and no illustrations at $19.95, in 1982: it is not clear from the correspondence where the copies without illustrations came from.

Reviews: *New York Herald Tribune*, 30 June 1964
Christian Science Monitor, 23 July 1964
Chicago Tribune, 26 July 1964
Saturday Review, 8 August 1964
National Review, 22 September 1964
Library Journal, 15 October 1964

A.29 A MAN FROM NOWHERE   1964

(a) First edition (1964)

A MAN FROM | NOWHERE | A Novel by | Elspeth Huxley | [at foot] 1964 | CHATTO & WINDUS | LONDON

Collation: [A] in 14s, B–I in 16s, K in 14s; 309,[310–312]p. 196 × 128mm.

Contents: p.[1] ht. and synopsis [2] "*By the same author*": 19 titles [3] tp. [4] "Published by | Chatto & Windus Ltd | ... | Clarke, Irwin & Co Ltd ... ©

72 A Books and pamphlets

ELSPETH HUXLEY 1964 | Printed in Great Britain | by Ebenezer Baylis & Son Ltd ... [5] 2nd ht. [6] blank 7–309,[310] text [311–312] blank.

Binding case: olive-green imitation cloth (120) gold-tooled down spine, "*A Man | from | Nowhere | [dec. flourish]* | ELSPETH | HUXLEY | [at foot] CHATTO | & WINDUS".

Dust-jacket: olive-green background; UC lettered in black shadow and black; jacket design by Patricia Davey; UF, blurb, 21s net; LC, notice of Elspeth Huxley's two most recent books; on LF, also by Elspeth Huxley : 12 titles, Chatto address.

Paper: Esparto antique wove.

Copies seen: EH

Notes: Published 11 June 1964 at 21s in edition of 8,852 of which 225/223 f. and c. sheets sold to Holt Jackson, 225/223 to Dunn and Wilson, 225/223 to Blunt: each library supplier used own bindings. In addition 82 page proofs were printed for sales purposes. The C&W copies were bound between 1964–8, as required.

This was the second occasion when EH consulted the Society of Authors about terms offered: as a result she queried the 50/50 split on paperback rights (C&W's special relationship with Penguin had ended by then) and asked for 60% to author and 40% to publisher. She also commented that by their asking for first option on her next book in every contract, she was going to be tied for life to C&W, but then added to NS 'I hasten to add that such bondage is always sweet to me, silken cords and all that, so this is an academic point really, but the theory faintly worries me!'

Peter Calvocoressi wrote to EH on 12 October 1963 suggesting possible libel of Kenyatta on p.277 of the MS as he felt that the character on that page was identifiable with him: this was referred to Rubinstein and Nash, book libel specialists, who saw little likelihood but wanted Kenyatta's name mentioned separately as the Prime Minister, which was done.

Reviews: TLS, 11 June 1964
New Statesman, 12 June 1964

(b) *First American issue (1965) – not seen.*

Notes: Published 10 September 1965 at $4.50 by William Morrow, print quantity not known. Rights reverted from Morrow on 10 November 1978.

Reviews: Library Journal, 15 October 1965
Saturday Review, 23 October 1965
National Review, 16 November 1965

(c) *First English paperback edition (1967)*

A MAN FROM | NOWHERE | Elspeth Huxley | [at foot, device] | HODDER AND STOUGHTON

Collation: A–K in 16s; 320p. 178 × 109mm.

Contents: p.[1] ht [2] "ELSPETH HUXLEY": 19 titles [3] tp. [4] "Hodder Paperback Edition 1967 | Printed in Great Britain for Hodder and | Stoughton Limited, St. Paul's House | Warwick Lane, London, E.C.4 by Cox | and Wyman Limited, London, Fakenham | and Reading . . . 5–320 text.

Wrappers: pictorial UW, Landrover, man with a shotgun, girl's face; spine no. 2871; LW, extracts from 3 reviews, United Kingdom 5/-.

Copies seen: EH

Notes: Published 23 October 1967 at 5s in edition of 10–15,000 – exact quantity not known. Hodder Paperback Division offered £250 against 7.5% royalty and received 3 year licence.

A.30   SUKI: A LITTLE TIGER   1964

(a) First edition (1964)

SUKI | A LITTLE TIGER | Photographed by | LAELIA GOEHR | Text by | ELSPETH HUXLEY | [at foot] CHATTO AND WINDUS | [rule] | LONDON

Collation: no signature marks; 46,[47–48]p. 270 × 229mm.

Contents: p.[1] ht. [2] list of illustrations [3] tp. [4] "Published by | Chatto and Windus Ltd . . . Clarke, Irwin & Co. Ltd . . . "Printed in France | by Intergraphic Ltd" [5] acknowledgements [6] illustration 7–46, [47–48] text.

Binding case: orange imitation cloth (48), gold-lettered down spine, on back cloth panel, "SUKI A Little Tiger ∗ *Laelia GOEHR & Elspeth HUXLEY*" [at foot] C & W".

Dust-jacket: orange and white with photographs on UC (not in text) and on LC (in text), 18s.net.

Copies seen: EH

Notes: Published 22 October 1964 at 18s in edition of 15,380 of which 11,679 were bound, 7,659 being sold to Morrow A.30(*b*). Remaining 3,581 quires were lost in 1968 by the Paris printer, Intergraphic, who had supplied paper, setting, printing and laminating.

EH was interviewed on Tonight BBC1 on 22 October 1964 (D.278)

Reviews: TLS, 26 November 1964
           Woman's Hour, 14 December 1964

(b) First American issue (1964) – not seen.

Notes: Published 25 November 1964 at $3.75 in edition of 7,659 (7,500 paid for) bound and jacketed books with Morrow imprint bought from C&W and sent direct from Intergraphic.

A.31 BACK STREET NEW WORLDS   1964

(a) First edition (1964)

BACK STREET | NEW WORLDS | [dec. rule] | A Look at Immigrants in Britain | [dec. rule] | BY ELSPETH HUXLEY | [at foot] CHATTO AND WINDUS | [rule] | PUNCH

Collation: [A] B–H in 8s; I in 4s; K in 16s; [1–7],8–168p. 195 × 127mm.

Contents: p.[1] ht. [2] *"By the same Author"*: 20 titles [3] tp [4] "Published by | Chatto and Windus Ltd | in association with | Punch | * | Clarke, Irwin & Co. Ltd | Toronto | © Elspeth Huxley 1964 | Printed in Great Britain by The Bradbury Agnew Press Limited" [5] contents [6] blank [7]–9 introduction 11–168 text.

Note on illustrations: on p.[10],21 signed: William Hewison; on p.43,102 signed: Barry Wilkinson; on p.58 signed: Micklewright; on p.71,121 signed: Wegner; on p.154 signed: H.

Binding case: red-pink imitation cloth (15), gold-lettered down spine, "BACK | STREET | NEW | WORLDS | [orn.] | Elspeth | Huxley | CHATTO | & WINDUS | [short rule] | PUNCH".

Dust-jacket: UC, illustration in black and white (as on p.102, reduced); lettered in red, black and blue on a semé pale blue background; on LC, Also by Elspeth Huxley: 6 titles.

Paper: Antique wove.

Copies seen: RC

Notes: Published jointly with *Punch* 12 November 1964 at 21s in edition of 6,029 of which 4,029 copies were bound between 1964–70 and 2,000 quires were remaindered to Murray Sales and Service.

This book was based on 12 articles on immigrants by EH published in *Punch* between 15 January and 1 April 1964 (C.551). EH writes to NS 'nearly all are a bit fuller than the articles themselves, there is an extra section about students and Africans, an introductory note and a bibliography and some appendices'. C&W offered 12.5% royalty split 5% to *Punch* and 7.5% to EH who did not agree as she was not aware that *Punch* had bought the copyright (having paid EH £500 for articles plus £132 travelling expenses). *Punch* finally accepted £150 with royalty of 4%.

Reviews: Times, 12 November 1964
 New Statesman, 27 November 1964
 TLS, 3 December 1964
 Manchester Guardian, 1964 – ndk

(b) First American issue (1965) – not seen.

Notes: Published 5 May 1965 at $4, print quantity not known. Morrow had planned to have an Introduction by Dr Kenneth B. Clarke but it did not materialise; offset from A.31(*a*).

Reviews: Library Journal, 15 March 1965
National Review, 24 August 1965

A.32 BRAVE NEW VICTUALS

(a) First edition (1965)

Brave New Victuals | AN INQUIRY INTO MODERN | FOOD PRODUCTION | By | ELSPETH HUXLEY | *With a Foreword by* | PETER SCOTT | [at foot] 1965 | CHATTO & WINDUS | LONDON

Collation: [A]–K in 8s, L in 6s; 167,[168]p. 196 × 128mm.

Contents: p.[1] ht. [2] "*By the same Author*": 20 titles [3] tp. [4] "Published by | Chatto and Windus Ltd | . . . Clarke, Irwin & Co Ltd . . . © Elspeth Huxley, 1965 | Foreword © Peter Scott, 1965 | Printed in Great Britain by | T.&A.Constable Ltd | Edinburgh" [5] quotations from John Woolman and Ronald Duncan [6] blank [7] contents [8] blank 9–13 author's note [14] blank 15–18 foreword by Peter Scott 19–167,[168] text.

Binding case: green imitation cloth (150), gold-lettered down spine, "Brave | New | Victuals | [orn.] | AN INQUIRY | INTO MODERN | FOOD | PRODUCTION | [orn.] | ELSPETH | HUXLEY | [at foot] Chatto | & Windus".

Dust-jacket: pictorial, a cockerel on a fork-lift truck in red and green on a white ground, design by William Hewison; on UF, blurb, 21s; LC, Also by Elspeth Huxley: 7 title; on LF, 5 titles.

Paper: Fortune Cartridge.

Copies seen: EH

Notes: Published 11 November 1965 at 21s in edition of 5,028 copies (10 lost in flood September 1968).

EH was offered £300 advance against 15% royalty to 10,000 and 17.5% thereafter.

Here's Health serialised the book in 14 monthly instalments starting January 1968 and ending October 1969 (C.648). EH was interviewed in 'On Your Farm' BBC Home Service 13 November 1965 (D.282).

Review: TLS, 1965

(b) First English paperback edition (1967)

Elspeth Huxley | Brave New Victuals | An inquiry into | modern food production | Foreword by Peter Scott | [at foot] A Panther Book

Collation: no signature marks; 125,[126–128]p. 178 × 108mm.

Contents: p.[1] quote from *The Guardian* [2] blank [3] tp. [4] "Panther edition published 1967 | . . . Printed in England by | C. Nicholls & Company Ltd., | The

Philips Park Press, Manchester, | and published by Panther Books Ltd., | 108 Brompton Road, London, S.W.3" [5] quotations [6] blank [7] contents [8] blank 9–11 author's note 12–14 foreword by Peter Scott 15–125 text [126] blank [127–128] Panther list.

Wrappers: pictorial, UW, photograph of a girl in a milking parlour with playing cards; Panther 3/6; spine, Panther Books, 2200; LW, extracts, quotation from review.

Copies seen: EH

Notes: Published in 1967 at 3s 6d. EH received £2,000 advance v. 7.5% royalty.

A.33   THEIR SHINING ELDORADO

(a) First edition (1967)

THEIR SHINING | ELDORADO | [dec. rule] | A Journey through Australia | [dec. rule] | ELSPETH HUXLEY | [at foot] 1967 | CHATTO & WINDUS | LONDON

Collation: A–M in 16s; [i–ii],382p. 215 × 137mm.

Contents: p.[i] ht [ii] "*By the same Author*": 21 titles [1] tp. [2] "Published by | Chatto and Windus Ltd | . . . Clarke, Irwin & Co. Ltd . . . © Elspeth Huxley 1967 | Printed in Great Britain by | Butler & Tanner Ltd . . . [3] "To | Isla and Nevil Stuart | Canberra, 1965" [4] "Their shining Eldorado | Beneath the southern skies . . . | *The Roaring Days* | by HENRY LAWSON" [5] contents [6] acknowledgements [7–8] list of illustrations, maps 9–382 text.

Note on illustrations: 20 plates, each with several illustrations; 7 maps, the last folded; loose erratum slip for p.10, line 8.

Binding case: greenish-blue imitation cloth (172), gold-lettered down spine, "THEIR | SHINING | ELDORADO | *A Journey through* | *AUSTRALIA* | * | Elspeth | Huxley | [at foot] CHATTO | & WINDUS".

Dust-jacket: pictorial across UC, spine and half LC from a painting by Donald Friend, "Explorer surprising a rare bird" in collection of Leslie Walford; lettered in black and white on blue (172); on UF, blurb, 42s net; LF, portrait and biography of EH.

Paper: Book wove.

Copies seen: RC

Notes: Published 11 May 1967 at 42s in an edition of 10,472 bound books plus 2,000 quires which were produced for the Australian market as Arthur Harrap of Australasian Publishing had expressed interest: these were not finally taken up and were pulped in 1972, 408 copies having been 'lost in flood' in C&W warehouse in September 1968.

EH was offered advance of £3,000, 50% of which to be offset against serial rights income.

Hicks Smith, C&W's Australian agent, pointed out an error in caption to Plate 6 as follows: 'The house pictured is not in a NSW county town but is Como, a National Trust property in South Yarra, Melbourne.'

The following erratum slip was inserted: '*Page 10, line 8*, the Australian dollar is worth 8s. in British currency not 7s. 9d.'

EH was interviewed about the book on BBC Home Service 16 May 1967 (D.285): also on Woman's Hour by Marjorie Anderson about her visit to Australia to collect material (D.286).

Reviews: *Times,* 18 May 1967
TLS, 25 May 1967
New Statesman, 7 July 1967

(b) First American edition (1967)

Their Shining | Eldorado: [5 above 4 type orns.] | A JOURNEY THROUGH | AUSTRALIA | [12 above 12 type orns.] | by Elspeth Huxley | WILLIAM MORROW | & COMPANY, INC. | NEW YORK 1967

Collation: signatures not established; 432p. 233 × 155mm.

Contents: p.[1] ht. [2] blank [3] By the same author: 22 titles [4] blank [5] tp. [6] "Copyright © 1967 by Elspeth Huxley" | acknowledgements | all rights reserved, "William Morris and Company, Inc., 425 | Park Avenue South, New York, N.Y.10016 | Printed in the United States of America", Library of Congress nos. [7] dedication [8] a note about the author [9] list of maps and illustrations [10] blank [11] contents [12] blank 13–14 foreword [15] 2nd ht. [16] quotation [17]–411 text 412–415 glossary 416–419 bibliography 420–432 index.

Note on illustrations: 30p. of photographic illustrations, 6 maps, plus 2 colour endpapers map of Australia which is the same as the last folded map in the UK edition.

Binding case: strong orange-yellow cloth (68), spine a strong red cloth (12); lettered on spine, [in white] "Elspeth | Huxley [double rule] | [in gold] THEIR | SHINING | ELDORADO: | A JOURNEY | THROUGH | AUSTRALIA | [double rule] | [in white] MORROW".

Dust-jacket: design on a mustard yellow and light yellow background over a purple base, lettered in back, white and red; on LC, a photograph of EH, biographical note and publisher's note; on UF, $6.95, quotes, blurb; jacket by Harsh-Finegold; LF, quotations, blurb continued, publisher's address.

Copies seen: photocopies and information by letter.

Notes: Published 25 May 1967 at $6.95, print quantity not known. The subtitle from the C&W edition, 'A Journey through Australia' was added both to the d.j. and title page. An edited extract entitled 'A Chicagoan designed Australia's Capital' was published in the *Chicago Tribune,* 10 September 1967 (C.643), and another entitled 'Australia's Very Foreign Fauna' appeared in *Venture* (USA) in November 1967 (C.646).

78   A Books and pamphlets

Released by Books on Tape Inc. in May 1990 at $96.

Reviews: Atlantic, 13 July 1967
Christian Science Monitor, 24 August 1967
Geographical Magazine, September 1967 (Professor A. J. Rose)
National Review, 3 October 1967

A.34   LOVE AMONG THE DAUGHTERS

(a) First edition (1968)

LOVE AMONG | THE DAUGHTERS | By | Elspeth Huxley | [at foot] 1968 | CHATTO & WINDUS | LONDON

Collation: 1–16 in 8s; [1–8],9–255,[256]p. 215 × 132mm.

Contents: p.[1] ht [2] *"By the same Author"*: 22 titles [3] tp. [4] "Published by | Chatto and Windus Ltd | . . . Clarke, Irwin & Co. Ltd . . . © Elspeth Huxley 1968 | Printed in Great Britain | by Ebenezer Baylis and Son Ltd . . . [5] "With love to the surviving daughters | P. and J." [6] blank [7] contents [8] blank 9–255 text [256] blank.

Binding case: greenish-blue imitation cloth (172), gold-tooled down spine, "LOVE | AMONG | THE | DAUGHTERS | [3 short rules] | Elspeth | Huxley | [at foot] CHATTO | & WINDUS".

Dust-jacket: pictorial design on yellow base on UC and spine by William Hewison; lettered in white and brown; on UF, blurb, SBN; LC, reviews of *The Flame Trees of Thika,* and *The Mottled Lizard;* on LF, also by Elspeth Huxley: 12 titles, Chatto address and Mackay, Chatham (printers).

Paper: Bedford antique wove.

Copies seen: RC

Notes: Published 12 September 1968 at 30s in edition of 7,555 of which 151 were sold to Morley Book Co. in f. and c. sheets. Reprinted 27 March 1969 on Foyle's paper (3,000 copies) for Foyle's Quality Book Club and sold at 6s.

Originally entitled *Nathan's Orchard* but changed before publication and agreed with Morrow who had already rejected *All Bitches Fight.*

The Queen published an extract entitled 'At the Thé Dansant' on 11 September 1968 (C.668):

EH was interviewed by Marjorie Anderson on Woman's Hour Radio 2 on 18 September 1968 (D.289) and by Sheridan Morley in Late Night Line-up 12 September 1969 (D.291).

Prunella Scales read 8 instalments on BBC Woman's Hour starting 12 March 1969, approx. 13 minutes each (D.290).

Reviews: Daily Mail, 12 September 1968
Evening Standard, 17 September 1968
Guardian, 20 September 1968
Scotsman, 21 September 1968
Daily Telegraph, 26 September 1968
Punch, 9 October 1968
TLS, 14 November 1968
Irish Times, 3 January 1969

(b) First American edition (1968)

Elspeth Huxley | [thick and thin rules] | *LOVE* | *Among the Daughters:* | *Memories of the Twenties* | *in England and America* | [small device] | William Morrow & Company, Inc. | NEW YORK 1968

Collation: no signature marks; 311,[312–313]p. 209 × 140mm.

Contents: p.[1] ht. [2] blank [3] "*By the same author*": 23 titles [4] blank [5] tp [6] "Copyright © 1968 by Elspeth Huxley | All rights reserved... | Printed in the United States of America." [7] 2nd ht. [8] blank 9–[311] text [312] blank [313] A note about the author.

Binding case: mottled yellow paper covered boards; one third bound green cloth; lettered across top of spine in white "Elspeth | Huxley | [thick and thin yellow rules: down spine in yellow] Love Among the Daughters [thick and thin yellow rules: across spine in white] Morrow | [device]".

Dust-jacket: yellow, lettered in green and red with design of blue petals above and below sub-title; on UF, jacket by Harsh-Finegold, blurb, $5.95; LF, blurb, photo of EH by East African Standard (Newspapers) Ltd.

Copies seen: Tiptree

Notes: Published 19 September 1968 at $5.95, print quantity not known. Morrow had played a major part in the choice of the final title.

Reviews: Library Journal, 8 July 1968
New York Times, 22 September 1968
Christian Science Monitor, 26 September 1968

A.35 THE CHALLENGE OF AFRICA 1971

(a) First edition (1971)

[Double-page pictorial title from picture by Thomas Baines, Livingstone sails up the Shire river, a trumpeting elephant to L. challenging a paddle steamer to R.; at head of R.hand page:] THE CHALLENGE OF AFRICA | BY ELSPETH HUXLEY | [at head of L.hand page:] ALDUS ENCYCLO-PEDIA OF | DISCOVERY AND EXPLORATION | [at foot, AD monogram] Aldus Books London

80   A   Books and pamphlets

Collation: [1–12] in 8s; 191,[192]p. 260 × 189mm.

Contents: p.[1] ht. [2-3] tp [4] list of technical credits, ISBN; "© 1971 Aldus Books Limited, London | First published in the United Kingdom | 1971 by Aldus Books Limited, | 17 Conway Street, London, W.1 | Printed in Yugoslavia by | Mladinska Knjiga, Ljubljana" [5] contents [6–7] list of maps, illustrations 8 map 9–191 text [192] blank.

Note on illustrations: p.190–191 contain a list of picture credits keyed to the layout of the book.

Binding case: quarter-bound in purplish-blue cloth (200) with pictorial laminated paper boards, gold-lettered down spine, "THE CHALLENGE OF AFRICA", horizontal at foot: AD monogram; and on UC, "ALDUS ENCYCLOPEDIA OF | DISCOVERY AND EXPLORATION | THE CHALLENGE | OF AFRICA".

Dust-jacket: none.

Copies seen: EH, RC

Notes: Published in 1971 by Aldus Books Limited, 17 Conway Street, London, a company started by Wolfgang Foges after the break-up of his working relationship with Walter Neurath (A.6). No records exist but it is believed to have been printed in excess of 50,000 copies, and bound by Mladinska Knijga, Ljubljana.

This book was one volume in an 18-volume 'continuity' series entitled the 'Aldus Encyclopaedia of Discovery and Exploration' which was sold in the USA as first American issue by Americana of Chicago and subsequently by Grolier of Danbury, C.T. primarily by mail-order.

In 1973 International Learning Systems Corporation Limited, London, bought an 'edition' with a cancel title page with their name replacing Aldus on the title page and reverse. Otherwise the text and illustrations remained the same: the binding was dark red Linson with a scene of an European explorer with two Africans, blocked on right foot of front cover.

(b) Second American issue (1973) – not seen.

Notes: Published in 1973 by Doubleday, New York as one of three titles under the title of *Africa and Asia: Mapping Two Continents*. The other two titles were *The Heartland of Asia* by Nathalie Ettinga and *Seas of Sand* by Paul Hamilton. This was part of a 5-volume 'History of Discovery and Exploration' which was a repackaging of the original 18-volume series. No publication date, price or print quantity are known; Mladinska Knjiga printed and bound all copies.

(c) Second English issue (1973)

Africa and Asia: | *Mapping Two Continents* | [at head of tp.] A HISTORY OF DISCOVERY AND EXPLORATION | [at foot of tp. AD monogram] Aldus Books/Jupiter Books | London

Collation: no signature marks; 488p. 258 × 190 mm.

Contents: p[1] ht. [2] introduction [3] tp. [4–5] contents: at foot of p.[4], "This edition published in 1973 by | Aldus Books and Jupiter Books, London" | SBN | "Distributed by Jupiter Books | 9–13 Cowcross Street, London EC1M 6DR" [copyright, publisher's and printer's imprint as in 1971 edition; text forms Part Two of the book:] p.[163] Part Two, ht. [164–165] double-page tp. as in 1971; at head of p.[165] "PART TWO | *The Challenge of Africa* | BY ELSPETH HUXLEY" 166 list of illustrations 167 foreword [168–321] text [322] blank.

Binding case: blue imitation cloth (182). gold-blocked on UC with illustration of an explorer with rifle over L. shoulder; gold-lettered spine, [rule] | [interlaced wavy orn.] | [rule] | A | HISTORY | OF | DISCOVERY | AND | EXPLORATION | [rule] | [interlaced wavy rule] | [rule] | [at foot] ALDUS | JUPITER | [rule] | [interlaced wavy orn.] | [rule]".

Dust-jacket: none.

Copies seen: BL

Notes: Published in 1973 by Aldus Books/Jupiter Books at £3.95 in the same form as A.35(*b*) under the title of *Africa and Asia*. Jupiter Books at that time largely concentrated on remainder books. No print quantity known.

Translation: German: *Nach Afrika-und Asien hinein . . . Sonderausg.* (Güterslok), Prisma Verlag 1977.

(d) Reader's Digest issue (1979)

Notes: The *Challenge of Africa* was reprinted with amendments by the Reader's Digest Association. The *Contents* were identical to 35 (a) except: at foot of left hand tp. Aldus imprint *replaced* by 'The Reader's Digest Association Limited, | London'. On p.[4] after the credits, the following was *added* 'This edition published in the UK by Reader's Digest Association Limited, London' and at the foot, 'Reprinted with amendments 1979 | First published in the United Kingdom | 1971 by Aldus Books Ltd. 17 Conway Street, London, W.1. | Printed in Great Britain | by Hunt Barnard Web | Offset Ltd, Aylesbury'.

A.36 THE KINGSLEYS

First edition (1973)

THE | KINGSLEYS | *A Biographical Anthology* | COMPILED BY | ELSPETH HUXLEY | [at foot] *London* | GEORGE ALLEN & UNWIN LTD | RUSKIN HOUSE MUSEUM STREET

Collation: no signature marks; 346p. 215 × 138mm.

Contents: p.[1–2] blank [3] ht. [4] "*Other works in the series*" [6] "First published in 1973"; copyright note; "© Allen & Unwin Ltd, 1973" | ISBN no. | [at foot] "Printed in Great Britain | in 11 pt Plantin, 1 pt leaded | by W.&J. Mackay Limited, Chatham" 7–9 preface [10] blank [11–12] contents [13]–346 text.

82   A   Books and pamphlets

Binding case: red cloth (16), silver-tooled down spine within a frame, "The Kingsleys | A BIOGRAPHICAL ANTHOLOGY | Compiled by ELSPETH HUXLEY | *George Allen & Unwin*".

Dust-jacket: photos on UC of Charles Kingsley, and on LC of Henry Kingsley, courtesy of The Mansell collection, lettered in green; on UF, blurb, Price net £5.50 in UK only; on LF, biographical anthologies, Belloc, Landon.

Copies seen: EH

Notes: Published in 1973 at £5.50 in edition of 2,500 copies (from the memory of the Publisher). Contains extracts from Charles (1819–75), Henry (1830–76) and George (1826–92) Kingsley.

Review: Times, 1973

A.37   LIVINGSTONE AND HIS AFRICAN JOURNEYS   1974

(a) First edition (1974)

LIVINGSTONE | And his African Journeys | Elspeth Huxley | [cartoon of Livingstone holding key in door in front of a map of Africa] | Introduction by Sir Vivian Fuchs | [at foot] Weidenfeld and Nicolson | London

Collation: no signature marks; 244p. 247 × 175mm.

Contents: p.[1] ht. and legend of frontispiece, tp. vignette and endpapers illustrations (identical) [2] portrait of Livingstone by Monson, 1851 [3] tp. [4] "To Charles, Frederica and Jos" | © Elspeth Huxley 1974 . . . *Designed by* Juanita Grout *for* | George Weidenfeld and | Nicolson Limited, | 11 St John's Hill, London SW11 | *Filmset by* | Cox & Wyman Ltd, | London, Fakenham | and Reading | . . . [5] contents 6 acknowledgements 7–9 introduction, signed, "V.E.Fuchs" [10]–224 text.

Note on illustrations: 16p of colour plates, 100 illustrations in text in black and white; endpapers green on white.

Binding case: yellow-green imitation cloth (137); gold-lettered down spine, LIVINGSTONE Elspeth Huxley"; across foot, "The Great | Explorers | [rule] | Weidenfeld | & Nicolson".

Dust-jacket: lettered in white and black over UC illustration from Thomas Baines, The great western wall, Victoria Falls, and LC, Charles Mellow, The grave of Archbishop Mackenzie at Malo Ruo; UF, blurb; LF, brief biography of EH and note on The Great Explorers Series published titles.

Copies seen: EH

Notes: Published 29 April 1974, at £2.95 'in UK only' in edition of 5,000 copies; this was part of the 'Great Explorers Series' under the general editorship of Sir Vivian Fuchs.

Review: TLS, 1974

Translations: Icelandic: *Livingstone og Afrikuferdir hans* (Reykjavik) Bókaṅtgatan 1977.
Japanese: Soshi-Sha (Tokyo) 1979.
Mexican: Lasser Press (Mexico City) 1988.

(b) First American issue (1974)

Title: as in A.37(*a*), save, omits "Introduction by Sir Vivian Fuchs" [but present in the text], and has as imprint, "Saturday Review Press | New York"

Collation: as in A.37(*a*).

Contents: as in A.37(*a*), save on p.[4] after "London SW11" adds "and | Saturday Review Press, | 201 Park Avenue South, | New York, N.Y.10003".

Illustrations and dust-jacket: as in A.37(*a*).

Binding case: as in A.37(*a*), save at foot instead of "The Great Explorers . . ." has "Saturday | Review | Press".

Copies seen: Hants CL

Notes: Published in 1974 at $12.50 by Saturday Review Press, a division of E. P. Dutton: offset from A.37(*a*) and printed by Cox & Wyman Ltd, to increased page height.

Released by Books on Tape Inc. in June 1989 at $36.

Reviews: Christian Science Monitor, 25 September 1974
New Yorker, 18 November 1974

A.38   FLORENCE NIGHTINGALE   1975

(a) First edition (1975)

[dec. caps] FLORENCE | NIGHTINGALE | [rom.caps.] BY | [dec. caps.] ELSPETH HUXLEY | [at foot, rom. caps WEIDENFELD AND NICOLSON | LONDON
Collation: no signature marks; 254p. 246 × 185mm.

Contents: p.[1] ht [2] blank [3] tp. [4] "© Elspeth Huxley 1975 | All rights reserved . . . | Designed by Anthony Cohen | for George Weidenfeld and Nicolson Ltd | Filmset by Keyspools Ltd, Golborne, Lancs | Printed in Great Britain by Tinling (1973) Ltd, Prescot, Merseyside | (a member of the Oxley Printing Group)" | ISBN no. [5] "*For Mama – another indomitable nonagenarian*" [6] acknowledgements; and, "The map on page 98 was designed by Manuel Lopez Parras. | Picture research by Pat Hodgson." [7] contents [8–9] double-page picture of Embley House, headed on R. hand page, "Bird in a Cage" 10–254 text.

84   A   Books and pamphlets

Note on illustrations: 8 plates containing 16 coloured illustrations and portraits; illustrations and portraits also in text; endpapers (identical): a double-page group photo of Florence Nightingale and her nurses.

Binding case: blue cloth (182), lettered in gold down spine, "FLORENCE [above] NIGHTINGALE ELSPETH HUXLEY [across foot] Weidenfeld | & Nicolson".

Dust-jacket: UC, a coloured engraving of Florence Nightingale (Royal College of Nursing); LC, a porcelain model of Florence Nightingale with a wounded soldier (Wellcome Historical Medical Museum); UF, blurb; LF, brief biography of EH.

Copies seen: BL

Notes: Published 27 March 1975 at £4.95 in edition of 6,000 copies. Purnell Book Services Book Club also published their edition in 1975: both issues were printed in UK.

Bounty Books, then part of the Hamlyn Group, published at £5.99 under their imprint of Chancellor Press in 1982: these copies were printed in Czechoslovakia.

EH interviewed on Woman's Hour by Teresa McGonagle on 26 March 1975 (D.294) and on Kaleidoscope by James Kellen on 1 April (D.295).

Reviews *Observer,* 25 May 1975
Sydney Morning Herald, 14 June 1975
Australian, 21 June 1975
Books and Bookmen, July 975 (Diana Mosley)
New Humanist, July 1975
Nursing Times, 31 July 1975

Translation: Japanese: Medical Friend Sha (Tokyo) 1981.

(b) First American issue (1975)

Title: identical to A.38(*a*) save that the imprint is that of: G.P. Putnam's Sons New York

Collation and Contents: identical to A.38(*a*) save that the verso of the tp. substitutes the SBN no., the Library of Congress no. and "All rights reserved" and is shorter.

Binding case: as in A.38(*a*).

Dust-jacket: not seen.

Copies seen: information by correspondence.

Notes: Published by G. P. Putnam & Sons, New York, at $15.75 in April 1975. This book was sold by Weidenfeld and Nicolson to Putnams, as printed and bound books at the same time as A.38(*a*).

Released by Books on Tape Inc. in December 1989 at $36.

US Reviews: *Library Journal,* 1 April 1975
New Yorker, 28 April 1975
National Review, 1 August 1975

(c) Second English issue

FLORENCE | NIGHTINGALE | BY | ELSPETH | HUXLEY | [at foot] PBS | BOOK CLUB EDITION

Collation: as in A.37(*a*).

Contents: as in A.37(*a*), save on p.[4] "This edition published by | Purnell Book Services | St Giles House, | 49/50 Poland Street, London W1A 2LG | by arrangement with | Weidenfeld and Nicolson Ltd".

Binding case: blue imitation cloth (177), gold-lettered down spine, "FLORENCE | NIGHTINGALE | ELSPETH HUXLEY | [across foot] FBS".

Dust-jacket: as in A.37(*a*).

Copies seen: EH

Notes: Published in 1975 by Purnell for their Book Club: this issue followed A.38(*b*).

(d) Third English issue (1982)

Title: as in A.37(*a*), save for imprint: "CHANCELLOR | PRESS"

Collation: as in A.37(*a*).

Contents: as in A.37(*a*), save, on p.[4] "This edition published by Chancellor Press | 59 Grosvenor Street | London W1 . . . Printed in Czechoslovakia".

Binding case: brown imitation cloth with an image of Florence Nightingale blocked in a panel on the UC.

Dust-jacket: on both UC and LC a 4-colour illustration from a painting in the National Portrait Gallery.

Copies seen: EH

Notes: Published in 1982 under the imprint of Chancellor Press, see A.38(*a*): no mention of year of publication is given in the book.

A.39 GALLIPOT EYES   1976

(a) First edition (1976)

ELSPETH HUXLEY | *Gallipot Eyes* | [thick and thin rule] | *A WILTSHIRE DIARY* | [at foot] | WEIDENFELD AND NICOLSON | LONDON

Collation: 1–6 in 16s, 7 in 10s; xii,198,[199–200]p. 232 × 152mm.

Contents: p.[i] ht. [ii] illustration [iii] tp. [iv] "Copyright © 1976 by Elspeth Huxley . . . Illustrated by Delia Delderfield | Designed by Simon Bell | for George

86　　A　Books and pamphlets

Weidenfeld and Nicolson Ltd | 11 St John's Hill, London SW1 | Printed and bound in Great Britain by | Morrison & Gibb Ltd, London and Edinburgh" [v] quotation from John Aubrey [vi] "*To Dolly and those other friends and neighbours | who helped me with my enquiries*" [vi]–ix contents [x] map [xi]–xii preface [1]–198 text [199–200] blank.

Note on illustrations: line illustrations in the text; with genealogical tables; the endpapers contain two different illustrations.

Binding case: yellow-brown imitation cloth (77); gold-lettered, "ELSPETH | HUXLEY | [down spine] GALLIPOT EYES A Wiltshire Diary | [across foot] Weidenfeld | & Nicolson".

Dust-jacket: colour illustration on UC and LC by Delia Delderfield; lettered in purple and black; on UF, blurb, price (in UK only) £4.25 net; on LF, brief biography of EH.

Copies seen: EH

Notes: Published 4 May 1976 at £4.25 in edition of 5,000 copies.

Turned down by C&W after their merger with Jonathan Cape this was the first time in 36 years that this had happened, but it was not to be the end of EH's relationship with C&W.

Readers' Union bought an edition in December 1976 for their readers.

Homes and Gardens published an extract of 1,600 words in May 1976, entitled 'The Fireman's Tale'. (C.708)

Review: Times, 27 May 1976

(b) Reader's Union issue (1976)

Title: as in A.39(*a*) save for imprint: READERS UNION | Group of Book Clubs | Newton Abbot 1976

Collation: no signature marks; [10],198p. 212 × 135mm.

Contents: as in A.39(*a*) save for note at foot of p.[4], "This edition was produced in 1976 for sale to its members | only by the proprietors, Readers Union Limited, | PO box 6, Newton Abbot, Devon, TQ12 2DW. | Full details of membership will gladly be sent on request | Reproduced and printed in Great Britain | by A.Wheaton & Co Exeter | for Readers Union".

A note on illustrations: as in A.39(*a*).

Binding case: yellowish-pink imitation cloth (26); gold-lettered down spine, "Gallipot Eyes Elspeth Huxley"; across foot, RU device.

Dust-jacket: UC, sepia illustration, lettered in brown and yellow; UF, blurb; LC, details of 3 other RU books; LF, details of RU.

Copies seen: RC

Notes: Published in 1976 by Readers' Union for their readers, being offset from W & N edition. No records now exist.

(c) First paperback issue (1988)

GALLIPOT EYES | A Wiltshire Diary | Elspeth Huxley | [illustration] | [at foot] CENTURY | London Melbourne Auckland Johannesburg | in association with The National Trust

Collation: as in RU issue; 216 × 134mm.

Contents: p.[1] note by author and brief biography [2] "Recently published in The National Trust Classics series": 13 titles [3] tp. [4] "First published in 1976 | Copyright © Elspeth Huxley 1988 . . . | Cover landscape painting by Alfred Clendening . . . | Printed in Great Britain by | Richard Clay | (The Chaucer Press) Ltd, | Bungay, Suffolk . . ." [v–vii] contents [viii] map [ix–x] preface [1]–198 text.

Wrappers: pictorial; on UW, "NATIONAL TRUST CLASSICS | Elspeth Huxley | GALLIPOT EYES | A Wiltshire Diary"; on LW, ISBN no., Century Hutchinson Limited; £5.95 net in UK.

Copies seen: EH

Notes: Published 24 April 1988 at £5.95 in edition of 4,580 copies, offset from W & N edition. Published in association with the National Trust as one of the National Trust Classics, who sold the book through their special outlets, while Century sold to the trade.

(d) Large Print edition (1995)

Gallipot Eyes | *A Wiltshire Diary* | Elspeth Huxley | ISIS | LARGE PRINT | Oxford, England

Collation: no signature marks; [16],309,[310–320]p. 233 × 150mm..

Contents: p.[1] ht [2] "Also available in this series": 30 titles [3] tp. [4] "Copyright © 1976 Elspeth Huxley | First published in Great Britain 1976 | by Weidenfeld and Nicolson | Published in Large Print 1995 by ISIS Publishing Ltd, | 7 Centremead, Osney Mead, Oxford OX2 OES, | by arrangement with Heather Jeeves | All rights reserved | The moral right of the author has been asserted" . . . Printed and bound by Hartnolls Ltd, Bodmin, Cornwall" [5] dedication [6] blank [7–11] contents [12] map [13–16] preface 1–309 text [311–317] ISIS addresses and lists [318–320] blanks.

Binding case: glazed boards, three-quarters UC, "a detail from The Village Street by Thomas Mackay, reproduced by arrangement with Sotheby's (Sussex)"; quarter-bound in yellow (69) with "Isis Reminiscence Series" on UC and LC; title and author in black on UC; blurb and ISBN in white panel on LC.

Dust-jacket: none.

Copies seen: RC

Notes: Published in May 1995 at £15.95 in edition of 550 copies. Isis became independent of Clio Press in July 1993. EH received advance of £850 against 10% royalty.

88   A   Books and pamphlets

A.40   TRAVELS IN WEST AFRICA   1976

(a) First edition (1976)

MARY H. KINGSLEY | TRAVELS IN | WEST | AFRICA | *Edited and introduced by* | ELSPETH HUXLEY | [Folio Society device, F.S. in scroll of white on black within an oval] | LONDON | THE FOLIO SOCIETY | 1976

Collation: no signature marks: [1–35, in 8s]; 276,[277–280]p. 246 × 148mm.

Contents: p.[1] tp. [2] "© *Introduction and Selection* | *The Folio Society Limited, 1976*" | [at foot] "PRINTED IN GREAT BRITAIN | *by Richard Clay (The Chaucer Press) Ltd, Bungay, Suffolk*" 3 contents 4 blank 5–6 list of illustrations 7–15 editor's introduction 16 blank 17–23 author's preface 24 blank 25–276 text [277] "Set in 11 point 'Monotype' Modern Extended leaded 1 point | with Scotch Roman for display. | Text printed by Richard Clay (The Chaucer Press) Ltd, Bungay | on Fineblade Cartridge paper. | Illustrations lithographed by W. & J. Mackay Ltd, Chatham | Bound by W. & J. Mackay Ltd | in printed cloth."

Note on illustrations: frontispiece-portrait of Mary Kingsley, and 14 illustrations (on 12 plates); end-papers map (identical) of West Africa in white on brown.

Binding-case: light-grey cloth printed with a picture of "The river port of Brazzaville" across LC, spine and UC in green (146); gold-lettered up spine, "Travels in West Africa" and across foot the Folio Society device in gold (a larger version of that on tp.); with a slip-case in yellowish-brown cloth (79).

Paper: Fineblade Cartridge.

Copies seen: Folio Society file copy.

Notes: Published October 1976 by the Folio Society at £5.95 in edition of 10,050 copies.

EH interviewed on Woman's Hour 30 April 1987 (D.318).

(b) First paperback edition (1987)

EVERYMAN [oval device] CLASSICS | [thick rule on each side of device] | MARY KINGSLEY | *Travels in West Africa* | Abridged and introduced by Elspeth Huxley | [at foot] Dent: London and Melbourne | EVERYMAN'S LIBRARY

Collation: no signature marks; [11],2–270,[271–274]. 189 × 123mm.

Contents: p.[1] oval device with thick rule on each side as on tp., Everyman motto, biographical notes on Mary Kingsley, 28 lines, and Elspeth Huxley, 10 lines [2] blank [3] tp. [4] "© Introduction and Selection, | The Folio Society Limited, 1976 | All rights reserved | Made in Great Britain by | Guernsey Press Co. Ltd, Guernsey C.I. for | J.M.Dent & Sons Ltd | Aldine House, 37 Welbeck Street, London W1M 8LX | First published as an Everyman Classic, 1987" | binding restriction, 4 lines | at foot, "No.1587 Paperback" ISBN No. [5] contents [6–7 & 8–9] 2 double-page maps [10] blank [11]–17 author's preface [18] blank [19]–270 text [271–274] list of Everyman titles.

Wrappers: cream, lettered in cream and white on black panel; UC illustration shows detail of water-colour by H.H. Johnston, courtesy of Royal Geographical Society, with inserted photograph of Mary Kingsley, courtesy of National Portrait Gallery; LC, blurb, GB £ net +003.95, ISBN no. and bar code.

Copies seen: BL

Notes: Published 30 April 1987 at £3.95 in Everyman Classics No. 1587. Reprinted in 1992 at £4.50 (2,500) with Charles E. Tuttle Co. Inc. Rutland; reprinted in 1993 at £5.99 (4,000). Each issue has a different cover: the first publication having detail from a watercolour by H. H. Johnston with Mary Kingsley photograph inset, the others with her photograph as the main design from the Mary Evans Picture Library.

A.41   SCOTT OF THE ANTARCTIC   1977

(a) First edition (1977)

SCOTT | OF THE ANTARCTIC | *Elspeth Huxley* | [at foot] WEIDENFELD AND NICOLSON | LONDON

Collation: no signature marks; xiv,303,[304]p. 233 × 153mm.

Contents: p.[i] ht. [ii] blank [iii] tp. [iv] "© Elspeth Huxley 1977 | Weidenfeld and Nicolson | 11 St John's Hill London SW11 . . . Printed in Great Britain by | Cox & Wyman Ltd, | London, Fakenham and Reading" [v] contents [vi–vii] double-page map [viii] *"For Cousin Peggy"* [ix] list of illustrations [x] blank [xi]–xii preface [xii]–xiv Personnel of the British Antarctic expeditions [1]–303 text [304] blank.

Note on illustrations: 16 plates containing 26 illustrations, and 3 maps.

Binding case: purplish-blue imitation cloth (196), gold-lettered down spine "SCOTT [above]OF[below] THE ANTARCTIC | [above] Elspeth [below] Huxley | [across foot] Weidenfeld | & Nicolson".

Dust-jacket: design by Grant Bradford, with photo of Scott on UC by Herbert Ponting; on LC, photo of Scott (Radio Times Hulton Picture Library); on UF, blurb, £6.95 net in UK only; on LF, synopsis, brief biography of EH.

Copies seen: EH

Notes: Published 7 November 1977 at £6.95 net (UK only) in edition of 6,000 copies.

An extract, 'Scott in Love' was published in the *The Times* Saturday Review on 29 October 1977 (C.711).

Reviews: Sunday Times, 6 November 1977
            Economist, 12 November 1977
            TLS, 10 February 1978
            TES, 21 December 1979

Translation: Mexican: *Capitan Scott: La Odisea del Antartico*; transl. Luz Maria Trejo de Hernandez, Lasser Press Mexicana, S.A. Mexico DF. 1979 (paperback and hardback).

90   A   Books and pamphlets

(b)   First American issue (1978)

Elspeth Huxley | SCOTT | OF THE | ANTARCTIC | [at foot] Atheneum NEW YORK 1978

Collation: as in A.41(*a*).

Contents: as in A.41(*a*) save, on p.[iv] Library of Congress CIP data; "Manufactured by Halliday Lithograph Corporation, | West Hanover and Plympton, Massachusetts | First American Edition".

Note on illustrations: as in A.41(*a*).

Binding case: Red cloth (16), lettered in silver down spine, "Elspeth Huxley * SCOTT OF THE ANTARCTIC * ATHENEUM".

Dust-jacket: as in UK edition, save for price: $12.50.

Copies seen: EH

Notes: Published in 1978 at $12.95 by Atheneum. Taken by the Book of the Month Club in 1978. Released by Books on Tape Inc. March 1990 at $96.

Reviews: New York Times, 16 April 1978
              Newsweek, 24 April 1978
              New Yorker, 22 May 1978
              Library Journal, 15 June 1978

(c)   First paperback edition (1979)

Elspeth Huxley | Scott | of the Antarctic | [at foot] Pan Books London and Sydney

Collation: no signature marks; [1–14],15–350,[2]p. 190 × 127mm.

Contents: p.[1] ht. and note on author, 7 lines [2] blank [3] tp. [4] "First published 1977 by Weidenfeld and Nicholson, | This edition published 1979 by Pan Books Ltd, | Cavaye Place, London SW10 9PG | © Elspeth Huxley 1977 | ISBN 0330 25861 3 | Set, printed and bound in Great Britain by | Cox & Wyman Ltd, Reading . . ." [5] contents [6–7] double-page map [8] dedication [9] list of illustrations [10–11] preface [12–13] "Personnel of the | British Antarctic Expedition" [14] blank 15–350,[351] text [352] note of two books by Ronald Lewinson and Henry Pelling published by Pan.

Note on illustrations: 4 leaves of plates containing 16 illustrations bound between p.176 and 177; maps on p.6–7, 79 and 282.

Wrappers: grey, UC illustration by Michael Leonard, Pan motif in top L corner, title in white, quote from *Publisher's Weekly* review; on LC, quotes from *Sunday Times, Evening Standard* and *The Economist* reviews, prices, including U.K. £1.95

Copies seen: BL (possibly cropped, no Pan Books no.)

Notes: Published by Pan Books 1 October 1979 at £1.95 in edition of 12,500: reprinted 5,000 copies at £2.50.

(d) First American paperback issue (1990)

Title: as in Atheneum issue, save imprint: "[at foot: Bison Book device] University of Nebraska Press. Lincoln"

Collation: as in Atheneum issue save size: 229 × 148mm.

Contents: as in Atheneum issue save on p.[iv] "Manufactured in the United States of America | First Bison Book printing: 1990 | More recent printing indicated by the first digit below: . . . Reprinted by arrangement with Heather Jeeves, representing Elspeth Huxley".

Note on illustrations: as in Atheneum issue.

Wrappers: on UW, photo of Scott (not the same as in the 1st edition); on LW: blurb.

Copies seen: EH

Notes: Published in February 1990 at $11.95 in edition of 3,152 copies in Bison Books. This was offset from A.41(*b*).

A.42 NELLIE: LETTERS FROM AFRICA   1980

(a) First edition (1980)

[Thin and thick rules] | NELLIE | *Letters from Africa* | [thin and thick rules] With a memoir by | ELSPETH HUXLEY | [at foot] Weidenfeld and Nicolson | London

Collation: no signature marks; x,326p. 214 × 137mm.

Contents: p.[i] ht [ii] blank [iii] tp. [iv] "*For Nellie's descendants: Charles,* | *Josceline, Hugh and Alexander* – | *not forgetting Frederica without* | *whom the last three would* | *not have existed.* | © Elspeth Huxley 1973 Trust, 1980 | Weidenfeld and Nicolson | 91 Clapham High Street | London SW4 . . . Printed in Great Britain by | Butler & Tanner Ltd, Frome and London" [v] contents [vi–vii] double-page map of Kenya [viii] blank ix–x foreword [1]–94 Memoir 95–326 Letters from Kenya 1937–65.

Note on illustrations: 8 pages.

Binding case: yellowish-green imitation cloth (137), gold-lettered down spine, "NELLIE [above] Letters from [below] Africa [above] Elspeth [below] Huxley | [across foot] Weidenfeld | & Nicolson".

Dust-jacket: sepia photo across UC, LC and spine; lettered in green and black; on UF, synopsis, price in UK only £8.95 net; on LF, brief biography of EH.

Copies seen: EH

Notes: Published 6 March 1980 at £8.95 in edition of 3,000 copies. Sold to Readers' Union in 1980. The author of the letters was Nellie Grant, EH's mother.

The American publisher changed the title to *Nellie's Story*.

92　A　Books and pamphlets

The Times published an extract on 23 February 1980 entitled 'Home among the Kikuyu' (C.720).

EH interviewed on Kaleidoscope 6 March 1980 (D.298).

Reviews:　Daily Telegraph, 6 March 1980
　　　　　Guardian, 6 March 1980
　　　　　Sunday Telegraph, 9 March 1980
　　　　　Birmingham Post, 13 March 1980
　　　　　Sunday Times, 15 March 1980
　　　　　Times, 20 March 1980 (Jan Morris)
　　　　　Scotsman, 22 March 1980
　　　　　Country Life, 10 April 1980
　　　　　Observer, 4 May 1980 (7 Dec. 1980, Book of the Year by Edward Crankshaw
　　　　　Spectator, 9 August 1980

(b)　First American issue (1981) – not seen.

Notes: Published in 1981 by W. Morrow at $12.95 under the title of *Nellie's Story*.

Reviews:　Winnipeg Tribune, 2 June 1981
　　　　　Toronto Sun, 22 June 1981

(c)　First paperback issue (1984)

Title, Collation, and Contents: as in 1980 edition, save, added on p.[4] "First published in paperback | Great Britain 1984".

Wrappers: as in 1980 dj save that LW has a blurb from the UC of the 1980 dj, plus a quotation from Alec Guinness, and £4.95 net in UK only.

Copies seen: EH

Notes: Published in 1984 at £4.95 in edition of 2,000 copies, and reprinted in same year at same published price (2,000).

A.43　WHIPSNADE: CAPTIVE BREEDING FOR SURVIVAL
1981

First edition (1981)

Whipsnade | CAPTIVE BREEDING FOR SURVIVAL | [2 type orns.] | ELSPETH HUXLEY | [at foot] COLLINS | St James's Place, London | 1981

Collation: no signature marks; i–xiv, [15]–159p. 222 × 145mm.

Contents: p.[i] ht. [ii] "*by the same author*": 15 titles [iii] tp. [iv] "William Collins Sons and Co Ltd | London.Glasgow.Sydney.Auckland | Toronto. Johannesburg . . .

First published 1981 | © Elspeth Huxley 1981 | Photoset in Lasercomp Ehrhardt | Made and printed in Great Britain by | William Collins Sons and Co Ltd, Glasgow" [v] contents [vi] blank [vi–viii] list of illustrations [ix]–x foreword [xi]–xiv introduction [15]–159 text.

Note on illustrations: 10 plates, 4 coloured.

Binding case: olive-green imitation cloth (128), gold-lettered down spine, "[above] Elspeth [below] Huxley Whipsnade Captive breeding for survival | [across foot] COLLINS".

Dust-jacket: coloured photo on dark green background; lettered in white and yellow; on UF, blurb, £8.95 net; on LF, brief biography of EH and "WHIPSNADE | ZOO | 50 | 1931–1981".

Copies seen: RC

Notes: Published in 1981 at £8.95 net. EH was interviewed about the book on Radio 2 by John Dunn on 27 April 1981 and by Bill Brecon on 22 May 1981 (D.300 & 301).

A.44   THE PRINCE BUYS THE MANOR   1982

First edition (1982)

THE PRINCE | BUYS THE MANOR | *An Extravaganza* | *By* | ELSPETH HUXLEY | [at foot] 1982 | CHATTO & WINDUS | LONDON

Collation: no signature marks; 215,[216]p. 198 × 125mm.

Contents: [1] ht. [2] "*By the same Author*": 33 titles [3] tp. [4] "Published by | Chatto & Windus Ltd . . . Clarke, Irwin & Co Ltd . . . © Elspeth Huxley 1982" [5] "For Norah, | silken spur, | incisive counsellor, and | warm-hearted friend" [6] blank [7]–215 text [216] at foot, "Typeset by T H Brickell & Son Ltd | Shaftesbury, Dorset | Printed by Redwood Burn Ltd | Trowbridge, Wiltshire".

Binding case: red-pink imitation cloth (16); gold-lettered on spine, "THE | PRINCE | BUYS | THE | MANOR | [dec. flourish] | [at foot] CHATTO | & | WINDUS".

Dust-jacket: UC and spine designed by John Sutcliffe, lettered in blue, red and black on a pink ground; UF, blurb, £6.95 net in UK only; LC, Also by Elspeth Huxley: 4 titles; LF, short biography of EH and photo by Tara Heinemann.

Paper: Kingsley antique wove.

Copies seen: RC

Notes: Published 4 October 1982 at £6.95 in edition of 8,930 copies of which Blunt and Holt Jackson each took 152 f. and c. sheets with 185 d.j.s and Askews bought 101 f. and c. sheets with 125 d.j.s. Leisure Circle took 4,000 copies from this printing on 26 July 1982 of which C&W took back 800 in April 1984 at 50p. 2,200 copies were subsequently remaindered outside UK and USA.

94 A Books and pamphlets

EH wrote 'I am a little worried about this being classified as a novel. The word conjured up a pretty serious image. Novels take matters seriously and readers expect the story to be credible and the characters true to life. This is the literary equivalent of a stage farce. Would the word extravaganza be better?' C&W agreed to describe it as such.

The incorporation of the Prince of Wales's Three Feather badge on the d.j. was refused as only used 'by tradesmen who hold a Royal Warrant of Appointment to his Royal Highness'. The book itself when presented to the Prince and Princess of Wales was refused as no gifts accepted.

C&W received a letter from Messrs Doolittle and Dalley of Kidderminster objecting to the use of their name in the book as quoted in an article in the *Daily Mail* of 8 September 1982. C&W is asked to withdraw the book for misusing their identity; a letter from Thursfield and Adams also asked for its withdrawal. C&W replied that the name in the novel related to an imaginary firm lying under the lea of the Cotswolds: an injunction was then threatened but did not happen.

EH dedicated the book to NS who was to die in 1984, as an indication of her respect and affection for her long-time publisher.

Reviews: Financial Times, 2 October 1982
    TLS, 29 October 1982

A.45 LAST DAYS IN EDEN   1984

(a) First edition (1984)

Last Days | in Eden | ELSPETH HUXLEY & HUGO van LAWICK | Harvill Press | 8 Grafton Street, London W1 | 1984

Collation: no signature marks; 192p. 232 × 194mm.

Contents: p.[1] ht. and photograph [2–3] double-page illustration; on p.[3] tp. [4] "Harvill Press Limited | is distributed by | William Collins Sons & Company Limited | London.Glasgow.Sydney.Auckland | Toronto. Johannesburg... | First published 1984 | Text © Elspeth Huxley 1984 | Photographs © Hugo van Lawick 1984... | This book was designed and produced by | George Rainbird Limited, | 40 Park Street, London W1Y 4DE... | Designer: Lee Griffiths... | Text filmset in Palatino by Wyvern Typesetting Limited, Bristol, England, | Colour origination by Gilchrist Brothers Limited, Leeds, England | Printed and bound by Brepols s.a., Turnhout, Belgium..." 5 contents .. 6 location map 7–192 text.

Binding case: orange-brown imitation cloth (58); gold-lettered down spine. "*LAST DAYS IN EDEN* [above] ELSPETH HUXLEY & [below] HUGO van LAWICK | [across foot] HARVILL | PRESS".

Dust-jacket: photographs from book on UC and LC; lettered in yellow and white; UF, blurb; sticker: Collins £9.95 LF, brief biographies of EH and van Lawick.

Copies seen: EH

Notes: The Harvill Press bought 10,000 copies from George Rainbird Limited and published in 1984 at £9.95. William Collins and Sons, the then owners of Harvill, are shown as the distributors on the reverse of title page; Hugo van Lawick is described as joint author but he was in fact the illustrator and he provided the inspiration for the book.

EH's comments by letter on her publisher were: 'Collins sat on the text for nearly 2 years, now want an extra 20,000 words which means virtually rewriting the book . . . this will deprove it not improve it'.

Translations: Dutch: *De Laatsten in de Hof van Eden,* tr. T. Kooij and H. J. M. Löffler, (Maastricht) Natuur en Techniek, 1984.

(b) First American edition (1984)

Title: as in A.45(*a*), save imprint: "THE AMARYLLIS PRESS | NEW YORK"

Collation: as in A.45(*a*), save size: 240 × 194mm.

Contents: as in A.45(*a*), save on p.[4] "The Amaryllis Press, Inc. | 219 West 79th Street | New York, N.Y. 10024"; Harvill Press imprint and BLCIP data omitted; Library of Congress catalog card no. and American ISBN substituted.

Binding case: dark-blue imitation cloth with no lettering.

Dust-jacket: on UC, photograph of two elephants butting, names of authors lettered in white; on LC, photograph of a stormy landscape, blurb lettered in white; on UF and LF blurb in American spelling; on UF, $28.00.

Copies seen: EH

Notes: Published in 1984 at $28.00 these books were manufactured by George Rainbird Limited with a different d.j. whose text is in American spelling; the page height is greater than A.45(*a*) by 8 mm, making it a better design.

A.46   OUT IN THE MIDDAY SUN   1985

(a) First edition (1985)

Out in the Midday Sun | My Kenya | by ELSPETH HUXLEY | [at foot] Chatto & Windus | LONDON

Collation: no signature marks; x,262p. 233 × 156mm.

Contents: p.[i] ht., orn. [ii] *"By the same author"*: 34 titles [iii] tp. [iv] "Published in 1985 by | Chatto & Windus Ltd . . . Copyright © Elspeth Huxley 1985 | . . . Typeset at The Spartan Press Ltd | Lymington, Hants | Printed in Great Britain at | Redwood Burn Ltd | Trowbridge | Wilts" v contents vi–vii list of illustrations [viii] map ix–x foreword 1–262 text.

96   A   *Books and pamphlets*

Note on illustrations: 8p. of plates containing 16 illustrations.

Binding case: red-pink cloth (12), gold-lettered down spine "OUT IN THE MIDDAY SUN.ELSPETH HUXLEY | [across foot] CHATTO | & WINDUS".

Dust-jacket: illustration from photograph of Mt Kenya by Granville Davies, lettered in orange-red outlined in blue, and white; on UF, blurb, £12.95 net in UK only; on LF, brief biography of EH and photograph by Tara Heinemann.

Paper: Redwood book wove.

Copies seen: EH

Notes: Published 7 November 1985 at £12.95 in edition of 5,899 copies of which 2,000 were sold to Westlands Sundries, Nairobi; reprinted December 1985 (2,042) without corrections. Reprinted February 1986 (1,987), subsequently at £14.95, with following corrections:

Prelims p.vi 6a: The Hill-Williams' house at Marindas, Molo circa 1909 *changed* to Typical settlers' house at Molo, circa 1920.

between pp.118–9 6a The Hill-Williams' house at Marindas, Molo circa 1909 *changed* to Typical settlers' house at Molo *but* 1909 was not changed to 1920.

p.95 l.7   seven pence *to* seven shillings
p.186 l.20   seven pence *to* seven shillings
p.258 & index   Cagnola *to* Cagnolo
p.202 l.1   Grandson *to* son
pp.127   Furze *to* Furse
p.128   *still* Furze
p.253   Furze *to* Furse
p.256   *still* Furze
p.259   *still* Furze
p.217 l.19   Lake Tanganyika *to* Lake Victoria
p.221 l.4   On a flight which started at Njoro *to* On a flight back home to Njoro.

For other textual changes see 45(c)

C&W paid advance of £5,000 against royalties of 10% of published price to 3,000 and 12.5% thereafter with export royalty on 50% discount sales of 10% of price received.

Merlin Unwin of George Allen and Unwin wrote complaining that the title and some of the contents – according to the author, Boris Gussman – had been lifted from his book which was by then out of print. Neither EH nor C&W took this seriously.

EH interviewed on Bookshelf in Radio 4, 3 September 1985 (D.317).

Reviews: Sunday Times, 22 December 1985
             Financial Times, 4 January 1986
             TLS, 31 January 1986

Translation: German; *In der Hitze des Mittags,* tr. F. A. Hofschuster, Bastei-Lubbe, 1989

(b) Large Print edition (1986)

ELSPETH HUXLEY | [swelled rule] | OUT IN THE | MIDDAY SUN | My Kenya | *Complete and Unabridged* | [castle device] | ULVERSCROFT | Leicester

Collation: OITMS [1]–36 in 8s; 549,[551–562]p. 214 × 135mm.

Contents: p.[1] 8-line poem © Janice James [2] blank [3] blurb [4] "*Books by Elspeth Huxley* | *in the Ulverscroft Large Print Series*": 3 titles [5] tp. [6] "First published in Great Britain in 1983. First Large Print Edition | published in November 1986 | by arrangement with | Chatto & Windus Ltd. | London | and | Viking Penguin Inc., | New York, N.Y. . . . Published by | F.A.Thorpe (Publishing) Ltd. | Anstey, Leicestershire | set by Rowland Phototypesetting Ltd | Bury St.Edmunds, Suffolk | Printed and bound in Great Britain by | T.J.Press (Padstow) Ltd., Padstow, Cornwall" [7–10] list of illustrations [11–14] foreword 1–549, [550] text [551–562] adverts. and list of Ulverscroft books.

Binding case: green and white laminated boards, coloured picture on UC of two Africans in green silhouette with animals walking from R. to L.; lettering in white and black; on LC, blurb and ISBN no.

Dust-jacket: none.

Copies seen: Hants CL

Notes: Published by F. A. Thorpe, Leicester, in their Ulverstock Large Print Books in November 1986 at £7.25 in edition of 1,750. Year of first publication on p.6 as 1983 was mistake for 1985.

(c) First American issue (1987)

Out in the | Midday Sun | [orn. of sun] | *My Kenya* | ELSPETH HUXLEY | [at foot] VIKING

Collation: as in A.46(*a*) 1985, save size: 232 × 154mm.

Contents: as in A.46(*a*) 1985, save on p.[iv] "VIKING | Viking Penguin Inc., . . . First American Edition. Published in 1987 | . . . Printed in the United States of America by | R.R.Donnelley & Sons Company, Harrisonburg, Virginia | Set in Sabon".

Binding case: buff cloth boards, quarter-bound in orange-brown cloth (39), goldlettered down spine, "Out in the Midday Sun. ELSPETH HUXLEY | [across foot, short rule above and below] VIKING".

Dust-jacket: mottled-yellow base with coloured photograph on UC (courtesy of the author); design by Irving Freeman; lettered in green and black; on UF, blurb; on UC, British reviews; on LF, brief biography of EH and photograph by Tara Heinemann, 1987.

Copies seen: EH, Tiptree

Notes: Published March 1987 at $18.95, print quantity not known. Viking offset their issue from C&W's 3rd impression at £3 per page: in addition to the corrections

98   A   Books and pamphlets

already made in that impression, Viking's editor spotted the following which were incorporated (except for three, see below):

between p.118–9 6a *changed* to The Poultons' house at Molo, circa 1920
p.128 l.1   Furze *to* Furse
p.129 l.1   Gander *to* Gandar
p.257 *Glossary*   Kekoi *to* Kikois
p.262 *Index*   Sherbrooke-Walker *to* Sherbroke-Walker

corrections missed:

p.199 l.4f.   Wauce *should* be Wouse
p.256 l.3f.   Furze *should* be Furse
p.259 *Index*   Gander *should* be Gandar see Dower

Viking paid $12,500 advance against royalties of 10% to 5,000, 12.5% to 10,000 and 15% thereafter.

Released by Books on Tape Inc. in April 1987 at $64.

Reviews: Library Journal, 1 February 1987
          New York Times, 22 March 1987
          National Review, 31 July 1987

(d)   First English paperback issue (1987)

Elspeth Huxley | Out in the Midday Sun | My Kenya | [at foot, Penguin device] PENGUIN BOOKS

Collation: as in A46(*a*), save size: 197 × 127mm

Contents: p.[i] brief biography of EH [ii] blank [iii] tp. [iv] "Published in Penguin Books 1987 | 7 9 10 8 . . . Printed in England by Clays Ltd, St Ives plc . . ." v contents [vi] blank [vii] list of illustrations [viii] to end, as in A46(*a*).

Wrappers: with cover illustration by Francesca Pelizzoli.

Copies seen: EH

Notes: Published 28 May 1987 at £3.95 in edition of 10,000, reprinted 29 June 1987 (15,000), 25 April 1988 at £4.50 (7,000), 10 October 1988 at £4.99 (5,000), 3 September 1990 at £5.99 (4,000), 11 November 1991 (5,000), in 1993 at £6.99 (3,000), 12 December 1994 (3,000).

Penguin offered advance of £5,000 against royalties of 7.5% and 6% to 20,000 home and export, and 10% and 8% thereafter.

Penguin offset from C&W's 3rd impression at fee of £3 per page: corrections were same as in that impression.

Illustrations were reduced to following 13, from 53 in C&W impressions, using C&W numbering:

1(a) (b) (c), 2 (c), 3(d), 4(a) (b), 5(a) (b), 6(b), 8(b) (c) (d).

(e) First American paperback issue (1988)

Notes: Published 5 April 1988 at $6.95 in edition of 10,000, imported from Penguin UK: further imports 25 April 1988 (3,000), 3 September 1990 published at $7.95 (3,000), 11 November 1991 at $10.00 (520), in 1993 at $10.95 (500).

Viking Penguin paid advance of $6.250 v. 7.5% to 50,000 and 10% thereafter.

A.47   NINE FACES OF KENYA   1990

(a) First edition (1990)

NINE FACES | OF KENYA | Compiled by | ELSPETH HUXLEY | [at foot, device] COLLINS HARVILL | 8 Grafton Street, London W1 | 1990

Collation: no signature marks; xxv,[xxvi],451,[452]p. 233 × 154mm.

Contents: p.[i] ht, [ii] "*By the same author*": 35 titles [iii] tp. [iv] "Collins Harvill | William Collins Sons and Co Ltd . . . First published by Collins Harvill 1990 | Introduction, chronology, commentary | and selection © Elspeth Huxley 1990 | For copyright in individual extracts | please see acknowledgements pages | Typeset in 10 on 11½ point Ehrhardt | by Rowland Phototypesetting Ltd | Bury St Edmunds, Suffolk | Printed and bound in Great Britain by | Hartnolls Ltd, Bodmin, Cornwall" [v] contents [vi] blank [vii] "For Michael Blundell | Citizen of Kenya | I have done the state some service – | *Othello*" [viii–xv] list of maps [xvi]–xxi chronology [xxii] blank [xxiii]–xxv introduction [xxvi] blank [1]–451 text [452] blank.

Binding case: purplish-red imitation cloth (257); spine gold-lettered in a black panel with dec. rules," ELSPETH HUXLEY | NINE | FACES OF | KENYA | [at foot, device] COLLINS | HARVILL".

Dust-jacket: photograph over UC, LC and spine by Christer Fredriksson, lettered in white and yellow; on UF, synopsis, £16.00 net; on LF, brief biography of EH and photograph by Lucinda Douglas-Menzies.

Copies seen: EH

Notes: Published 20 September 1990 at £16 in edition of 5,000 under the imprint of Collins Harvill, 8 Grafton Street; Readers' Union bought 150 of these copies. £12,000 advance was paid.

EH discussed background to book reported in *The Times,* 22 August 1990 (C.752); also appeared on the Gloria Hunniford Show, on Radio 2, interviewed on her life in Africa and about the book, 20 September 1990 (D.319).

Reviews: *TLS,* 12 October 1990
         Sunday Times, 9 December 1990

(b) First American issue (1991)

Title: as in A.47(*a*) save, imprint at foot: "VIKING"

100   A   Books and pamphlets

Collation: as in A.47(*a*) save, size: 227 × 150mm.

Content: as in A.47(*a*), save imprint on p.[iv] "VIKING | Published by the Penguin Group . . . | First American Edition | Published in 1991 by Viking Penguin, a division of Penguin Books USA Inc. | 1 3 5 7 9 10 8 6 4 2 | Copyright © Elspeth Huxley, 1990 | All rights reserved | Pages 428–30 constitute an extension of this copyright page . . . | Printed in the United States of America . . ."

Binding case: grey paper boards, quarter-bound in black cloth, gold-lettered, "ELSPETH HUXLEY | [rule, down spine] NINE FACES [orn.] OF KENYA | [rule, across spine] VIKING [rule]".

Dust-jacket: grey, with photograph; design by Neil Stuart; lettered in orange outlined in black, and black; on UF, blurb; on LC, extract from introduction; on LF, short biography of EH, and photograph by Tara Heinemann, 1987, $24.95.

Copies seen: EH

Notes: Published 25 July 1991 at $24.95 in edition of 8,000 copies. Advance of $10,000 paid by Viking, a member of the Penguin Group in USA. No mention is made of the original publisher on the reverse of the title page.

This was offset from the Collins Harvill edition.

Reviews: Library Journal, 15 May 1991
Christian Science Monitor, 29 August 1991

(c)   *First English paperback issue (1991)*

Elspeth Huxley | NINE FACES OF | KENYA | An Anthology | [at foot, device] HARVILL | *An Imprint of* Harper Collins *Publishers*

Collation: as in A.47(*a*), save size: 213 × 132mm.

Contents: as in A.47(*a*), save imprint on p.[iv] "This paperback edition first published 1991 | by Harvill | an imprint of Harper Collins Publishers . . . Printed and Bound in Great Britain by | Hartnolls Limited, Bodmin, Cornwall".

Wrappers: on UW a black and white design of a zebra with green stripes, from a lithograph (1943) by Victor Vasarely; on UW and LW, extracts from reviews; on LW, UK £8.99 net.

Copies seen: EH

Notes: Published in October 1991 at £8.99 under the imprint of Harvill, an imprint of Harper Collins Publishers, 77/85 Fulham Palace Road, London; reprinted 1992 at £9.99 (2,000). The colour of the vertical stripes on cover were changed from green to red in the second impression; there is no mention of this reprint on title page reverse.

(d)   *First American paperback issue (1992)*

Title: as in A.47(*a*) save: "[at foot, device] PENGUIN BOOKS"

Collation: as in first edition, save size: 215 × 138mm.

Contents: as in first edition, save on p.[iv] "Published in Penguin Books 1992 . . . | Printed in the United States of America" and after text, p.[452–454] adverts for Penguin Books.

Wrappers: cover design by Paul Buckley; cover photograph © Burt Glenn | Magnum Photos; on LW, U.K. £6.99 (export only); USA $12.00.

Copies seen: EH

Notes: Published by Penguin USA in 1992 at $12.00 in edition of 6,500 copies of which 500 were exported to UK. This issue was offset from Viking copy, A.47(*b*).

(e) Second English paperback issue (1992)

Notes: Published in August 1992 at £6.99: 500 copies were imported from Viking Penguin without any changes to the cover or prelims, which had both US and UK prices on back cover, but no UK ISBN or CIP.

A.48   PETER SCOTT: PAINTER AND NATURALIST   1993

(a) First edition (1993)

PETER SCOTT | *Painter and Naturalist* | [illustration] | ELSPETH HUXLEY | with an introduction by Sir David Attenborough | [at foot] ff | *faber and faber* | LONDON. BOSTON

Collation: no signature marks; xx,361p. 233 × 152mm.

Contents: p.[i] ht. [ii] "*by the same author*": 9 titles [iii] tp. [iv] "First published in 1993 | by Faber and Faber Limited | 3 Queen Square London WC1N 3AU | Photoset by Parker Typesetting Service, Leicester | Printed in England by Clays Ltd, St Ives plc | All rights reserved | © Elspeth Huxley, 1993 . . ." [v] contents [vi] blank vii–viii list of illustrations ix–x introduction xi–xiv acknowledgements xv–xx chronology 1–361 text.

Note on illustrations: 16pp of plates containing 46 illustrations.

Binding case: green imitation cloth (145), lettered in silver within a frame of rules, "ff | PETER | SCOTT | Elspeth | Huxley | [at foot: two swans]".

Dust-jacket: green, with photograph by Philippa Scott on UC of 'Peter Scott with 2 Koala bears, Australia 1956'; photograph on LC of 'Peter Scott with Nenes'; on UF, blurb, UK £17.50 net. Canada $35.00 on LF, brief biography of EH.

Copies seen: EH

Notes: Published 25 October 1993 at £17.50 ($35 in Canada) in edition of 10,000 copies.

EH was interviewed by Dea Birkett in *The Scotsman* on 22 November 1993 about the book (C.760).

102   A   Books and pamphlets

Reviews: Sunday Telegraph, 17 October 1993 (Derrick Turner)
Sunday Express, 17 October 1993 (Jonathan Porritt)
Daily Mail, 23 October 1993 (Selina Hastings)
Times, 25 October 1993 (Derwent May)
Financial Times, 30 October 1993 (Francesca Greenoak)
Sunday Times, 7 November 1993 (Louisa Young)
Independent on Sunday, 7 November 1993 (Chris Barker)
TES, 17 December 1993
The Field, December 1993
Country Life, 20 January 1994 (David Tomlinson)
BBC Wildlife, January 1994 (Keith Shackleton)

(b) First English paperback issue (1995)

Title: as in first edition

Collation: as in A.48(a); xx,361,[362–364]p. 215 × 136mm.

Contents and illustrations: as in A.48(a) save, p.[i] brief blurb and biography of EH [iv] additional line after Faber address, "This paperback edition first published in 1995" [362–364] blanks.

Wrappers: on UW, enlargement of section of photograph by Philippa Scott as on dj of A.48(a), with lettering in black in a black-framed buff panel, "ff | PETER SCOTT | Elspeth Huxley | [quote from *Sunday Times* review] | Introduction by Sir David Attenborough"; spine lettered in black on a buff panel, "[rule] | ff | [rule] | [down spine] PETER SCOTT Elspeth Huxley | [rule]"; on LW, extracts from 6 reviews, UK £9.99 net, Canada $18.99; ISBN.

Copies seen: RC

Notes: Published 7 August 1995 at £9.99.

(c) Readers' Digest Condensed Book edition (1995) – not seen.

Notes: Published in August 1995 for subscribers, as part of the 'Today's Best Non-Fiction' series of which five are published each year.

(d) First American edition (1995)

Peter Scott | PAINTER AND NATURALIST | ELSPETH HUXLEY | Introduction by | Sir David Attenborough | [at foot: Fulcrum device] | FULCRUM PUBLISHING | Golden, Colorado

Collation: no signature marks; xix,[xx], 326,[6]p. 228 × 150mm.

Contents: p. [i] ht [ii] blank [iii] tp [iv] "First published in 1993 | by Faber and Faber Limited | ... | Copyright © 1993 Elspeth Huxley | Copyright © 1995 Fulcrum

Publishing" | ... | [Library of Congress CIP data] | "Cover design by Heidi Herndon | Printed in the United States of America | 0 9 8 7 6 5 4 3 2 1 | Fulcrum Publishing | 350 Indiana Street, Suite 350 | Golden, Colorado 80401-5093 | 8090/992-2908" [v] contents [vi] blank vii–viii introduction ix–xii acknowledgments xiii–xiv chronology [xx] blank 1–326 text [followed by 5 blank pages, then a page containing an advert for the World Wide Fund for Nature]

Note on illustrations: no plates; on p.149 a sketch of the "Proposed layout for Wildfowl Reserve ... designed by Peter Scott November 1967".

Binding case: Quarter-bound in yellowish-green imitation cloth (138) with cream paper boards, gold-lettered down spine "PETER SCOTT Elspeth Huxley", across foot: Fulcrum device | "FULCRUM"

Dust-jacket: in green and cream, as on binding case, lettered in green and cream; on UC illustration of two swans and the WWF logo (in black and white); UF, "bibliography" and price, "$24.95; LF ISBN, illustration of a dolphin, brief biography of EH, notes on Fulcrum; on LC, 3 flying swans, extract from introduction, Fulcrum address.

Copies seen: EH

Notes: Published in 16 October 1995 at $24.95 in edition of 3,785 copies, by Fulcrum Publishing under the same title. It has been reset with American spelling and some other changes. No illustrations.

B. Books Edited or with Contributions by Elspeth Huxley

B.1   THE BRITISH EMPIRE   1947–8

Description: The British Empire, edited by Hector Bolitho, with contributions by J. B. Archer, Kenneth Bradley, O. T. Dusseck, Wilfrid Egglestone, W. J. Grant, Elspeth Huxley, Ludovic Kennedy, Sir Harry Luke, D. E. McKenzie, Robert Marrs, Julian Mockford, James Pope-Hennessy, Owen Rutter, Neville Thomson, Bella Sidney Woolf (Lady Southorn).
London, New York, Totonto, Sydney: B. T. Batsford, Ltd., [1947–8]

"East Africa by Elspeth Huxley", p.142–156, with 3 leaves of plates containing 13 illustrations numbered 131–144, and a sketch map in the text

Copy seen: BL

Notes: "First published, winter, 1947–8" (verso of tp.) "This book was first planned towards the end of the War and the majority of the chapters were contributed at that time. The text has since been revised to include post-war developments in the Commonwealth and Empire up to the early months of 1947 . . ." (publisher's note, p.vii)

Batsford confirms that this book was published in Winter 1947 at 21s in edition of 10,000 copies (according to a handwritten record): it contained 256 pp. of text, 8 plates in colour and over 170 illustrations from photographs.

B.2   LE TRAVAIL EN AFRIQUE NOIR   1952

Description: Le Travail en Afrique Noir. (Présence africaine, 13) [Paris]: aux Éditions du Seuil, [1952]

"Visite à l'Est africain en 1946. Par Helspeth [sic] Huxley", p.180–185. Traduit de l'anglais par P. Naville.

Copy seen: RH

Notes: This book was published in April 1952. The chapter by EH was originally written in 1946, based on articles she wrote for *Time and Tide* entitled 'African Vista', C.273–5.

B.3   WHITE AFRICANS   1955

Description: White Africans, by J. F. Lipscomb, with an introduction by Elspeth Huxley.

London: Faber and Faber Limited, [1955].

"Introduction" (unsigned), p.9–15.

Copy seen: BL

Notes: Facsimile reprint by Greenwood Press, publishers, Westport, Connecticut, 1974.

B.4   PRINCES OF ZINJ   1957

Description: Princes of Zinj, the Rulers of Zanzibar. Genesta Hamilton. Foreword by Elspeth Huxley.
London: Hutchinson of London, [1957]

"Foreword", p.13–15, facsimile signature of "Elspeth Huxley".

Copy seen: Hants CL

B.5   I WAS A SAVAGE   1958

Description: I was a savage, by Prince Modupe. Foreword by Elspeth Huxley. Ilustrations and sketch map by Rosemary Grimble.
London: Museum Press, [1958]

"Foreword by Elspeth Huxley", p.ix–xi.

Copy seen: BL

B.6   A NEW HOME IN KENYA   1962

Description: A new home in Kenya, by Campbell K. Finlay, with a foreword by Elspeth Huxley.
London, Toronto, Wellington, Sydney: George G. Harrap & Co. Ltd, [1962]

"Foreword", p.[5]–8

Copy seen: RH

B.7   THEY MADE IT THEIR HOME   1962

Description: They made it their home. Presented by the East Africa Women's League. Introduction by Elspeth Huxley.
Nairobi: East African Standard Limited, 1962.

"Introduction" signed "ELSPETH HUXLEY" and dated "July, 1961", p.[7–11]

Copy seen: EH

106   B   Books Edited or with Contributions by Elspeth Huxley

Notes: The story of early settlement in Kenya illustrated by the Kenya Embroidery Panels (50 coloured plates of embroidery panels, worked by each of the branches of the East Africa Women's League).

B.8   THE CATECHIST   1965

Description: The Catechist, by Joseph W. Abruquah, with a foreword by Elspeth Huxley.
London: George Allen & Unwin Ltd, [1965]

"Foreword by Elspeth Huxley", p.11–14

Copy seen: BL

Notes: "This book is based on a framework of reality – my father's life. Much of the detail, but not all of it, is fiction" (author's preface); Catechist – "a failed and underpaid Minister who could not baptise, marry or bury members of his flock" (from EH's foreword).

B.9   THE FLAG-WAGGER   1974

Description: The flag-wagger, by Harry Franklin, with an introduction by Elspeth Huxley.
[London]: Shepheard-Walwyn, [1974]

"Introduction", p.ix–xi, dated "October 1973"

Copy seen: RH

Notes: Published 28 March 1974 at £3.95 in edition of 4,000 copies (this quantity is based on the publisher's memory).

B.10   CARGOES OF THE EAST   1978

Description: Cargoes of the East: the ports, trade and culture of the Arabian Seas and Western Indian Ocean, [By] Esmond Bradley Martin and Chrysee Perry Martin. Foreword by Elspeth Huxley.
London: Elm Tree Books, [1978]

"Foreword", p.ix–xi.

Copy seen: Hants CL

B.11   THE SEARCHING SPIRIT   1978

Description: The Searching Spirit: an autobiography [by Joy Adamson]. With a foreword by Elspeth Huxley.
London: Collins and Harvill Press, 1978.

"Foreword" signed "Elspeth Huxley", p.13–15

Copy seen: BL

Notes: Published 13 November 1978 at £6.95.

B.12   OUT OF AFRICA   1980

Description: Out of Africa, [by] Karen Blixen. Introduction by Elspeth Huxley. Lino-cuts by Peter Pendrey.
London: The Folio Society, 1980.

"Introduction", p.[7]–12

Copy seen: RH

Notes: Published in October 1980 at £8.95 in edition of 5,000 copies.

B.13   PIONEER'S SCRAPBOOK   1980

Description: Pioneer's scrapbook: reminiscences of Kenya 1890 to 1968. Edited by Elspeth Huxley and Arnold Curtis. Foreword by H.R.H. Princess Alice, Duchess of Gloucester.
London: Evans Brothers Limited, [1980]

Copy seen: EH

Notes: Published in 1980 at £8.50 in edition of 7,000 copies and reprinted in 1981 (2,000).
Copyright by the East Africa Women's League.

B.14   RUN RHINO RUN   1982

Description: Run rhino run, [by] Esmond and Chrysee Bradley Martin, with an introduction by Elspeth Huxley, photographs by Mohamed Amin.
London: Chatto & Windus, 1982

"Introduction" signed "Elspeth Huxley", p.7–9

Copy seen: BL

Notes: Published at £19.95.

B.15   THE CARRIER CORPS   1986

Description: The Carrier Corps: military labor in the East African campaign, 1914–1918, [by] Geoffrey Hodges. Introduction by Elspeth Huxley. (Contributions in Comparative Colonial Studies, Number 18).
New York, Westport, Connecticut, London: Greenwood Press, [1986].

"Introduction by Elspeth Huxley", p.[xvii]–xx.

Copies seen: RH, BL

B.16   MEMORIES OF KENYA   1986

Memories of Kenya: stories from the pioneers. Edited by Arnold Curtis, with an introduction by Elspeth Huxley.
[London, Nairobi, Ibadan]: Evans Brothers Limited, [1986].

"Introduction by Elspeth Huxley", p.xiii–xvi.

Copies seen: BL, RH

Notes: Published in 1986 at £14.50 in edition of 4,000 copies. Copyright by East Africa Women's League.

B.17   THE LAST OF THE MAASAI   1987

Description: The last of the Maasai, [by] Mohamed Amin, Duncan Willetts, John Eames. Foreword by Elspeth Huxley.
London: The Bodley Head, [1987].

"Foreword by Elspeth Huxley", p.13–15

Copy seen: RH

Notes: Published on 3 September 1987 at £22.50 in edition of 10,000 copies.

B.18   AN AFRICAN SKETCHBOOK   1988

Description: An African sketchbook: drawings & watercolours of Kenya by Ray Nestor with extracts from his memoirs.
[Tolworth, Surrey]: Fountain Press, [1988].

"Foreword", signed "Elspeth Huxley May 1988," p.6–7.

Copy seen: Hants CL

Notes: Published on 27 October 1988 at £14.95 in edition of 6,000 copies. Designed by Grant Bradford.

B.19   A ROVING SCOT   1991

Description: A roving Scot, by Douglas Hutton.
Edinburgh, Cambridge, Durham: the Pentland Press Ltd., [1991].

"Foreword" signed in facsimile signature "Elspeth Huxley", p.vii–viii.

Copy seen: BL

B.20 JOMO'S JAILOR 1993

Description: Jomo's jailor: grand warrior of Kenya. The life of Leslie Whitehouse, by Elizabeth Watkins. Foreword by Elspeth Huxley.
[Calais]: Mulberry Books, [1993].

"Foreword by Elspeth Huxley", p.ix–xi, dated "Malmesbury, England 1992".

Copy seen: RH

Notes: Published in 1993 at £8.50 in sewn paperback (hardbacks to order only). This book has been retitled *Wouse.*

B.21 OSCAR FROM AFRICA 1995

Description: Oscar from Africa: the biography of Oscar Ferris Watkins, 1877–1943. [By] Elizabeth Watkins.
London, New York: The Radcliffe Press, [1995].

"Foreword by Elspeth Huxley", p.xvii–xx.

Copy seen: RC

Notes: Published 23 March 1995 at £24.50.

C. Contributions to newpapers and periodicals

Mrs. Huxley had kept cuttings of many of her articles in periodicals, including those on polo which she had pasted into a book, and also those she had written while working for the Empire Marketing Board (EMB) which were syndicated throughout the British Empire. All these can be seen in the Rhodes House Library, Oxford. Those articles which were not traceable as to date or provenance, have been placed in the Appendix under E.1. This section also includes EH's short stories.

1921

C.1   Country Sport – Makuyu Hunt & Polo Club. Mr. Swift's Accident. *East African Standard.* 10 December 1921

1922

C.2   Polo in Kenya – clubs throughout the country in full swing (by 'Bamboo'). *Kenya Sunday Times & Sporting News.* 17 February 1922

C.3   Hunting in Kenya – signed L.S. p.433. v.CXXlX. no.3614. *The Field.* 1 April 1922

C.4   In Kenya – signed L.S. v.CXL. no.3636. *The Field.* 2 September 1922

C.5   Polo in Kenya – Successful Cole Cup Tournament at Nyeri (by 'Bamboo'). *Kenya Sunday Times & Sporting News.* 1 October 1922

C.6   Polo in Kenya – Close of the Nyeri Tournament (by 'Bamboo'). *Kenya Sunday Times & Sporting News.* 8 October 1922

C.7   Polo in Kenya – Is it for the Many or the Few? (by 'Bamboo'). *Kenya Sunday Times & Sporting News.* 22 October 1922

C.8   Polo in England – the International Trial Matches (by 'Bamboo'). *Kenya Sunday Times & Sporting News.* 29 October 1922

C.9   Polo in Kenya – Possibility of a new Club in the Country (by 'Bamboo'). *Kenya Sunday Times & Sporting News.* 5 November 1922

C.10 Weather causes hell in Polo – The Hunting begins (by 'Bamboo'). *Kenya Sunday Times & Sporting News.* 12 November 1922

C.11 Polo in Kenya – Arrangements for Christmas Tournaments (by 'Bamboo'). *Kenya Sunday Times & Sporting News*. 19 November 1922

C.12 Polo in Kenya – programme for Polo Week at Makuyu (by 'Bamboo'). *Kenya Sunday Times & Sporting News*. 26 November 1922

C.13 Polo – Entries & Details of the Cranworth Cup. *Kenya Sunday Times & Sporting News*. 30 November 1922

C.14 Polo in America – Result of the National Open Championship. *Kenya Sunday Times & Sporting News*. 3 December 1922

C.15 Polo – The Origin and Development of the Game (by 'Bamboo'). *Kenya Sunday Times & Sporting News*. 10 December 1922

C.16 Polo in England – Introduction, Development & Expansion (by 'Bamboo'). *Kenya Sunday Times & Sporting News*. 17 December 1922

C.17 Polo in Kenya – Further details of MacMillan Cup (by 'Bamboo'). *Kenya Sunday Times & Sporting News*. 24 December 1922

1923

C.18 Nairobi Polo Week – Competitions for Cranworth & L.S.T.Cups (by 'Bamboo'). *East African Standard*. 5 January 1923

C.19 Makuyu Week – Hunting and the First Day's Polo. (From our own correspondent). *East African Observer*. 8 January 1923

C.20 L.S.T. Polo Cup – remarkably good Tournament between the banks (by 'Bamboo'). *East African Standard*. 9 January 1923

C.21 Makuyu Week – First Matches in the Polo Tournament. *East African Standard*. 13 January 1923

C.22 Makuyu Week – Makuyu and Rift Valley win the Cups. (From our own correspondent). *East African Observer*. 16 January 1923

C.23 Makuyu Polo Week – A full round of Sporting Events. *East African Standard*. 17 January 1923

C.24 Polo in Kenya – new arrangements for the Tournament (by 'Bamboo'). *East African Standard*. 24 January 1923

C.25 Polo in Kenya – A Review of the Past Season. *East African Observer*. 24 January 1923

C.26 Polo in Kenya – A few do's and don'ts for Players. *East African Standard*. 31 January 1923

C.27 Polo in Kenya – More hints for the would-be player (by 'Bamboo'). *East African Standard*. 8 February 1923

C.28 Polo in Kenya – Prospective games at Nanyuki Gymkhana (by 'Bamboo'). *East African Standard*. 14 February 1923

C.29 Polo Notes – (From our own correspondent). *East African Observer*. 17 February 1923

C.30 Polo Notes – The Expense of Polo in Kenya. *East African Observer*. 22 February 1923

C.31 Polo in Kenya – Points to Remember when purchasing a Pony (by 'Bamboo'). *East African Standard*. 1 March 1923

C.32 Polo Notes. (From our own Polo Poet). Adapted from a list of Hints made out by Capt. Ward for beginners. *East African Observer*. 1 March 1923

C.33 Polo in Kenya – Notes on the Training of Young Ponies (by 'Bamboo'). *East African Standard*. 6 March 1923

C.34 Polo in Kenya – Notes on the Education of a Polo Pony (by 'Bamboo'). *East African Standard*. 15 March 1923

C.35 Polo Notes – The History of the Game. (contributed). *East African Observer*. 17 March 1923

C.36 Polo in Kenya – concluding notes on the Training of ponies (by 'Bamboo'). *East African Standard*. 20 March 1923

C.37 Polo – A Possible Kenya Polo Team in London (by 'Bamboo'). *East African Standard*. 6 April 1923

C.38 Polo Notes – The Early History of Polo in England. *East African Observer*. 7 April 1923

C.39 Thika Notes – Weather, Sport & Politics. (From our own correspondent). *East African Observer*. 7 April 1923

C.40 In Kenya (polo article). v.CXLl. no.3668. Illustrated with 2 photographs. *The Field*. 12 April 1923

C.41 Thika Notes – Thika District Association splits into Two. (From our own correspondent). *East African Observer*. 21 April 1923

C.42 Polo Notes. (From our own correspondent). *East African Observer*. 5 May 1923

C.43 Thika Notes – Golf Course now being constructed. *East African Observer*. 19 May 1923

C.44 Thika Notes – A Wedding at the Makuyu Chapel. (From our own correspondent). *East African Observer*. 23 June 1923

C.45 Polo in Kenya – Particulars of the Fawcus Polo Cup at Njoro to be played this month (by a special correspondent). *East African Observer*. 30 June 1923

C Contributions to newspapers and periodicals 113

C.46 Polo Notes – Teams scratch in the Fawcus Cup owing to Horse-sickness. (By our own correspondent). *East African Observer*. 30 June 1923

C.47 Polo Notes – Horse-sickness at Njoro: further details. (From a special correspondent). *East African Observer*. 7 July 1923

C.48 Polo Notes – Probable Teams for July Tournament (by 'Bamboo'). *East African Standard*. 20 July 1923

C.49 Polo Notes – Particulars of This Week's Tournament (by 'Bamboo'). *East African Standard*. 24 July 1923

C.50 Nairobi Polo Week – Makuyu win the Cranworth Cup. *East African Standard*. 30 July 1923

C.51 Nairobi Polo Week – Surprising Game in the Cavalry Cup. *East African Standard*. 31 July 1923

C.52 Nairobi Polo Week – Concluding Game of the Tournament. *East African Standard*. 1 August 1923

C.53 Polo Notes – Visit of a Team to Zanzibar this week. *East African Standard*. 8 August 1923

C.54 Thika Notes – Thika versus Makuyu Cricket Match. (From our own correspondent). *East African Observer*. 11 August 1923

C.55 Polo in England – The Indian Tigers Team at Hurlingham. *East African Standard*. 21 August 1923

C.56 Polo in Zanzibar – The Visit of the Up-country Team. *East African Standard*. 25 August 1923

C.57 The Polo Tournament at Nyeri. *East African Standard*. 15 September 1923

C.58 Polo Notes – Poor Entries for the Cole Cup at Nyeri. *East African Standard*. 17 September 1923

C.59 Thika Notes – Buffalo seen near the Thika Sports Ground. *East African Observer*. 22 September 1923

C.60 Polo in England – British Army Team now in America. *East African Standard*. 24 September 1923

C.61 Successful Polo Week at Nyeri – Local Team wins the Cole Cup. *East African Standard*. 25 September 1923

C.62 Polo Notes – some remarks on the Nyeri Tournament. *East African Standard*. 4 October 1923

C.63 The Makuyu Hunt, Kenya Colony, signed E.G. v.CXLII. no.3693. Illustrated with 3 photographs. *The Field*. 4 October 1923

C.64 Polo in Kenya – the Nairobi New Year Polo Week. *East African Standard*. 12 December 1923

C.65 The Nairobi Week – details of the Coming Tournaments. *East African Standard*. 22 December 1923

C.66 Nairobi Polo Week – Details of First Round of the Connaught Cup. *East African Standard*. 31 December 1923

1924

C.67 Polo Week in Nairobi – Matches for the Various Competitions described. *East African Standard*. 3 January 1924

C.68 The Banks Cup – The First Tie in the L.S.T. Tournaments. *East African Standard*. 4 January 1924

C.69 Polo week in Nairobi – Nyeri in the Connaught Cup. *East African Standard*. 5 January 1924

C.70 The Banks Cup – Strength and Weaknesses of the Teams. *East African Standard*. 7 January 1924

C.71 Polo in England – the Team to visit America this Year (by 'Bamboo'). *East African Standard*. 28 June 1924

C.72 Polo Notes – The Forthcoming Tournament Week (by 'Bamboo'). *East African Standard*. 5 July 1924

C.73 This Week's Polo Tournament – Teams for Cavalry Cup. *East African Standard*. 22 July 1924

C.74 Polo Week in Nairobi – Criticism of First Day's Play. *East African Standard*. 25 July 1924

C.75 Success of the Polo Tournament – How Nyeri won the Cavalry Cup. *East African Standard*. 28 July 1924

C.76 End of the Polo Tournament – Meru wins Cranworth Cup on Handicap. *East African Standard*. 29 July 1924

C.77 International Polo Test – Teams for the American Visit. *East African Standard*. 15 August 1924

1927

C.78 'I'll tell the World!' – impressions of an American university. Signed E.J.G. pp.11–13. v.XXVI. no.1. *Tamesis*. Autumn Term 1927

1929

C.79 'Science War on Locusts'. *Times*. 12 January 1929

C.80 'The Most Modern Traveller'. *Observer*. 13 January 1929

C.81 'Biologist for the Empire'. *Times*. 26 January 1929

C.82 'Poultry & Eggs Research. Marketing Board Grants.' *Times*. 28 January 1929

C.83 'Great Need for more Trained Biologists' (EMB). *Daily Gleaner* (Jamaica). 5 February 1929

C.84 'Export of Cattle. Progress at Quarantine Station'. p.8. *Times*. 7 February 1929

C.85 'Virus Disease Problems' (EMB). *The Field*. 21 February 1929

C.86 'Safety First in Oranges – the Tale of an Arab's Fingernail'. *Tit Bits*. 23 March 1929

C.87 'Empire Marketing – colour affects prices' (EMB). *News* (Adelaide). 3 April 1929

C.88 'Fruit Problems' (EMB). *News* (Adelaide). 3 April 1929

C.89 'Research at Rothamsted' (EMB). *West Australian* (Perth). 29 April 1929

C.90 'What do Insects eat?' (EMB). *West Australian* (Perth). 15 June 1929

C.91 'Grass & Meat: doubling the Yield'. *Times*. 1 July 1929

C.92 'Fruit Doctors of the Harbour' (EMB). *Cape Times*. 5 July 1929

C.93 'The Grasslands of South Africa' (EMB). *Cape Times*. 25 July 1929

C.94 'A Tide in the Affairs of Mice' (EMB). *Calgary Daily Herald*. 3 August 1929

C.95 'Pasture Deficiencies in the Empire. The Work in Kenya' (EMB). *East African Standard*. 10 August 1929

C.96 'Fatal Banana Wilt: fruit destroyed by parasite'. Panama disease. *Daily Telegraph*. 16 August 1929

C.97 'Fur-bearing Animals found to Fluctuate in Even Cycles' (EMB). *Daily Star* (Montreal). 20 August 1929

C.98 'The Significance of Weather: insect & rodent pests'. *Manchester Guardian*. 3 September 1929

C.99 'Effect of Cold on Meat. New Zealand Mutton Trade.' A Scientific Survey. *Times*. 28 September 1929

C.100 'Scientists Help the Sports Craze'. Games they win in the laboratory. (On Professor Stapleton). *Tit Bits*. 23 October 1929

C.101 'Fruit Tree Behaviour' (EMB). *Farm & Home* (Vancouver). 5 November 1929

C.102 'Behind the Scenes at Kew' (EMB). *Cape Argus*. 22 November 1929

C.103 'Pedigree Pastures. Breeding blue blood grasses'. *Manchester Guardian*. 5 December 1929

116   C   *Contributions to newspapers and periodicals*

C.104   'Hard Cheese' (EMB). *The Sun* (Sydney). 5 December 1929
C.105   'Top-Hat Trees' (EMB). *The Sun* (Sydney). 18 December 1929
C.106   'Tung-Oil and its uses in Industry' (EMB). *Natal Mercury.* 21 December 1929
C.107   'Weather is helpful in Control of Farmers' Pests' (EMB). *Baltimore Sun.* 22 December 1929
C.108   'Science at Slough'. Investigating habits of insect pests (EMB). *Newcastle Daily Journal.* 30 December 1929

1930

C.109   'Bringing the Tropics to the Thames' (EMB). *East African Standard.* 11 January 1930
C.110   'Parasite Zoo kills Canada's Crop Pests' (EMB). *Vancouver Sun.* 4 February 1930
C.111   'From Wales. Seeds for Australia' (EMB). *The Sun* (Sydney). 6 February 1930
C.112   'Beetle Battles' (EMB) *The Sun* (Sydney). 26 February 1930
C.113   'Caged Cannibals in English Village' (EMB). *Manitoba Free Press.* 11 March 1930
C.114   'With Graphs – Scientific Farming' (EMB). *The Sun* (Sydney). 12 March 1930
C.115   'Improving Grasses of the Empire. Seeds from Welsh Farms for Africa' (EMB). *East African Standard.* 15 March 1930
C.116   'Mouse Maps to Help Farmers' (EMB). *Melbourne Herald.* 20 March 1930
C.117   'Glass Gardens' (EMB). *The Sun* (Sydney). 30 March 1930
C.118   'Empire Woods Favoured' (EMB). *Telegraph-Journal* (St. John, New Brunswick). 1 April 1930
C.119   'Flowering under Artificial Sun'. Field of Research for Scientists. Tracking disease (EMB). *Manchester Evening News.* 16 April 1930
C.120   'Strange Tasks for the Scientists! – An Insect Police Force'. p.21. *Daily Mail.* 28 April 1930
C.121   'Women support Empire Shopping?'. *Western Press & Review* (Bristol) 29 April 1930
C.122   'Strange Tasks for the Scientists. 2 – Finding New Bananas'. p.21. *Daily Mail.* 5 May 1930
C.123   'Strange Tasks for the Scientists. 3 – Enemies too Small To be Seen' p.17. *Daily Mail.* 13 May 1930

C Contributions to newspapers and periodicals

C.124 'Strange Tasks for the Scientists! 4 – Growing Special Grasses'. p.17. *Daily Mail*. 20 May 1930

C.125 'Strange Tasks for the Scientist! 5 – Floating Farmyards'. p.19. *Daily Mail*. 28 May 1930

C.126 'Strange Tasks for the Scientist! 6 – Apples All-Alive-O'. p.19. *Daily Mail*. 10 June 1930

C.127 'An Insect War against a Weed – Australia's effort. Salving 60,000 acres.' *Manchester Guardian*. 12 July 1930

C.128 'Insect Migrants' (EMB). *The Sun* (Sydney). 13 August 1930

C.129 'Cold Cargoes. The Freezing of Empire Food – Research during 50 Years'. (Cold station in Ditton Lab. built with aid from EMB. at East Malling, Kent). *Times*. 14 August 1930

C.130 'Luxury Homes for Insects'. Article on new wing of Natural History Museum – built by EMB to house insects from all parts of the world. *The Star*. 21 August 1930

C.131 'The New Insect Museum'. *Manchester Guardian*. 22 August 1930

C.132 'Millions from Grass' British Farming Enterprise. Pedigree crop experiment. *Morning Post*. 28 August 1930

C.133 'Frozen Cargo Problems' (EMB). *Natal Mercury*. 18 September 1930

C.134 'Hair-raising mysteries – Marvels at research H.Q. Measuring by squeaks. Imitating the human finger'. *Liverpool Echo*. 25 September 1930

C.135 'Pedigree Grasses for Natal' (EMB). *Natal Mercury*. 2 October 1930

C.136 'The Nature of Wool' (EMB). *Cape Times*. 29 October 1930

C.137 'How Science helps the Woolgrower' (EMB). *Natal Mercury*. 11 November 1930

C.138 'Safe Transport for Empire Fruit' (EMB). *Cape Times*. 13 November 1930

C.139 'Scheme for Empire Development' (EMB). *Times of India*. 20 November 1930

C.140 'Wizards of Science build Ship's Hold in Orchard to solve Apple Storage Riddles' (EMB). *Vancouver Sun*. 6 December 1930

C.141 'Ship's Hold in an Orchard' (EMB). *Farmers' Weekly* (Bloemfontein). 10 December 1930

C.142 'Milk-fed Rats for Research'. Dairying Institute for experiments. *Daily Express*, Scottish edition. 31 December 1930

1931

C.143 'Science takes an Apple – and liquifies the Aroma: Solving the Secret of Flavour.' *Morning Post*. 8 January 1931

C.144 'Empire's Insect Foes' (EMB). *Rhodesia Herald*. 12 January 1931

C.145 'Fruit Trees in Desert Soil' (EMB). *Cape Times*. 13 January 1931

C.146 'Quest for T.B.Freedom'. *Farmer & Stockbreeder & Agricultural Gazette*. 19 January 1931

C.147 'Artificial Orchards' (EMB). *Natal Witness*. 19 January 1931

C.148 'Plant Plagues: A New Campaign on Kew Green – Microscopic Foes of Empire' (re new Imperial Mycological Institute with aid from EMB). *Times*. 7 February 1931

C.149 'Behaviour of Bananas' (EMB). *Ceylon Observer*. 9 February 1931

C.150 'Safe from T.B. Scourge' (EMB). *Daily Telegraph* (Sydney). 17 February 1931

C.151 'How Fruit Commits Suicide' (EMB). *Melbourne Herald*. 21 February 1931

C.152 'Liquified Aromas' (EMB). *Daily Telegraph* (Sydney). 23 February 1931

C.153 'Empire Insects' (EMB). *Dominion* (Wellington N.Z.). 3 March 1931

C.154 'Battle of the Bugs' (EMB). *Trinidad Guardian*. 25 March 1931

C.155 'An Empire Workshop' (EMB). *Manchester Guardian*. 27 March 1931

C.156 'Plant Doctors of the Empire' (EMB). *Cape Times*. 30 March 1931

C.157 'Empire Plant Doctors' (EMB). *Farmers' Weekly* (Bloemfontein). 1 April 1931

C.158 'Bottled Smoke for Kippers. Secret of colour and fragrance. Search for right sawdust blend.' *Morning Post*. 6 April 1931

C.159 'The House that Jerry Built – novel experiments in war against dry rot'. *Evening Standard*. 17 April 1931

C.160 'Deep Sea Fish. The New Nets of Science. Two Empire Research Stations' – from a correspondent. *Times*. 1 May 1931

C.161 'Britishers deal Death Blow to Warble Fly Pest' (EMB). *Vancouver Daily Province*. 2 May 1931

C.162 'Bright Lights under the sea'. Solving mystery of the ocean bed. Curing haddocks to colour shades (EMB). *Northern Evening Dispatch*. 4 May 1931

C.163 'Better Hides for Britain' (EMB). *The Statesman* (Calcutta). 14 May 1931

C   *Contributions to newspapers and periodicals*   119

C.164 'Wheat–stem 'Sawfly' under Attack' (EMB). *Calgary Daily Herald*. 16 May 1931

C.165 'Stopping the Rot' (about pit props). *New Statesman*. 17 May 1931

C.166 'New Ways of Deep Sea Fishing' (EMB). *Ceylon Observer*. 31 May 1931

C.167 'Grass to Combat Drought' (EMB). *Cape Times*. 2 June 1931

C.168 'A House For Beetles' (EMB). *Daily Telegraph* (Sydney). 9 June 1931

C.169 'The Myth of the Healthy Savage' by E.J. Grant. *Weekend Review*. 20 June 1931

C.170 'Empire Fruit Research' (EMB). *Daily Telegraph* (Sydney). 24 June 1931

C.171 'The Sociable Apple: how it thrives better in company'. Gas storage system. (Department of Scientific and Industrial Resources at Cambridge). *Observer*. 5 July 1931

C.172 'Foodstuffs and Disease' (EMB). *Farmers' Weekly* (Bloemfontein). 8 July 1931

C.173 'Diet and Disease' (EMB). *Bloemfontein Friend*. 11 July 1931

C.174 'New Successes of Food Experts' (EMB). *Cape Argus*. 14 July 1931

C.175 'Gas Attack on Fruit Storage' (EMB). *Farmers' Weekly* (Bloemfontein). 15 July 1931

C.176 'Gas Storage of Fruits' (EMB). *Daily Telegraph* (Sydney). 21 July 1931

C.177 'Ousting Foreign Timbers' (EMB). *Farmers' Weekly* (Bloemfontein). 29 July 1931

C.178 'A Plant which makes Horses Bald' (EMB). *Manchester Guardian*. 31 July 1931

C.179 'Voyage in Hold of Steamer' (EMB). *Natal Mercury*. 4 August 1931

C.180 'Buried Treasure' (EMB) *Times of India*. 11 August 1931

C.181 'Magicians seek for Empire Buried Treasure' (EMB). *Trinidad Guardian*. 14 August 1931

C.182 'Woman Scientist's Great Discovery' (EMB). *Ceylon Observer*. 30 August 1931

C.183 'How Scientists help Pilots. Testing Schneider Trophy Planes' (EMB). *Cape Times*. 15 September 1931

C.184 Imperial & Foreign News. 'Locust Danger' A conference in Rome. *Times*. 29 September 1931

C   Contributions to newspapers and periodicals

C.185   'What Faraday did for Women' (EMB). *Telegraph-Journal* (St John, New Brunswick). 6 October 1931
C.186   'War on the Tsetse' by E.J.Grant. pp.569–70. *Weekend Review*. 25 October 1931
C.187   'Carton Beef Plan Mooted' (EMB). *Kamloops Sentinel* (British Columbia). 26 October 1931
C.188   Knowledge for Use – 1. 'The Tap Root of Industry' by E.J.Grant. *The Times – Trade & Engineering Supplement*. 14 November 1931
C.189   'Wool for Women's Faces' (EMB). *New Daily/Chronicle* (Georgetown, B.G.). 30 November 1931
C.190   'Better Meals for Animals' (EMB). *Cape Argus*. 2 December 1931
C.191   Knowledge for Use – 2. 'Science & Wool' by E.J.Grant. *Times – Trade & Engineering Supplement*. 5 December 1931
C.192   'New Grasses which defy Drought. Important discovery in South Africa' (EMB). *East African Standard*. 26 December 1931

1932

C.193   Knowledge for Use – 3. 'Tracking Troubles in the Cotton Industry' by E.J.Grant. *Times – Trade & Engineering Supplement*. 2 January 1932
C.194   'Africa Improving Hill Grazing. Experiments in Wales. Ploughing Plynlymmon'. *Times*. 4 January 1932
C.195   'Romance in a Blue Book. Sugar Cane & Scientists' by E.J.Grant. *Daily Telegraph*. 8 January 1932
C.196   'Process of Milk Manufacture remains Dairy Cow's Trade Secret' (EMB). *Melbourne Countryman*. 8 January 1932
C.197   'The Cow and the Man of Science. How Research helps the Dairy Industry' (EMB). *East African Standard*. 23 January 1932
C.198   'New Opportunities for Sheep Farmers. Fishing boots: leather goods made from wool' (EMB). *East African Standard*. 6 February 1932
C.199   Knowledge for Use – 4. 'Watchdogs of Food Quality' by E.J.Grant. *Times – Trade & Engineering Supplement*. 6 February 1932
C.200   Knowledge for Use – 5. 'New Metals for New Industries' by E.J.Grant. *Times – Trade & Engineering Supplement*. 5 March 1932
C.201   'British Chocolate keeps its Freshness' (EMB) (by a correspondent). *Glasgow Evening Times*. 16 March 1932
C.202   'The Chocolate Scientist' (EMB). *Times of India*. 18 March 1932

C   *Contributions to newspapers and periodicals*   121

C.203 'Scientific Sweets' (EMB). *Cape Times*. 19 March 1932

C.204 'Helping Empire Cotton to grow Straight' (EMB). *The Star* (Johannesburg). 22 March 1932

C.205 'Neps gives in to Research' (EMB). *Farmers' Weekly* (Bloemfontein). 23 March 1932

C.206 'The Chocolate Scientist' (EMB). *The Argus* (Melbourne). 26 March 1932

C.207 'The Newest Frocks'. *Dominion* (Wellington N.Z.). 31 March 1932

C.208 'Scientists seek to track Deadly Disease Viruses' (EMB). *The Gazette* (Montreal). 31 March 1932

C.209 'New Model Frocks'. *Dominion* (Wellington N.Z.). 1 April 1932

C.210 Knowledge for Use – 6. 'Mathematics of the Foot' by E.J. Grant. *Times – Trade & Engineering Supplement*. 2 April 1932

C.211 'Crop and Animal Diseases studied by Empire Board' (EMB). *Saskatoon Star-Phoenix*. 9 April 1932

C.212 'A New Light on the Invisible' by E.J.Grant. pp.478–9. *Weekend Review*. 16 April 1932

C.213 Knowledge for use – 7. 'Chemical Research' by E.J. Grant. *Times – Trade & Engineering Supplement*. 7 May 1932

C.214 'Aiding Empire Cotton to go straight. Scientists discover the Secret of Neps' (EMB). *East African Standard*. 21 May 1932

C.215 Knowledge for Use – 8. 'The Chemist looks ahead' by E.J.Grant. *Times – Trade & Engineering Supplement*. 4 June 1932

C.216 Knowledge for Use – 9. 'Teamwork in Imperial Research' by E.J.Grant. *Times – Trade & Engineering Supplement*. 2 July 1932

C.217 Knowledge for Use – 10. 'New Outlets for Rubber' by E.J.Grant. *Times – Trade & Engineering Supplement*. 6 August 1932

C.218 Knowledge for Use – 11. 'Scientific Instruments' by E.J.Grant. *Times – Trade & Engineering Supplement*. 3 September 1932

C.219 Knowledge for Use – 12. 'Flax & Linen' by E.J.Grant. *Times – Trade & Engineering Supplement*. 1 October 1932

C.220 'The Future of the Empire Marketing Board. Complete Abolition recommended'. *East African Standard*. 8 October 1932

C.221 Industrial Research Abroad – 1. 'Scientific Structure in the United States by E.J.Grant. p.155. *Times – Trade & Engineering Supplement*. 3 November 1932

C.222 Industrial Research Abroad – 2. 'American Companies' by E.J. Grant. *Times – Trade & Engineering Supplement*. 3 December 1932

1933

C.223 Industrial Research Abroad – 3. 'American Achievments' by E. J. Grant. *Times – Trade & Engineering Supplement.* 7 January 1933

C.224 Industrial Research Abroad – 4. 'Germany's Lead' by E.J.Grant. *Times – Trade & Engineering Supplement.* 4 February 1933

C.225 Industrial Research Abroad– 5. 'Germany – Iron & Engineering' by E.J.Grant. *Times – Trade & Engineering Supplement.* 4 March 1933

C.226 Gold Rush in Kenya – 1. Prospecting at Kakamega. (From a special correspondent). *Times.* 21 March 1933

C.227 Gold Rush in Kenya – 2. Miners & Natives. (From a special correspondent). *Times.* 22 March 1933

C.228 Industrial Research Abroad – 6. 'Germany – Chemicals & Light Metals' by E.J.Grant. *Times – Trade & Engineering Supplement.* 1 April 1933

1935

C.229 ' A New deal for Farmers' – 1. The American Experiment. pp.17–18. *Times.* 16 April 1935

C.230 'A New Deal for Farmers' – 2. Scenes beyond Washington. pp.15–16. *Times.* 17 April 1935

C.231 'In the New South: An American Experiment'. pp.163–172. v.1. is.3. *Geographical Magazine.* July 1935

1936

C.232 'The Nature of the Native' p.15. *Times.* 28 July 1936

C.233 'Soil erosion in America' p.10. *Times.* 11 September 1936

C.234 'Resettling the small farmer'. The Bare Lands of America. *Times.* 16 December 1936

1937

C.235 'The Story of Njombo' – notes & photographs. pp.157–168. v.4. is.3. *Geographical Magazine.* January 1937

C.236 'The Story of the Mississippi Floods'. *East African Standard.* 12 February 1937

C.237 'Making Deserts' 1. The Other Aspect of Agriculture. *Times.* 10 June 1937

C.238 'Making Deserts' 2. The Exhausted Pasture. *Times*. 11 June 1937
C.239 'The Dead Cities of Ceylon'. pp.225–240. v.5. is.4. *Geographical Magazine*. August 1937
C.240 'Erosion 1: America's distressed areas'. pp.297–312. v.5.is.5. *Geographical Magazine*. September 1937

1938

C.241 'Tropical Soils'. Letter. p.15. *Times*. 14 July 1938
C.242 'Erosion 2: Man the desert makers'. pp.297–312. v.6. is.5. *Geographical Magazine*. August 1938
C.243 'America on the Highway'. pp.299–320. v.7. is.5. *Geographical Magazine*. September 1938

1939

C.244 'The Wish of the People: Measuring opinion: A new American Technique'. p.15–16. *Times*. 2 May 1939
C.245 'Locust Horde sweeps Africa' Photo–essay. pp.33–35. *Pix*. December 1939

1940

C.246 'Camera Safari' article and photographs by Elspeth and Gervas Huxley. pp.10–11. *New York Times Magazine*. 11 February 1940

1941

C.247 'Blitz–seeing in a Tea–car'. p.15. *The Argus Week-end Magazine* (Melbourne). 4 January 1941
C.248 'Farms from the Desert: Land reclamation in the U.S.A.' pp.86–97. v.3. is.2. *Geographical Magazine*. June 1941

1942

C.249 'The Only Woman in the Lifeboat'. The story of Mary Cornish taken from *Atlantic Ordeal* (A.8). pp.113–125. v. 184. *Harper's Magazine*. January 1942
C.250 'Did you hear that?' Microphone miscellany featuring Home Service report about the WAAF. p.73. v.28. no.705. *The Listener*. 16 July 1942

C.251 'Did you hear that?'. Home Service report on the WRENS. p.138. v.28. no.707. *The Listener.* 30 July 1942

C.252 'Did you hear that?' Report on the WRENS. (Wrongly ascribed to Elizabeth Hughes, but indexed under Elspeth Huxley). p.395. v.28. no.715. *The Listener.* 24 September 1942

1943

C.253 'Did you hear that?' Report of 'Jeeps and Sprouts' broadcast on American soldiers. p.266. v.29. no.738. *The Listener.* 4 March 1943

C.254 'East Africa & the Future'. pp.14–23. v.16. is.1. *Geographical Magazine.* May 1943

C.255 'Did you hear that?' Report on Buried Cities of Ceylon. p.685. v.29. no.752. *The Listener.* 10 June 1943

C.256 'A challenge to all of us: two views on the responsibilities of colonial empire.' Report of Home Service broadcast with Leonard Woolf. pp.180–181. v.30. no.761. *The Listener.* 12 August 1943

C.257 'The Grouping of Colonies'. pp.1016–1017 v.24 no.50. *Time & Tide.* 11 December 1943

1944

C.258 'A Plan for Africa'. p.45. v.25. no.3. *Time & Tide.* 15 January 1944

C.259 'The Empire Conference & the Colonies' 1. p.413 v.25 no.20. *Time & Tide.* 13 May 1944

C.260 'The Empire Conference & the Colonies' 2. pp.438–9 v.25 no.21. *Time &Tide.* 20 May 1944

C.261 'Flesh & Paper Africa' – review of *African Conversation Piece* by Sylvia Leith-Ross. p.750 v.25. no.35. *Times & Tide.* 26 August 1944

C.262 'Blue-print for Belly-aches' – review of *Welfare in the British Colonies* by L.P.Mair. p.971 v.25 no.45. *Time & Tide.* 4 November 1944

C.263 'Self-rule for Ceylon'. pp.1125–6 v.25 no.52. *Time & Tide.* 23 December 1944

1945

C.264 'The Rebuilding of Burma' 1. pp.137–8 v.26 no.7. *Time & Tide.* 17 February 1945

C Contributions to newspapers and periodicals   125

C.265 'The Rebuilding of Burma' 2. pp.158–9 v.26 no.8. *Time & Tide.* 24 February 1945

C.266 'Mandates' – review of *Tanganyika Territory* by C. Leubuscher. pp.231–2. v.26 no.11. *Time & Tide.* 17 March 1945

C.267 Review of *The African as Suckling and as Adult* by J.F.Ritchie. Rhodes-Livingstone Papers No.9. pp.87–88. v.44. no.175. *African Affairs.* April 1945

C.268 'Democracy: an African Experiment'. pp.493–4 v.26 no.24. *Time & Tide.* 16 June 1945

C.269 'Colonial Universities'. pp.644–5. v.26. no.31. *Time & Tide.* 4 August 1945

C.270 'Trouble in Uganda'. p.790. v.26. no.38. *Time & Tide.* 22 September 1945

C.271 'A New Start in Malaya'. p.853. v.26. no.41. *Time & Tide.* 13 October 1945

C.272 'Tour of East Africa: in Tanganyika discussions on formation of literature bureau'. *Times* 21 November 1945

1946

C.273 African Vista: 1. 'Two Sides of the Continent'. pp.151–2. v.27. no.7. *Time & Tide.* 16 February 1946

C.274 African Vista: 2. 'The Twilight of Peasantry'. p.174. v.27. no.8. *Time & Tide.* 23 February 1946

C.275 African Vista: 3. 'The Spring of Discontent'. p.198. v.27. no.9. *Time & Tide.* 9 March 1946

C.276 'East Africa Revisited: 1. Growth of population on poorer soil – political temper sharpened'. p.5. *Times* 25 March 1946

C.277 'East Africa Revisited: 2. Need for new industries and sure markets – a country without towns'. p.5. *Times.* 26 March 1946

C.278 'Proposed East African literature bureau.' *Times.* 29 April 1946

C.279 The future of the colonies: a discussion between a questioner (Edward Higgins), an administrator, H. M. Grace (missionary) & E H. p.712–713. v.35. no.907. *The Listener.* 30 May 1946

C.280 'Social Anthropology' – review of *The Dynamics of Cultural Change* by Bronislaw Malinowski. p.710. v.27. no.30 *Time & Tide.* 27 July 1946

C.281 Reflections on Colonial Policy: 1 'Palestine, India & the Colonies'. p.773. v.27. no.33. *Time & Tide.* 17 August 1946

126   C   Contributions to newspapers and periodicals

C.282   Reflections on Colonial Policy 2: 'The Mirage of "Common Citizenship".' pp.799–800. v.27. no.34. *Time & Tide*. 24 August 1946

C.283   Reflections on Colonial Policy 3: 'The Future of Divided Colonies'. pp.820–1. v.27. no.35. *Time & Tide*. 31 August 1946

1947

C.284   'Malayan Federation'. p.4. v.28. no.1. *Time & Tide*. 4 January 1947

C.285   'Imperial Small Talk' – review of *Tour of Duty* by Stewart Symes, and *Malayan Landscape* by Katharine Sim. p.84. v.28. no.3. *Time & Tide*. 18 January 1947

C.286   'Economic Weakness in East Africa: Mrs. Huxley's warning' (Report of talk to Royal African Society and Royal Empire Society). p.7. *Times*. 31 July 1947

C.287   'Game slaughter in Africa: the tsetse menace: Plea for intensified research'. Letter. p.5. *Times*. 16 September 1947

C.288   'Some Impressions of East Africa Today.' pp. 197–207. v.46. no.185. *African Affairs*. October 1947

1948

C.289   'Groundnuts and the Gogo'. p.634 v.29. no.25. *Time & Tide*. 19 June 1948

C.290   'The Gold Coast Disturbances'. pp.828–9. v.29. no.33. *Time & Tide*. 14 August 1948

C.291   Review of 'Nairobi: Master plan for a colonial capital' by Professor L.W.Thornton White. pp.251–2. v.47. no.189. *African Affairs*. October 1948

C.292   'The African Conference'. pp.1043–4. v.29. no.42. *Time & Tide*. 16 October 1948

C.293   'Whither in Africa? Some reflections on the Gold Coast Report'. pp.439–448. v.131. no.789. *The National Review*. November 1948

C.294   'Whither in Africa? The choice before us.' pp.548–556. v.131. no.790. *The National Review*. December 1948

1949

C.295   Review of *The Sky and the Forest* by C.S.Forester. p.82. v.48. no.190. *African Affairs*. January 1949

C Contributions to newspapers and periodicals

C.296 'Rome in Africa: Days of Service to an Empire'. Letter. p.5. *Times*. 13 January 1949

C.297 'The Tsetse Fly: Progress in modern methods of attack'. p.5. *Times*. 9 February 1949

C.298 'Notes on the Way'. pp.147–8. v.30. no.7. *Time & Tide*. 12 February 1949

C.299 'The Malayan Crisis'. p.244–5. v.30. no.11. *Time & Tide*. 12 March 1949

C.300 Letter 'E.H.'s Notes on the Way'. p.274. v.30. no.12. *Time & Tide*. 19 March 1949

C.301 'Tombo and his people 1: A Masai Boyhood'. pp.460–469. v.21. is.12. *Geographical Magazine*. April 1949

C.302 'Books new and old: a human document' Review of *Cry the Beloved Country* by Alan Paton. pp.449–453. v.132. no.794. *The National Review*. April 1949

C.303 'Tombo and his people 2. Tombo's schooldays'. pp.1–8. v.22. is.1 *Geographical Magazine*. May 1949

C.304 'Greater Rhodesia'. pp.227–233. v.39. no.155. *Round Table*. June 1949

C.305 'Colonial Cockayne'. pp.639–40. v.30. no.26. *Time & Tide*. 25 June 1949

C.306 'Land problems in Africa: Cambridge Conference'. (Report of E.H. as speaker giving talk 'Must Africa starve?'). p.3. *Times*. 29 August 1949

C.307 'Collectives without Tears' pp.880–1 v.30. no.36. *Time & Tide*. 3 September 1949

C.308 'British Aims in Africa' pp.43–55. v.28. no.1. *Foreign Affairs*. October 1949

C.309 'Must Africa Starve?' An abbreviation of an address given by Mrs. Elspeth Huxley to the Cambridge Summer Conference. pp.15–17. v.1. no.10. *Corona*. November 1949

C.310 'Gold Coast Plan' pp.1108–9 v.30. no.45. *Time & Tide*. 5 November 1949

C.311 Travels in Kenya' – review of *Last Chance in Africa* by Negley Farson, and of *Karamojo Safari* by W.D.M.Bell. pp.1234–5 v.30. no.49. *Time & Tide*. 3 December 1949

C.312 'From Lake Success to the Zambesi'. pp.1260–1. v.30. no.50. *Time & Tide*. 10 December 1949

1950

C.313 'On Clearing Out' – review of *Self Government in the Colonies* by W.R.Crocker. p.139. v.31. no.6. *Time & Tide*. 11 February 1950

C.314 'Seretse Khama'. p.153 v.31. no.7. *Time & Tide*. 18 February 1950

C.315 'First British Colonial Capital City'. pp.233–235. *South African Railways & Harbours Magazine*. April 1950

C.316 'In Face of Fear'. p.385. v.31. no.16. *Time & Tide*. 22 April 1950

C.317 'Native Africa' – review of *Africa: Britain's Third Empire* by George Padmore, and of *Black Man's Country* by Isobel Ryan. pp.423–4. v.31. no.17. *Time & Tide*. 29 April 1950

C.318 'The Rise of the African Zealot'. pp.163–166. v.2. no.5. *Corona*. May 1950

C.319 'Tomorrow's Hope or Yesterday's Dream?' p.12. v.99. no.33,734. *New York Times Magazine*. 4 June 1950

C.320 'The Groundnut Fiasco'. p.597. v.31. no.24. *Time & Tide*. 17 June 1950

C.321 'Our Mission in Africa. Earning Natives' Loyalties'. Letter. *Daily Telegraph*. 23 June 1950

C.322 'The Cold War & the Colonies'. A critique of the Colombo Plan. pp. 1–9. v.CXLVIII. no.881. *The Nineteenth Century & After*. 1 July 1950

C.323 'Africa's Tomorrow'. pp.28–34. v.41. no.227. *Progress*. Summer 1950

C.324 'Dusty Answer' – review of *White Man Boss* by 'Adamaster'. pp.1056–7. v.31 no.42. *Time & Tide*. 21 October 1950

C.325 'Africa's Tomorrow' (extract from an article in *Progress*). pp.442–443. v.2. no.12. *Corona*. December 1950

C.326 'An Olive Branch for Africa'. pp.1296–7. v.31. no.51. *Time & Tide*. 23 December 1950

1951

C.327 'Experiment in Africa'. p.92. v.32. no.5. *Time & Tide*. 3 February 1951

C.328 'Fear in South Africa' – review of *The People of South Africa* by S.G.Millin. p.302. v.32. no.14. *Time & Tide*. 7 April 1951

C.329 'Central African Federation'. p.590. v.31. no.25. *Time & Tide*. 23 June 1951

C.330 'A Madeira Holiday'. pp.267–274. v.24. is.6. *Geographical Magazine*. October 1951

1952

C.331 'Two nations of the Gold Coast'. p.5. *Sunday Times*. 6 January 1952

C.332 'The Future of the Gold Coast'. p.172. v.33. no.8 *Time & Tide*. 23 February 1952

C.333 'African Story' – review of *The Palm-wine Drunkard* by Amos Tutuola. p.491–2. v.33. no.19. *Time & Tide*. 10 May 1952

C.334 'A Plan for Central Africa'. p.674–5. v.33. no.25. *Time & Tide*. 21 June 1952

C.335 'Africa All Over'. p.754–5. v.33. no.27. *Time & Tide*. 5 July 1952

C.336 'Democracy in Gold Coast. Giving full power to Africans'. Letter. *Daily Telegraph*. 6 August 1952

C.337 'Three Nigerias'. *Time & Tide*. 8 August 1952

C.338 'Unrest and Crime in Kenya. Basic cause is Social Revolution – too much too soon.' *Daily Telegraph*. 17 September 1952

C.339 'West Africa in Transition'. pp.310–320. v.25. is.6. *Geographical Magazine*. October 1952

C.340 'The Lion needs the Jungle'. pp.1159–60. v.33. no.41. *Time & Tide*. 11 October 1952

C.341 'Terrorism in Kenya – Jomo Kenyatta's Significance'. *Daily Telegraph*. 1 November 1952

C.342 'The Roots of Mau Mau'. pp.1321–2. v.33. no.46. *Time & Tide*. 15 November 1952

1953

C.343 'A Last Chance in Central Africa'. p.10. v.34. no.1. *Time & Tide*. 3 January 1953

C.344 'Mau Mau' (Men & Books). pp.21–2. v.34. no.1. *Time & Tide*. 3 January 1953

C.345 'An area of light in the Dark Continent'. p.20. v.102. no.34,686. *New York Times Magazine*. 11 January 1953

C.346 'On Central African Federation'. *Times*. 15 January 1953

C.347 'Remedies for Kenya'. pp.133–4. v.34. no.5. *Time & Tide*. 31 January 1953

C.348 'Africa at the Crossroads'. pp.202–3. v.34. no.7. *Time & Tide*. 14 February 1953

C.349 'Last seen Johannesburg' – review of *Blanket Boy's Moon* by P.Lanham & A.Mopeli-Paulus. p.214. v.34. no.7. *Time & Tide*. 14 February 1953

- C.350 'The Gikuyu's Lament' – review of *Facing Mount Kenya* by Jomo Kenyatta. p.278. v.34. no.9. *Time & Tide*. 28 February 1953
- C.351 'Confusion in Kenya'. p.502. v.34. no.16. *Time & Tide*. 18 April 1953
- C.352 'Should Seretse return?' pp.678–9. v.34. no.21. *Time & Tide*. 23 May 1953
- C.353 'General Erskine's Problems'. pp.778–9. v.34. no.24. *Time & Tide*. 13 June 1953
- C.354 'Agricultural wages'. Letter. p.9. *Times*. 23 July 1953
- C.355 'Personalities and Policies in Nigerian Breakdown'. *Daily Telegraph*. 29 July 1953
- C.356 'The Roots of Mau Mau'. pp.88–92. v.141. no.846. *The National and English Review* (formerly the *National Review*). August 1953
- C.357 'First Aid for Nigeria'. pp.1010–1. v.34. no.31. *Time & Tide*. 1 August 1953
- C.358 'African Oyster' (Men & Books) reviews of *Africa – a Study in Tropical Development* by Dudley Stamp; *The Fon & his Hundred Wives* by R. Reyner; *Who Killed Kenya?* by C. Wills; *The Nardi of Kenya* by G.W.B. Huntingford; *Return to Goli* by P. Abraham. p.1073. v.34. no.37. *Time & Tide*. 15 August 1953
- C.359 'Decisions on Nigeria'. pp.1170–1. v.34. no.37. *Time & Tide*. 12 September 1953
- C.360 'Memorial to Lord Delamere'. Letter p.9. *Times*. 23 September 1953
- C.361 'Nairobi Balance Sheet'. p.1299. v.34. no.41. *Time & Tide*. 10 October 1953
- C.362 'Notes from Nairobi'. p.1416–7. v.34. no.44. *Time & Tide*. 31 October 1953
- C.363 The Kenya Scene 1. 'A Raid against Mau Mau'. pp.1539–40. v.34. no.48. *Time & Tide*. 28 November 1953
- C.364 The Kenya Scene 2. pp.1569–70. v.34. no.49. *Time & Tide*. 5 December 1953
- C.365 'Kenya Screening'. pp.1695–6. v.34. no.52. *Time & Tide*. 26 December 1953

1954

- C.366 'The Kenya Scene: a summing up'. pp.107–8. v.35. no.4. *Time & Tide*. 23 January 1954
- C.367 'Lyttleton in Kenya'. p.266. v.35. no.9. *Time & Tide*. 27 February 1954

C.368 'Development in Kenya'. pp.325–6. v.35. no.11. *Time & Tide*. 13 March 1954

C.369 'The Gamble that failed'. pp.501–2. v.35. no.16. *Time & Tide*. 17 April 1954

C.370 'What life is like for a settler in Kenya?' p.12. v.103. no.35,197. *New York Times Magazine*. 6 June 1954

C.371 'On the Demise of Colonialism' (Men & Books) review of *An African Afterthought* by Sir Philip Mitchell. pp.789–90. v.35. no.24. *Time & Tide*. 12 June 1954

C.372 'The vast challenge of Africa'. p.10. v.103. no.35,239. *New York Times Magazine*. 18 July 1954

C.373 *A Thing to Love* – first Br. serial rights. 1st inst. pp.7–10 & 32–37. *John Bull*. 14 August 1954

C.374 'Man against Man' – review of *Colour Bar* by Learie Constantine. pp.1057–8. v.35. no.32. *Time & Tide*. 17 August 1954

C.375 *A Thing to Love* – 2nd inst. pp.7–9 & 35–42. *John Bull*. 21 August 1954

C.376 'A Thing to Love' – 3rd inst. pp.12–15 & 32–39. *John Bull*. 28 August 1954

C.377 *A Thing to Love* – 4th inst. pp.24–26 & 42–46. *John Bull*. 4 September 1954

C.378 *A Thing to Love* – 5th inst. pp.24–26 & 29–34. *John Bull*. 11 September 1954

C.379 *A Thing to Love* – 6th inst. pp.23–25 & 28–30. *John Bull*. 18 September 1954

C.380 'Under African Skies' – review of *Return to Laughter* by E. Smith Bowen. p.1271. v.35. no.39. *Time & Tide*. 25 September 1954

C.381 'The Dark and the Light in Kenya'. pp.1406–7. v.35. no.43. *Time & Tide*. 23 October 1954

C.382 'Race' – review of *An Essay on Racial Tension* by Philip Mason. p.1422. v.35. no.43. *Time & Tide*. 23 October 1954

C.383 'Africa and Us' – review of *Must we lose Africa?* by Colin Legum. p.1458. v.35. no.44. *Time & Tide*. 30 October 1954

C.384 'Black Cauldron' – review of *Riot* by John Wyllie. pp.1487–8. v.35. no.45. *Time & Tide*. 6 November 1954

C.385 'Africa Past and Present' – reviews *The Heart of Africa* by A. Campbell; *Defeating Mau Mau* by L.S.B.Leakey; *African Bush Adventures* by J. Hunter & D. Mannix. pp.1581–2. v.35. no. 48. *Time & Tide*. 27 November 1954

1955

C.386 'Beyond Recall?' – reviews of *Thro' Malan's Africa* by Robert St.John and *The Numbered Days* by Stuart Jackman. p.21. v.36. no.1. *Time & Tide*. 1 January 1955

C.387 'The Demon with Long Fingernails' – fiction. *Evening Standard*. 20 January 1955

C.388 'Kenya Amnesty'. p.126. v.36. no.5. *Time & Tide*. 20 January 1955

C.389 'Aims in East Africa'. Letter. p.9. *Times*. 11 February 1955

C.390 'Realities in Kenya'. p.226. v.36. no.8. *Time & Tide*. 19 February 1955

C.391 'The Paramount Chief's Revenge' – fiction. *Evening Standard*. 15 March 1955

C.392 'Reflections of our World?' pp.468 & 470. v.36. no.15. *Time & Tide*. 9 April 1955

C.393 'Land in Kenya'. pp.554–5. v.36. no. 18. *Time & Tide*. 30 April 1955

C.394 'The Mikongo Tree' – review of the Trial of Jomo Kenyatta. p.646. v.36. no.20. *Time & Tide*. 14 May 1955

C.395 'Gladstonian cure for Africa's Ills. Adam Smith might have signed Dow report – but it has courage'. *Sunday Times*. 12 June 1955

C.396 'East African Ferment'. pp.790–1. v.36. no.25. *Time & Tide*. 18 June 1955

C.397 'Economic Man in East Africa: some reflections on the Dow Report'. pp.323–3. v.45. no.180. *Round Table*. September 1955

C.398 'Tobermory Treasure'. pp.1130–1. v.36. no.36. *Time & Tide*. 3 September 1955

C.399 'Drop in the Ocean' – review of *The Problem of South Africa* by Herbert Tingsten. p.1144. v.36. no. 36. *Time & Tide*. 3 September 1955

C.400 'Sanctas Simplicitas' – review of *African Journeys* by Fenner Brockway. pp.226–230. v.145. no.872. *The National and English Review*. October 1955

C.401 'Africa & Us'. pp.1375–6. v.36. no.43. *Time & Tide*. 22 October 1955

C.402 'Two Serpents from One Egg' – Did it Happen? series. *Evening Standard*. 15 November 1955

C.403 'African Independence and After; some reflections on "S.G."' pp.17–26. v.46. no.181. *Round Table*. December 1955

C *Contributions to newspapers and periodicals* 133

C.404 'Who Killed Indirect Rule?' pp.1642–3. v.36. no. 50. *Time & Tide*. 10 December 1955

1956

C.405 'Tribute to the late Lord Altrincham'. p.10–11. v.146.no.875. *The National and English Review*. January 1956

C.406 'Expensive Victory'. p.39. v.37. no.2. *Time & Tide*. 14 January 1956

C.407 'Kenya faces her New Chance'. *Daily Telegraph*. 18 January 1956

C.408 'Year of Decision for Nigeria'. *Daily Telegraph*. 23 January 1956

C.409 'Nigeria Welcomes the Queen'. pp.98–100. v.37. no.4. *Time & Tide*. 28 January 1956

C.410 Notes on the Way. 'Farming Efficiency'. pp.324–5. v.37. no. 27. *Time & Tide*. 24 March 1956

C.411 'Ghana'. p. 610. v.37. no.21. *Time & Tide*. 26 May 1956

C.412 'Convention at Salina'. pp.739–40. v.37. no. 25. *Time & Tide*. 23 June 1956

C.413 'To Rule in Hell' (Men & Books). pp.879–80. v.37. no.29. *Time & Tide*. 21 July 1956

C.414 'The Year of Ghana'. pp.898–9. v.37. no. 30. *Time & Tide*. 28 July 1956

C.415 'Colonialism psycho-analysed' – review of *Prospero and Caliban* by O. Mannoni translated by Pamela Powesland. pp.96–98. v.147. no.882. *The National and English Review*. August 1956

C.416 'Gluckstein of the Guards' – short story. pp.18–20, 41–42. v.100. no.2615. *John Bull*. 11 August 1956

C.417 'Prickly Crown'. pp.1142–3. v.37. no. 39. *Time & Tide*. 29 September 1956

C.418 'Son of Calypso' – short story. pp.16–17,48,50. v.100. no.2623. *John Bull*. 6 October 1956

C.419 'Empire of a Lifetime' (Men & Books) – review of *Lugard. The Year of Adventure* by Margery Perham. pp.1303–4. v.37. no.43. *Time & Tide*. 27 October 1956

C.420 'The Birth of Ghana'. pp.48–56. v.47. no.185. *Round Table*. December 1956

C.421 'Kenya's Pipeline to Freedom'. *Daily Telegraph*. 7 December 1956

C.422 'Building a New Kikuyuland'. *Daily Telegraph*. 19 December 1956

134   C   Contributions to newspapers and periodicals

1957

C.423   'African Quarrel'. p.31. v.38. no.2. *Time & Tide*. 12 January 1957

C.424   'Questioning Apparitions' – review of *Ghosts of Versailles* by Lucille Iremonger. p.74. v.38. no. 3. *Time &Tide*. 19 January 1957

C.425   'Time of Hope'. p.1223 v.38. no. 5. *Time & Tide*. 2 February 1957

C.426   'Independence Day'. pp.242–3. v.38. no.9. *Time & Tide*. 2 March 1957

C.427   'The Red Cockerel' – review of *Autobiography of Kwame Nkrumah*. pp.322–3. v.38. no. 11. *Time & Tide*. 14 March 1957

C.428   'Two Elections' p.343. v.38. no.12. *Time & Tide*. 23 March 1957

C.429   'Two revolutions that are changing Africa'. p.9. v.106. no.36,345. *New York Times Magazine*. 19 May 1957

C.430   'Red Queen's Conference'. pp.670–1. v.38. no.22. *Time & Tide*. 1 June 1957

C.431   'The Crisis of Piebald Africa' 1. p.802. v.38. no. 26. *Time & Tide*. 29 June 1957

C.432   'The Crisis of Piebald Africa' 2. pp.834–5. v.38. no.27. *Time & Tide*. 6 July 1957

C.433   'The £50 Rolls' – fiction. *Evening Standard*. 19 July 1957

C.434   'Africa's lions go out like lambs'. p.11. v.106. no.36,345. *New York Times Magazine*. 28 July 1957

C.435   'Rock or Sand'. p.958. v.38. no.31. *Time & Tide*. 3 August 1957

C.436   'Kicks for the Sacred Cow'. p.1014. v.38. no.33. *Time & Tide*. 17 August 1957

C.437   'Clouds over the Black Continent'. *New York Times Magazine*. 1 September 1957

C.438   'Spades & Jumbles' – review of *City of Spades* by Colin McInnes. p.1116. v.38. no.36. *Time & Tide*. 7 September 1957

C.439   'Mr. Eduser & Mr. Bing'. p.1152,. v.38. no.38. *Time & Tide*. 21 September 1957

C.440   'The Way of the Country' – short story. pp.28–30,51. v.102. no.2675. *John Bull*. 5 October 1957

C.441   'The Wizard of Arusha' – Did it Happen? series. *Evening Standard*. 22 October 1957

C.442   'No Through Road in Nairobi'. pp.1326–7. v.38. no.43. *Time & Tide*. 26 October 1957

C.443   'Stillborn out of Deadlock'. p.1418. v.38. no.46. *Time & Tide*. 16 November 1957

C.444 'A Woman of Sentiment' – short story. pp.22–23,34. v.102. no.2683. *John Bull*. 30 November 1957

C.445 'Shockable Age'. pp.1482–3. v.38. no.48. *Time & Tide*. 30 November 1957

1958

C446 'Moonshine & Mr. Mboya'. pp.118–9. v.39. no.5. *Time & Tide*. 1 February 1958

C.447 'Islam in Zinj'; 1. The Somali Line. *Sunday Times*. 2 March 1958

C.448 'Islam in Zinj': 2. Greater Somalis. *Sunday Times*. 9 March 1958

C.449 'Islam in Zinj': 3. Awakening Zanzibar. *Sunday Times*. 16 March 1958

C.450 Notes on the Way. 'The Game of Human Grab'. pp.347–8. v.39. no.12. *Time & Tide*. 22 March 1958

C.451 'Islam in Zinj': 4. Cairo's Treble Chance. *Sunday Times*. 23 March 1958

C.452 'Africa's testing ground on race relations'. p.14. v.117. no.36,618. *New York Times Magazine*. 27 April 1958

C.453 'Black Destiny?' pp.538–9. v.39. no.18. *Time & Tide*. 3 May 1958

C.454 'Nasser's African Design – 1. Serpent of Racialism'. p.11. *Sunday Times*. 11 May 1958

C.455 'Misunderstood Toes' – reviews of *The Treason Cage* by Anthony Sampson and *Sea Never Dry* by Anthony Smith. pp.618–9. v.339. no.20. *Time & Tide*. 17 May 1958

C.456 'Nasser's African Design – 2. The Gentle Voice of Hate'. p.15. *Sunday Times*. 18 May 1958

C.457 'Signed Print' Can this little pig.....? p.13. no.1634. *Kenya Weekly News*. 23 May 1958

C.458 'Nasser's African Design – 3. Fanning the Flame of Islam'. p.20. *Sunday Times*. 25 May 1958

C.459 'East African Birds'. Letter p.11. *Times*. 10 July 1958

C.460 'South of Cairo'. pp.908–9. v.39. no.30. *Time & Tide*. 26 July 1958

C.461 'Africa's wild life: need to preserve game sanctuary'. p.9. *Times*. 19 August 1958

C.462 'Kenya after Mau Mau'. pp.101–10. v.7. no.5. *Optima*. September 1958

C.463 'No Parrots' Eggs in Nigeria'. pp.1070–1. v.39. no.36. *Time & Tide*. 6 September 1958

136   C   *Contributions to newspapers and periodicals*

C.464   'Wild life in Tanganyika'. Letter. p.9. *Times*. 9 September 1958

C.465   'Democracy or Government?' p.1183. v.39. no.40. *Time & Tide*. 4 October 1958

C.466   'Under a Hopeful Star'. p.1307. v.39. no.44. *Time & Tide*. 1 November 1958

C.467   'The Falling Altars'. p.1390. v.39. no.47. *Time & Tide*. 22 November 1958

C.468   'Elastic Mansion'. p.1417. v.39. no.48. *Time & Tide*. 29 November 1958

C.469   'The Older People' – review of *The Lost World of the Kalahari* by Laurens van der Post. p.1430. v.39. no.48. *Time & Tide*. 29 November 1958

1959

C.470   'The High Jump' – short story. pp.10–12. v.105. no.2744. *John Bull*. 31 January 1959

C.471   'The Nationalist tide sweeps Africa'. p.11. v.108. no.36,912. *New York Times Magazine*. 15 February 1959

C.472   'And the Waters Prevailed' – Kariba Dam. *Sunday Times*. 26 April 1959

C.473   'Time runs out in Africa – 1.' p.13. *Sunday Times*. 3 May 1959

C.474   'The Threat to the Federation – 2.' p.13. *Sunday Times*. 10 May 1959

C.475   'Signed Print. Sand turns to gold'. p.15. no.1685. *Kenya Weekly News*. 15 May 1959

C.476   'Transformation Scene in Kenya – 3.' p.13. *Sunday Times*. 17 May 1959

C.477   'Science, psychiatry – or witchery?' p.17. v.108. no.37,017. *New York Times Magazine*. 31 May 1959

C.478   'East African Witness: 1. Can Partnership work in Kenya?' pp.13–14. v.3. no.1. *Central African Examiner*. 6 June 1959

C.479   'East African Witness: 2. Kenya isn't really looking south'. pp.15–16. v.3. no.2. *Central African Examiner*. 20 June 1959

C.480   'The Listener's book chronicle': *No Room in the Ark* by Alan Moorehead. Review. pp.1119. v.61. no.1578. *The Listener*. 25 June 1959

C.481   'The Issue in Africa'. p.820 v.40. no.31. *Time & Tide*. 1 August 1959

C.482 'African Water Engineers.' pp.170–175. v.32. is.4. (Ch.2. 'In the Kerio Valley' from *A New Earth*, edited and considerably cut) *Geographical Magazine*. 8 September 1959

C.483 The Road to 1984: 'Not so Dark Continent'. pp.260–3 v.CCXXXVII no.6210. *Punch*. 7 October 1959

C.484 'Wildlife – another African tragedy'. p.21. v.109. no.37,150. *New York Times Magazine*. 11 October 1959

C.485 'Threat to game in Africa'. pp.7,14. *Times*. 24 October 1959

C.486 'Drums of change beat for Africa's tribes'. p.24. v.109. no.37,199. *New York Times Magazine*. 29 November 1959

C.487 'Portrait Gallery – The Central African Enquiry'. p.31 (and photo). *Sunday Times*. 29 November 1959

1960

C.488 'The African at the Door'. p.49. v.41. no.3. *Time & Tide*. 16 January 1960

C.489 'For many Africans white men are still Red Strangers'. p.15. *Times*. 30 June 1960

C.490 'Freedom in Africa: the next stage'. pp.350–371. v.36. no.3. *Virginia Quarterly Review*. Summer 1960

C.491 'Science and the peasant farmer'. p.11. *Times*. 25 July 1960

C.492 'Ahead with dictators... Tribal wars... Red influence' (interview with E.H.) pp.82–87. no.11. v.49. *US News and World Report*. 12 September 1960

C.493 'Africa's first loyalty'. p.14. v.110. no.37,493. *New York Times Magazine*. 18 September 1960

C.494 'Africa's First Loyalty: The Tribe.' (article condensed from *The New York Times Magazine*, 18 September 1960) pp.124–127. *Reader's Digest*, USA. December 1960

C.495 'The Ethos of Negro Africa'. pp.7–14. v.51. no.201. *Round Table*. 1 December 1960

1961

C.496 'Tribal Challenge to the New Africa' (article condensed from *The New York Times Magazine*, 18 September 1960). pp. 80–83. *Reader's Digest*, UK. January 1961

C.497 'Kenya tour'. Letter p.13. *Times*. 2 March 1961

C.498 'Two tribes tell Africa's story'. p.14. no.37,717. *New York Times Magazine*. 14 April 1961

C.499 'What Future for Africa?' 1. Thomas Hodgkin pp.3–8. 2. Elspeth Huxley pp.8–20 vol.xvi. no.6. *Encounter*. June 1961. Later edited and included in *Forks and Hope*

C.500 'Retreat from Africa'. *Kenya Weekly News*. 2 June 1961

C.501 'The Next-to-Last Act in Africa'. pp.655–69. v.39. no.4. *Foreign Affairs*. July 1961

C.502 'What Future for Africa?' A reply to Edward Shils. pp.69–72. vol.xvii. no.3. *Encounter*. September 1961

C.503 'Out of Africa' – review of *The Heart of the Hunter* by Laurens van der Post, and *African Genesis* by Robert Ardrey. pp.666 & 669. v.66. n.1700. *The Listener*. 26 October 1961

C.504 'The Queen of Ghana'. *Kenya Weekly News*. 27 October 1961

C.505 The Crowded World: 'The Fruitful Primitives' pp.740–3. v.CCXLI. no.6324. *Punch*. 22 November 1961

1962

C.506 'Africa's struggles with democracy'. p.10. v.111. no.37,983. *New York Times Magazine*. 21 January 1962

C.507 The Second Sex: 'No Surrender'. pp.670–3. v.CCXLII no.6347. *Punch*. 2 May 1962

C.508 'France's Face-lift'. *Kenya Weekly News*. 4 May 1962

C.509 'Kenya Settlers'. Joint letter with Margery Perham. p.13. *Times*. 5 July 1962

C.510 'The Listener's book chronicle – Review of *The Blue Nile* by Alan Moorehead. p.107. v.68. no.1738. *The Listener*. 19 July 1962

C.511 'The Dragon in Africa'. pp.113–20. v.12. no.3. *Optima*. September 1962

C.512 'The White Africans'. General Overseas broadcast on Kenya. pp.342–343. v.68. no.1745. *The Listener*. 6 September 1962

C.513 'Visas refused for conference.' p.10. *Times*. 25 September 1962

C.514 'Visas refused for conference.' p.12. *Times*. 26 September 1962

C.515 Keeping: 'More Crafts, Less Malaise'. pp.512–514. v.CCXLIII. no.6370. *Punch*. 10 October 1962

C.516 'Kenya's White Highlands: the end of an Experiment'. pp.414–424. v.35. is.7. *Geographical Magazine*. November 1962

C.517 Children's Classics revisited: 'A New Review of *Uncle Tom's Cabin*'. pp.784–6. v.CCXLIII no.6377. *Punch*. 28 November 1962

C.518 'Some Observations on the African Personality'. pp.79–95. no.1. v.38. *Virginia Quarterly Review*. Winter 1962

C   *Contributions to newspapers and periodicals*   139

C.519   Report from Redbrick: 'Getting In'. pp.820–822. v.CCXLIII. no.6378. *Punch*. 5 December 1962

C.520   Report from Redbrick: 'Getting On'. pp.867–869. v.CCXLIII. no.6379. *Punch*. 12 December 1962

C.521   Report from Redbrick: 'Getting Out'. pp.896–899. v.CCXLIII. no.6380. *Punch*. 19 December 1962

1963

C.522   'Report from Redbrick. Getting In'. (Article previously appeared in *Punch*. 5 December 1962) *A.C.A.C. Journal*. Fall 1963

C.523   Kenya Today. 'Kenya's Clouded Future. Can the Europeans Survive?' *Daily Telegraph*. 1 March 1963

C.524   'Professor in the Hills'. pp.76–7. v.44. no.10. Illustration by Drake Brookshaw. *Homes & Gardens*. April 1963

C.525   Kenya Today. 'Picking Kenya to Pieces. Can the country survive the drastic surgery now being carried out in the name of a regional policy?' *Daily Telegraph*. 8 April 1963

C.526   Kenya Today. 'The Threat of Tribalism'. *Daily Telegraph*. 17 April 1963

C.527   Kenya Today. 'Back to Peasant Farming'. *Daily Telegraph*. 18 April 1963

C.528   'Wildlife becomes Big Business'. *Daily Telegraph*. 10 May 1963

C.529   'The Million-acre Scheme'. *Kenya Weekly News*. 10 May 1963

C.530   'Wildlife becomes Big Business'– 2. The cost of preservation. *Daily Telegraph*. 11 May 1963

C.531   'Kenya and her Neighbours'. *Kenya Weekly News*. 17 May 1963

C.532   'Kenya tries to put the clock ahead'. p.18. v.112. no.38,466. *New York Times Magazine*. 19 May 1963

C.533   'Land Hungry in Kenya – Small plots cannot provide a living'. Letter. *Daily Telegraph*. 20 May 1963

C.534   'Beasts & Men' pp.814–7. v.CCXLIV. no.6404. *Punch*. 5 June 1963

C.535   Mine own Exchequer: 'Penny Pincher'. The Finances and Financial Career of E.H. pp.890–3. v.CCXLIV. no.6406. *Punch*. 19 June 1963

C.536   'Lamuria' (later in *Forks & Hope*). pp.82–86. v.294. no.1773. *Blackwoods Magazine*. July 1963

C.537   Africana: 'Kings & Commoners', Kampala. pp.4–6. v.CCXLV. no.6408. *Punch*. 3 July 1963

140   C   *Contributions to newspapers and periodicals*

C.538   Africana: 'Forks & Hope', Dar es Salaam. pp.40–3. v.CCXLV. no.6409. *Punch*. 10 July 1963

C.539   Africana: 'Tribal Drums', Kabeve, Kenya. pp.76–9. v.CCXLV. no.6410. *Punch*. 17 July 1963

C.540   Africana: 'Happy Valley, New Style', Nairobi. pp.112–5. v.CCXLV. no.6411. *Punch*. 24 July 1963

C.541   Foreword. pp.1–4. v.1. *East African Wildlife Journal*. August 1963

C.542   'Breach of Contract. Britain's Duty to the Kenya Farmers'. Letter. *Daily Telegraph*. 30 August 1963

C.543   'The Future of Africa'. Letter p.11. *Times*. 24 September 1963

C.544   'The Happiest Bond' – a famous author analyses qualities which make a successful marriage. pp.70–1. v.45. no.4. Photograph by J. March-Penney. *Homes & Gardens*. October 1963

C.545   'My Friend Jackie Fox' – (1st episode) pp.9,93–98. *Woman's Own*. 26 October 1963

C.546   'My Friend Jackie Fox' – (2nd episode). pp.75–84. *Woman's Own*. 2 November 1963

C.547   'Dateline Africa: Kenya's cauldron'. pp.437–457. v.15. no.20. *National Review* (New York). 19 November 1963

C.548   Extract from forthcoming article in *Sunday Telegraph*. *Daily Telegraph*. 6 December 1963

C.549   Extract from forthcoming article in *Sunday Telegraph*. *Daily Telegraph*. 7 December 1963

C.550   'Smoke over Kenya' – extract from *Forks & Hope*. *Sunday Telegraph*. 8 December 1963

1964

C.551   Settlers in Britain: 'Tents of Israel'. pp.80–8. v.CCXLVI. no.6436. *Punch*. 15 January 1964

C.552   Settlers in Britain: 'Poles to Dinner'. pp.116–9. v.CCXLVI. no.6437. *Punch*. 22 January 1964

C.553   'African Affairs: no flowers for Welensky's baby'. pp.65–66. v.16. no.4. *National Review* (New York). 28 January 1964

C.554   Settlers in Britain: 'Blacks Next Door'. pp.154–7. v.CCXLVI. no.6438. *Punch*. 29 January 1964

C.555   'To Travel Hopefully'. pp.64–5. v.45. no.8. Illustration by Hugh Marshall. *Homes & Gardens*. February 1964

C.556   Settlers in Britain: 'Coconuts in Ladbroke Grove'. pp.190–2. v.CCXLVI. no.6439. *Punch*. 5 February 1964

C.557 *Forks & Hope* 1st inst. of serialisation. *Liverpool Daily Post.* 10 February 1964

C.558 *Forks & Hope* 2nd inst. *Liverpool Daily Post.* 11 February 1964

C.559 *Forks & Hope* 3rd inst. *Liverpool Daily Post.* 12 February 1964

C.560 Settlers in Britain: 'The Silent Italian'. pp.222–4. v.CCXLVI. no.6440. *Punch.* 12 February 1964

C.561 *Forks & Hope* 4th inst. *Liverpool Daily Post.* 13 February 1964

C.562 *Forks & Hope* 5th inst. *Liverpool Daily Post.* 14 February 1964

C.563 *Forks & Hope* 6th inst. *Liverpool Daily Post.* 15 February 1964

C.564 *Forks & Hope* 7th inst. *Liverpool Daily Post.* 17 February 1964

C.565 *Forks & Hope* 8th inst. *Liverpool Daily Post.* 18 February 1964

C.566 *Forks & Hope* 9th inst. *Liverpool Daily Post.* 19 February 1964

C.567 Settlers in Britain: 'Bubble & Squeak'. pp.260–2. v.CCXLVI. no.6441. *Punch.* 19 February 1964

C.568 *Forks & Hope* 10th inst. *Liverpool Daily Post.* 20 February 1964

C.569 *Forks & Hope* 11th inst. *Liverpool Daily Post.* 21 February 1964

C.570 *Forks & Hope* 12th inst. *Liverpool Daily Post.* 22 February 1964

C.571 'The rise and fall of the Watusi'. p.10. v.113. no.38,746. *New York Times Magazine.* 23 February 1964

C.572 Settlers in Britain: 'Punjab in Middlesex'. pp.296–8. v.CCXLVI. no.6442. *Punch.* 26 February 1964

C.573 Settlers in Britain: 'Uprooted Men'. pp.336–8. v.CCXLVI. no.6443. *Punch.* 4 March 1964

C.574 'Witches' Brew'. pp.191–192. v.16. no.10. *National Review* (New York). 10 March 1964

C.575 Settlers in Britain: 'Clocking In'. pp.368–70. v.CCXLVI. no.6444. *Punch.* 11 March 1964

C.576 Settlers in Britain: 'Climbing the Ladder'. pp.404–6. v.CCXLVI. no.6445. *Punch.* 18 March 1964

C.577 Settlers in Britain: 'Dark Glasses' pp.440–2. v.CCXLVI. no.6446. *Punch.* 25 March 1964

C.578 Settlers in Britain: 'Some Conclusions'. pp.480–3. v.CCXLVI. no.6447. *Punch.* 1 April 1964

C.579 'The Rise and Fall of the Watusi' p.6–7. *Johannesburg Sunday Chronicle.* 26 April 1964

C.580 'Leading Ladies' – Mrs. Harold Wilson & Lady Douglas-Home interviewed by E.H. pp.70–1. v.45. no.11. *Homes & Gardens.* May 1964

142   C   *Contributions to newspapers and periodicals*

C.581   'Mammal migration poses problems in Tanganyika's Serengeti National Park'. pp.10–14. *National Parks Magazine* (Washington D.C.). May 1964

C.582   'African Affairs: The road to Johannesburg'. p.351. v.16. no.18. *National Review* (New York). 5 May 1964

C.583   E.H.'s Favourite Vice: 'The Whole Hog'. pp.782–784. v.CCXLVI. no. 6455. *Punch*. 27 May 1964

C.584   'Clues to the African personality'. p.18. v.113. no.38,844. *New York Times Magazine*. 31 May 1964

C.585   'The Face behind the Mask: some thoughts on revolutions'. pp.59–67. v.14. no.2. *Optima*. June 1964

C.586   'African Affairs: Aid for the needy – the need for a new look'. p.351–352. v.16. no.26. *National Review* (New York). 30 June 1964

C.587   'African Affairs: Will he, won't he, will he, won't he...?' pp.651–652. v.16. no.30. *National Review* (New York). 28 July 1964

C.588   'In my Garden'. pp.56–7. v.46. no.3. Illustration by M.Wilson. *Homes & Gardens*. September 1964

C.589   *Forks and Hope* 1st inst. p.4. *Johannesburg Sunday Chronicle*. 13 September 1964

C.590   *Forks and Hope* 2nd inst. p.4. *Johannesburg Sunday Chronicle*. 20 September 1964

C.591   *Forks and Hope* 3rd inst. p.4. *Johannesburg Sunday Chronicle*. 27 September 1964

C.592   *Forks and Hope* 4th inst. p.4. *Johannesburg Sunday Chronicle*. 4 October 1964

C.593   'African Affairs: The long spoon of Peking'. pp.868–869. v.16. no.40. *National Review* (New York). 6 October 1964

C.594   A fresh eye on the Election. 'Democracy playing at Home. Some of the New Nations think our rules quite of date. Why are we Britons still so good at the Westminster Code?' *Sunday Telegraph*. 11 October 1964

C.595   The Price of Plenty: 'The Feeding of the 3,000,000'. pp.558–60. v.CCXLVII. no.6475. *Punch*. 14 October 1964

C.596   The Price of Plenty: 'Agribusiness'. pp.596–8. v.CCXLVII. no.6476. *Punch*. 21 October 1964

C.597   The Price of Plenty: 'The Stalled Ox'. pp.634–6. v.CCXLVII. no.6477. *Punch*. 28 October 1964

C *Contributions to newspapers and periodicals* 143

C.598 'Controversial Subjects' (on manly sports). pp.92–3. v.46. no.5. Illustration by Rosalind Hoyle. *Homes & Gardens.* November 1964

C.599 The Price of Plenty: 'Sweat & Fears'. pp.674–6. v.CCXLVII. no.6478. *Punch.* 4 November 1964

C.600 The Price of Plenty: 'What turns into Miss T.' pp.728–30. v.CCXLVII. no.6479. *Punch.* 11 November 1964

C.601 The Price of Plenty: 'Chemical Warfare'. pp.766–8. v.CCXLVII, no.6480. *Punch.* 18 November 1964

C.602 The Price of Plenty: 'Fouling our Nest'. pp.806–8. v.CCXLVII. no.6481. *Punch.* 25 November 1964

C.603 'Bringing home the Hippo'. p.134. v.114. no.39,026. *New York Times Magazine.* 29 November 1964

C.604 The Price of Plenty: 'It's no good asking the Computer'. pp.830–2. v.CCXLVII. no.6482. *Punch.* 2 December 1964

C.605 'African Affairs: As Nigeria goes'. pp.1105–1106. v.16. no.50. *National Review* (New York). 15 December 1964

C.606 'Exploding Population. Case for taxation of large Families'. *Daily Telegraph.* 28 December 1964

1965

C.607 'Controversial Subjects –Teenagers'. pp.28–9. v.46. no.7. Illustration by Rosalind Hoyle. *Homes & Gardens.* January 1965

C.608 'African Affairs: Red China's year in Africa.' pp.95. v.17. no.6. *National Review* (New York). 9 February 1965

C.609 'A Cottage on a Hillside' (in index 'A Cottage with a View'). pp.84–5. v.46. no.10. Illustration by Gavin Rowe. *Homes & Gardens.* April 1965

C.610 'Australia's aborigines step out of the Stone Age.' p.10. v.114. no.39,229. *New York Times Magazine.* 20 June 1965

C.611 'The Four Pillars' – a summary of our aims. Essay specially written for 'The Launching of a New Ark', the first report of the International Trustees of the WWF. pp 3–5. *World Wildlife News.* Summer 1965.

C.612 'My Next Husband'. pp.200–2. v.CCXLIX. no.6518. *Punch.* 11 August 1965

C.613 'A Bead on Roos'. *New York Times Magazine.* 24 October 1965

144   C *Contributions to newspapers and periodicals*

1966

C.614   'As I see it: Crushing the Mouse'. p.28. *Building Materials.* January 1966

C.615   'Making Space for the Multitude'– impressions of 'The Countryside in 1970' conference. pp.178–184. v.8. no.7. *Animals.* 18 January 1966

C.616   'African Affairs: Death in Nigeria'. pp.163–164. v.18. no.8. *National Review* (New York). 22 February 1966

C.617   'Letter from Africa: The rope that hanged Nkrumah'. pp 268–270. v.18. no.12. *National Review* (New York). 22 March 1966

C.618   'Beasts and Men'. pp.4–8. (This article had previously appeared in *Punch* 5 June 1963). *Black Lechwe.* April 1966

C.619   'Letter from Africa: the end of King Freddie'. p.569. v.18. no.24. *National Review* (New York). 14 June 1966

C.620   'Much to be Immodest about' – E.H. on Social Behaviour. p.186–8. v.251. no.6569. *Punch.* 3 August 1966

C.621   'African Affairs: Naked emperor'. pp.877–878. v.18. no.30. *National Review* (New York). 6 September 1966

C.622   'My Favourite Town; Malmesbury'. pp.94–7. v.48. no.4. *Homes & Gardens.* October 1966

C.623   'African Affairs: Seven days' humiliation'. p.989. v.18. no.40. *National Review* (New York). 4 October 1966

C.624   'Nine Lost Sheep'. Elspeth Huxley investigates the flight from the churches. pp.92–3. v.48. no.5. Illustration by Michael Grimsdale. *Homes & Gardens.* November 1966

C.625   'Rhodesian legality'. Letter. p.15. *Times.* 9 December 1966

1967

C.626   'The Gambling Bonanza'. pp.32–3. v.48. no.8. Illustration by Michael Grimsdale. *Homes & Gardens.* February 1967

C.627   'Reading for Pleasure'. pp.44–5. v.48. no.9. Illustration by Michael Grimsdale. *Homes & Gardens.* March 1967

C.628   Growing Up in Britain: 1. 'Under 5'. pp.290–2. v.252. no.6599. *Punch.* 1 March 1967

C.629   'Sanctions against Rhodesia'. p.9. v.116. no.39,852. *New York Times.* 5 March 1967

C.630   Growing Up in Britain: 2. 'Fun with Fractions'. pp.331–4. v. 252. no.6600. *Punch.* 8 March 1967

C Contributions to newspapers and periodicals

C.631   Growing up in Britain: 3. 'Revolution in the Primary School'. pp.371–4. v.252. no.6601. *Punch*. 15 March 1967

C.632   Growing up in Britain: 4. 'Streaming & Creaming'. pp.407–10. v.252. no.6602. *Punch*. 22 March 1967

C.633   Growing up in Britain: 5. 'Into Hospital'. pp.445–7. v.252. no.6603. *Punch*. 29 March 1967

C.634   'Going Comprehensive'. pp.80–1. v.48. no.10. *Homes & Gardens*. March 1967

C.635   Growing up in Britain: 6. 'An Inspector calls'. pp.489–93. v.252. no.6604. *Punch*. 5 April 1967

C.636   Growing up in Britain: 7. 'In Care'. pp.527–31. v.252. no.6605. *Punch*. 12 April 1967

C.637   Growing up in Britain: 8. 'Handicapped'. pp.557–60. v.252. no.6606. *Punch*. 19 April 1967

C.638   'Two women in the clean, lean, hungry country'. (Interview, with Judith Wright by Patricia der Joux). p.9. *Times*. 5 May 1967

C.639   'African Affairs: A confusion of colonels'. pp.466–467. v.19. no.17. *National Review* (New York). 7 May 1967

C.640   'Personal impressions of Pommie in Australia'. Letter p.15. *Times*. 18 May 1967

C.641   'African Affairs: Biafra libre?' pp.896. v.19. no.33. *National Review* (New York). 22 August 1967

C.642   'Welsh Magic'. pp.38–9. v.49. no.3. Illustration by Allan Cracknell. *Homes & Gardens*. September 1967

C.643   'A Chicagoan designed Australia's Capital'. Edited extract from *Their Shining Eldorado* p.28. section 1. *Chicago Tribune*. 10 September 1967

C.644   Autumn Books. 'West Side Story'. review of *La Vida* by Oscar Lewis. pp.521. v.253. no.6630. *Punch*. 4 October 1967

C.645   'A Venture in the Algarve'. pp.82–3. v.49. no.5. Illustration by Allan Cracknell. *Homes & Gardens*. November 1967

C.646   'Australia's Very Foreign Fauna' extract from *Their Shining Eldorado*. pp.67–76. Illustrations by Betty Fraser. *Venture*. 10 November 1967

C.647   'Books: arts: manners: Blundering into danger' – review of *Crisis over Rhodesia* by Charles Burton Marshall. pp.1339–1340. v.19. no.47. *National Review* (New York). 28 November 1967

1968

C.648 'Brave New Victuals' (condensed from *Brave New Victuals*). pp.41–45. v.12. no.137. *Here's Health*. January 1968

C.649 'Letter from Africa: Entering 1968'. pp.33. v.20. no.2. *National Review* (New York). 16 January 1968

C.650 'Life Sentence' (condensed from *Brave New Victuals*). pp.83–89. v.12. no.138. *Here's Health*. February 1968

C.651 'Defiant Daughters'. pp.28–9. v.49. no.8. Illustration by Michael Grimsdale. *Homes & Gardens*. February 1968

C.652 'The Great broiler gamble' (condensed from *Brave New Victuals*). pp.83–88. v.12. no.139. *Here's Health*. March 1968

C.653 'Rhodesia's Obvious Independence'. *Daily Telegraph*. 12 March 1968

C.654 'Who represents Rhodesia's Africans?' *Daily Telegraph*. 13 March 1968

C.655 'Churchill in the Liberal party'. pp.302–303. v.20. no.12. *National Review* (New York). 26 March 1968

C.656 'Does cooking destroy the chemicals?' (condensed from *Brave New Victuals*). pp.85–88. v.12. no.140. *Here's Health*. April 1968

C.657 'Letter from Rhodesia: To crush a mouse'. pp.335–336. v.20. no.14. *National Review* (New York). 9 April 1968

C.658 'What happens when you eat an additive?' (condensed from *Brave New Victuals*). pp.103–107. v.12. no.141. *Here's Health*. May 1968

C.659 'Age shall not Weary Them' pp.80–1. v.49. no.11. Illustration by Robert Broomfield. *Homes & Gardens*. May 1968

C.660 Letter re British policy towards Rhodesia. *Times*. 14 May 1968

C.661 'Lion Tamer' – short story. pp.12–13,33–56. *Woman' Own*. 18 May 1968

C.662 'Pearls before swine' (condensed from *Brave New Victuals*). pp.63–66. v.12. no.142. *Here's Health*. June 1968

C.663 'Phantom Commonwealth' *Daily Telegraph Magazine*. 7 June 1968

C.664 'The Whiter than white business' (condensed from *Brave New Victuals*). pp.85–89. v.12. no.143. *Here's Health*. July 1968

C.665 'African Affairs: The castle of apartheid'. pp.854. v.20. no.34. *National Review* (New York). 27 August 1968

C.666 'The Bloodsports Row'. pp.21,22. v.431. no.5653. *The Queen*. 28 August 1968

C.667 'Goodbye, Farmer Giles!' (condensed from *Brave New Victuals*). pp.99–103. v.12. no.145. *Here's Health*. September 1968

C.668 'At the Thé Dansant' extract from *Love among the Daughters* pp.64,65. v.431. no.5654. Illustration by May Routh. *The Queen*. 11 September 1968

C.669 'African Affairs: Sacred cow'. pp.962. v.20. no.38. *National Review* (New York). 24 September 1968

C.670 'Plant above Falls in Uganda'. Letter. *Daily Telegraph*. 1 October 1968

C.671 'Living in Towers' pp.84–5. v.50. no.4. Illustration by Richard Reid. *Homes & Gardens*. October 1968

C.672 'Towards rebuilding One Nigeria'. *Daily Telegraph*. 15 October 1968

C.673 'Can we rear enough to eat?' (condensed from *Brave New Victuals*). pp.63,65–66. v.12. no.147. *Here's Health*. November 1968

C.674 'African Affairs: The emperor Wilson'. pp.1110. v.20. no.44. *National Review* (New York). 5 November 1968

C.675 'I Love Christmas'. pp.46–9. v.50. no.6. Illustration by Jenny Williams. *Homes & Gardens*. December 1968

C.676 Before there was a Christmas – Far out Feasts'. pp.802–7. v.255. no.6691. *Punch*. 4 December 1968

1968

C.677 'Stress in the animal kingdom' (condensed from *Brave New Victuals*). pp.95–100. v.13. no.149. *Here's Health*. January 1969

C.678 'Gaps in the Welfare State'. pp.48–9. v.50. no.7. Illustration by Michael Grimsdale. *Homes & Gardens*. January 1969

C.679 'When will the Clash come?' Elspeth Huxley examines the South African dilemma. pp.26,27. v.432. no.5662. *The Queen*. 8 January 1969

C.680 'But – What gets left out?' (condensed from *Brave New Victuals*). pp.53–57. v.13. no.152. *Here's Health*. April 1969

C.681 'Things are'nt what they used to be.' pp.46.–7. v.50. no.10. Illustration by Michael Grimsdale. *Homes & Gardens*. April 1969

C.682 'Letter from London: The Powell enigma'. pp.328–330. v.20. no.13. *National Review* (New York). 8 April 1969

C.683 Judy: 'Blame the Beast' pp.568. v.256. *Punch*. 16 April 1969

C.684 'There's gold in those pesticides!' (condensed from *Brave New Victuals*). pp.61–66. v.13. no.154. *Here's Health*. June 1969

148   C   Contributions to newspapers and periodicals

C.685   'Are British Women Emanicipated?' pp.72–3. v.50. no.12. *Homes & Gardens*. June 1969
C.686   Judy: 'Benevolent Bwanas' pp.830–1. v.256. *Punch*. 4 June 1969
C.687   'Chemistry takes over' (condensed from *Brave New Victuals*). pp.61–65. v.13. no.156. *Here's Health*. August 1969
C.688   'The Vanishing Village'. pp.48–9. v.51. no.2. *Homes & Gardens*. August 1969
C.689   'Elephants in Danger'. *Observer Magazine*. 10 August 1969
C.690   'The World in the Morning'. pp.17–27. v.6. no.7. Illus. by Betty Fraser. *Venture*. September 1969
C.691   'Will nature's bank run out?' (condensed from *Brave New Victuals*). pp.51–56. v.13. no.158. *Here's Health*. October 1969
C.692   'The Skin Game'. pp.80–1. v.51. no.4. *Homes & Gardens*. October 1969
C.693   'Animals preyed upon for Fur Collection'. Letter. *Daily Telegraph*. 13 November 1969
C.694   'Back to Nature: not just for Cranks'. *Daily Telegraph*. 27 November 1969
C.695   'Letter from London: Sniping at Springboks'. pp.1265–1266. v.21. no.49. *National Review* (New York). 16 December 1969

1970

C.696   'Why do Women Shop?' pp.48–9. v.51. no.8. Illustration by Michael Grimsdale. *Homes & Gardens*. February 1970
C.697   'On the Beaver's Back'. pp.36–45. v.20. no.1. *Optima*. March 1970
C.698   'What's Your Poison?' pp.64–5. v.51. no.10. *Homes & Gardens*. April 1970
C.699   'Farming in England'. pp.123–29. v.20. no.3. *Optima*. September 1970

1971

C.700   'Water shortage'. Letter. p.13. *Times*. 6 August 1971
C.701   'Colonialism: the credit side'. pp.170–6. v.21. no.4. *Optima*. December 1971

1972

C.702   'Scarring the Future'. *Daily Telegraph Magazine*. 21 January 1972

C.703 'Uganda expulsions as a precedent'. Letter. p.13. *Times*. 23 August 1972

C.704 'General Amin's move: England faces the great migration'. pp.1124–1125. v.24. no.40. *National Review* (New York). 13 October 1972

1973

C.705 'Treatment of Uganda regime's opponents'. Letter. p.15. *Times*. 14 April 1973

1974

C.706 'The End of the Elephants' Road?' *Guardian*. 22 April 1974

1976

C.707 Review of *Malindi: the Historic Town on Kenya's Coast* by Esmond Bradley Martin. pp.25–27. v.6 no.1. *Africana*. April 1976

C.708 'The Fireman's Tale' – extract from *Gallipot Eyes*. pp.108–110. v.57. no.11. *Homes & Gardens*. May 1976

C.709 'Ban on Rhodesian Cricketers'. Letter. p.15. *Times*. 17 May 1976

C.710 'Porridge while you walk'. Letter. p.11. *Times*. 4 October 1976

1977

C.711 'Scott in love' (Extract from *Scott of the Antarctic*). p.6. *Times – Saturday Review*. 29 October 1977

1978

C.712 'Behaving like animals'. Letter. p.15. *Times*. 17 January 1978

C.713 'Supporting a Rhodesian settlement'. Letter. p.17. *Times*. 19 April 1978

C.714 'British policy on Rhodesia'. Letter. p.19. *Times*. 30 June 1978

C.715 *Evelyn Baring: the last Proconsul* by Charles Douglas-Home. Review. p.929. *Times Literary Supplement*. 18 August 1978

C.716 'A baby born in space'. Letter. p.13. *Times*. 2 October 1978

C.717 *David Livingstone* by Oliver Ransford. Review. p.1346. *Times Literary Supplement*. 17 November 1978

C.718   E. H. on Dhows – 'The Ocean Butterfly – for romantics who see the beauty of form but not the dung on which it feeds'. pp.32–34. v.6. no.10. *Africana*. December 1978

1979

C.719   Review of *Zanzibar: Tradition and Revolution* by Dr. Esmond Bradley Martin. p.24. v.6. no.11. *Africana*. March 1979

1980

C.720   'Home among the Kikuyu' (Extract from *Nellie*). p.6. *Times – Saturday Review*. 23 February 1980

C.721   'From Africa to Whipsnade'. no.181. *Sunday Telegraph Magazine*. 9 March 1980

C.722   Extract from *Pioneers' Scrapbook* ed. by Elspeth Huxley and Arnold Curtis. *Sunday Telegraph*. 29 June 1980

C.723   'Breeding animals in zoos'. Letter. p.15. *Times*. 10 September 1980

1981

C.724   'The Zoo Trap'. Opinion. *Sunday Telegraph Magazine*. 26 April 1981

C.725   'An Edwardian Childhood in Africa' (on filming of *Flame Trees of Thika*) pp.36,38–41. *Observer Magazine*. 30 August 1981

C.726   'Food for Thought'. Letter to the editor on watching people eat on TV. p.687–688. v.106. no.2738. *The Listener*. 3 November 1981

1984

C.727   'Farewell to the Oaksey Lilly'. *Western Daily Press*. 25 April 1984

C.728   'Just so'. Letter on use of word 'animals'. p.13. *Times*. 14 December 1984

1986

C.729   Saturday Matters 'Trowel and Error'. *Daily Telegraph*. 21 June 1986

C.730   'Us and them'. Letter on substitution of word 'taxpayer' for 'government'. p15. *Times*. 3 July 1986

C.731   My Kind of Life. *Daily Telegraph*. 14 July 1986

C   *Contributions to newspapers and periodicals*   151

C.732   My Kind of Life. *Daily Telegraph*. 4 August 1986
C.733   My Kind of Life. 'The village shop is where you pick up local news and pass rumours'. *Daily Telegraph*. 1 September 1986
C.734   My Kind of Life. *Daily Telegraph*. 29 September 1986
C.735   My Kind of Life. *Daily Telegraph*. 27 October 1986

1987

C.736   Country View. 'Extending the Field of Vision'. *Daily Telegraph*. 3 January 1987
C.737   Country View. 'Winter: the season of our greatest content'. *Daily Telegraph*. 24 January 1987
C.738   Country View. 'Booking a place at the Mobile'. *Daily Telegraph*. 14 February 1987
C.739   Country View. 'Nurturing a growing addiction'. *Daily Telegraph*. 7 March 1987
C.740   'My Time of Life' (article on people at their various ages). photograph by Evelyn Hofer. pp.59–61. *Sunday Times Magazine*. 26 April 1987
C.741   Country View. 'On the road to ruin.' *Daily Telegraph*. 30 May 1987
C.742   'Kenya's First Flying Doctor' – review of *Different Drum: Reflections on a changing Africa* by Michael Wood. *Daily Telegraph*. 19 June 1987
C.743   Friday Matters. 'Its hard work being an Old Lady with Mousy Hair.' *Daily Telegraph*. 24 July 1987
C.744   Country View. 'Picking out the Plums'. *Daily Telegraph*. 29 August 1987

1988

C.745   Article on 'Cockie' Hoogterp (died aged 96). *Daily Telegraph*. 13 December 1988

1989

C.746   'Winter, Season of Content' (article condensed from *The Daily Telegraph*. 24 January 1987). pp.70–71. *Reader's Digest*. (UK edition). February 1989
C.747   Letter on book characters. p.17. *Times*. 13 March 1989

152   C   *Contributions to newspapers and periodicals*

C.748   'Man's Avarice threatens the Noblest Species of All'. *Daily Telegraph.* 22 May 1989

C.749   'An Embellished Hero'. Article on Richard Meinertzhagen. *Daily Telegraph.* 17 July 1989

C.750   'The Fête Accomplished'. p.42. *Sunday Times Magazine.* 20 August 1989

C.751   Review of *Where Giants Trod: the Saga of Kenya's Desert Lake* by Monty Brown. *Daily Telegraph.* 25 November 1989

1990

C.752   *Nine Faces of Kenya.* E.H. discusses background to her latest book. Photograph. *Times.* 22 August 1990

1991

C.753   'Steps to lowering interest rates'. Letter. p.11. *Times.* 19 February 1991

1992

C.754   Review of *Enigmatic Proconsul: Sir Philip Mitchell and the Twilight of Empire* by Richard Frost. *Daily Telegraph.* 31 October 1992

1993

C.755   'Well done Jock'. Letter. *Daily Telegraph.* 2 March 1993

C.756   'Heartless BMA?' *Daily Telegraph.* 1 July 1993

C.757   'Eternal quest for Other Worlds' – review of *Rider Haggard and the Lost Empire* by Tom Pocock. *Daily Telegraph.* 21 August 1993

C.758   'Legend of their Lions' – review of *The Great Safari: the Lives of George and Joy Adamson* by Adrian House. *Daily Telegraph.* 18 September 1993

C.759   Letter querying reasons why *A Suitable Boy* by Vikram Seth was not shortlisted for the Booker Prize. *Sunday Times.* 3 October 1993

C.760   E.H. interviewed by Dea Birkett about *Peter Scott: Painter and Naturalist. The Scotsman.* 22 November 1993

1994

C.761　Letter commenting on review on 3 July 1994 of *The Hidden Huxley* (ed. David Bradshaw). *Sunday Times*. 14 August 1994

1995

C.762　'The Flames Still Burn' – article about a recent return visit to Kenya pp.1–2. *Daily Telegraph Weekend Supplement*. 24 June 1995

D. Radio and television appearances by Elspeth Huxley

This list has mainly been compiled on the basis of information from the BBC Archives. When an entry is asterisked the BBC Sound Library and Archive holds a recording. In the case of serial readings of EH's books, one number is attached to the first reading only.

1929

D.1 The Nation's Milk Supply (1). National. 12 June 1929

D.2 The Nation's Milk Supply (2). National. 19 June 1929

D.3 The Nation's Milk Supply (3). National. 26 June 1929

D.4 The Nation's Milk Supply (4). National. 3 July 1929

D.5 The Nation's Milk Supply (5). National. 10 July 1929

D.6 The Nation's Milk Supply (6). National. 17 July 1929

1938

D.7 'Dust Bowl' – a dramatic presentation of the causes and results of soil erosion in the Middle West. National, Schools. 25 February 1938

D.8 History in the making. 'Soil Erosion in the Middle West – Dust Bowl'. National, Schools. 22 March 1938

D.9 Senior Geography. 'Misunderstanding Climate: the Dust Bowl'. National, Schools. 8 December 1938

D.10 Senior Geography. 'America: Mud and Flood: the Mississippi, friend or enemy?' National, Schools. 15 December 1938

1939

D.11 Travel Talks. 'A Boy's Life in Kenya' for children aged 9–11. Dialogue between a boy of 12 and a writer. Home, Schools. 8 December 1939

D.12 Travel Talks. 'A Pride of Lions' dialogue on lions. Home, Schools. 15 December 1939

D Radio and television appearances by Elspeth Huxley

1940

D.13 Travel Talks. 'Farms turned to Dust'. Home, Schools. 4 October 1940

D.14 Meet the Empire – 'Bill & Bob at the BBC'. Forces. 9 October 1940

D.15 Travel Talks. 'If you were a cowboy'. Home, Schools. 11 October 1940

D.16 Meet the Empire – 'Bill & Bob at the BBC'. Forces. 16 October 1940

D.17 Meet the Empire – 'Bill & Bob at the BBC'. Forces. 23 October 1940

D.18 Senior Geography. 'Science fights the Tsetse Fly', written in the character of a fairly young tsetse fly officer working in Tanganyika. Home, Schools. 24 October 1940

D.19 Travel Talks. 'Where films are made', written in the character of a Hollywood camera-man. Home, Schools. 25 October 1940

D.20 Meet the Empire – 'Bill & Bob at the BBC'. Forces. 30 October 1940

D.21 Meet the Empire – 'Bill & Bob at the BBC'. Forces. 6 November 1940.

D.22 Meet the Empire – 'Bill & Bob at the BBC'. Forces. 13 November 1940

D.23 Meet the Empire – 'Bill & Bob at the BBC'. Forces. 20 November 1940

D.24 Meet the Empire – 'Bill & Bob at the BBC'. Forces. 27 November 1940

D.25 Meet the Empire – 'Bill & Bob at the BBC'. Forces. 4 December 1940

D.26 Meet the Empire – 'Bill & Bob at the BBC'. Forces. 11 December 1940

D.27 Meet the Empire – 'Bill & Bob at the BBC'. Forces. 18 December 1940

1941

D.28 Meet the Empire – 'Bill & Bob at the BBC'. 1 January 1941

D.29 Meet the Empire – 'Bill & Bob at the BBC'. Forces. 8 January 1941

D.30 British History. Movements and Men. 1875 to the present day. Stories from West Africa. For children aged 11–15. (1) 'White Man and Black Man'. Home, Schools. 26 June 1941

D.31 British History. Movements and Men. 1875 to the present day. Stories from West Africa. For children aged 11–15. (2) 'Indirect Rule'. Home, Schools. 3 July 1941

156   D   Radio and television appearances by Elspeth Huxley

D.32   Radio Reconnaissance. 'The United States and Ourselves', including 2 feature flashes: 'Why some Americans think we're slow' by William Vandivert. Forces. 9 October 1941

D.33   Life over here. 'The Village rolls up its sleeves'. Overseas, Empire Eastern Transmission. 15 October 1941

D.34   Senior Geography. 'Building the Transcontinental Railway'. Home, Schools. 23 October 1941

D.35   Radio Reconnaissance. 2 dramatic interludes illustrate the talks 'Two Democracies but different' in the series 'The United States and ourselves'. Forces. 6 November 1941

D.36   Radio Reconnaissance. 'An American looks at the World'. 3 character studies on Americans living in different parts of the States, and attitudes to Canada, South America, Japan.' Forces. 20 November 1941

1942

D.37   Senior Geography. 'Ths United States: Combating Soil Erosion'. Home, Schools. 12 February 1942

D.38   Senior Geography. 'Making the Americas the United States: Out on the Range'. Home, Schools. 26 February 1942

D.39   Senior Geography. 'Power for New Industries'. Home, Schools. 19 March 1942

D.40   'Work of the WAAF'. Home. 14 June 1942

D.41   Second talk on WAAF. 'Fighter Station'. Home. 28 June 1942

D.42   'The ATS'. Home. 6 July 1942

D.43   'Work of the ATS'. Home. 10 July 1942

D.44   'WAAF – Bomber Operations'. Home. 12 July 1942

D.45   'Work of the WRENS'. Home. 15 July 1942

D.46   'The WRENS'. Home. 20 July 1942

D.47   Calling South Africa. 'The WAAF'. Overseas. 24 July 1942

D.48   Calling Africa. 'WRENS'. Overseas, Africa. 3 September 1942

D.49   Women and War. Talks. (1) 'Balloons'. Overseas, Pacific. 17 September 1942

D.50   Women and War. Talks. (2) 'WAAF'. Overseas, Pacific. 24 September 1942

D.51   Women generally speaking. 'Women's Land Army'. Overseas, Eastern. 4 November 1942

D   *Radio and television appearances by Elspeth Huxley*   157

D.52 'North and Central America. Cow Country'. Semi-dramatic. On ranching in the foothills of the Rockies. Home, Schools. 13 November 1942

1943

D.53 Senior History. 'Some North American questions: the Undefended Frontier'. Home, Schools. 4 February 1943

D.54 'Jeeps and Sprouts'. American troops help to grow vegetables in Great Britain. Home. 24 February 1943

D.55 'Story of a Dutch Naval Air Squadron'. Home. 26 February 1943.

D.56 'ATS' Wireless Operators. Home. 21 March 1943

D.57 The World goes by. 'Uganda'. Forces. 31 March 1943

D.58 Radio Newsreel. EH on Locust Control. Overseas, African. 31 March 1943

D.59 'Eternity in an Hour'. Radio play. Home. 21 April 1943

D.60 Senior English 1. Book talk. *Jock of the Bushveld*. Home, Schools. 7 May 1943

D.61 The World goes by. 'Ceylon'. Forces. 2 June 1943

D.62 'War against the locust'. Home. 5 June 1943

D.63 'Campaign against the locust'. Home. 19 July 1943

D.64 'War against the Bush: the building of the Kenya-Uganda Railway'. Home. 23 July 1943

D.65 'Red on the Map: Colonial Empire'. Home. 3 August 1943

D.66 'War against the Bush'. Arabic translation. With Audrey Jones. Overseas, Near East. 6 October 1943

D.67 The World goes by. 'Locusts'. Forces. 6 October 1943

D.68 Calling East Africa. 'Working in London'. Overseas, African. 5 December 1943

1944

D.69 Schools Geography. British Africa. 'Settlers of the Kenya Highlands'. Home, Schools. 2 March 1944

D.70 Calling East Africa. 'Political Comparisons between West and East Africa'. Overseas, African. 21 May 1944

D.71 London Calling. No.247. 'Hands across the Jungle'. Overseas. 1 June 1944

D.72 Senior History 11. 'International science combats an international pest'. (Original script 'War against the Locust'). With Edward Livesey. Home, Schools. 29 June 1944

D.73 Brush up your Empire. 'East Africa'. With Lionel Gamlin. Home, Talks. 31 July 1944

D.74 Calling East Africa. Kenya. 'Kenya's Political Future'. With F. J. Couldrey. Overseas, African. 13 August 1944

1945

D.75 Travel Talks. India and her neighbours. 'Indian shopkeepers'. About the Indian population of East Africa. Home, Schools. 2 March 1945

1946

D.76 Calling East Africa. 'Revisiting East Africa'. Overseas, African. 10 March 1946

D.77 Calling East Africa. 'East Africa Revisited – The African People'. Overseas, African. 24 March 1946

D.78 Adapted *Jock of the Bushveld* (Sir Percy Fitzpatrick). Home. 29 March 1946

D.79 Questions in the air. 'The Colonial empire'. Scripted discussion with three other speakers. Home. 17 May 1946

D.80 'England after Africa'. Agricultural and colonial settlement in Africa as they might affect West Country people. Home, West. 5 June 1946

1947

D.81 'The practical potentialities of development in East Africa'. Overseas, European. 25 March 1947

D.82 Travel Talks. How the world lives. 'Cattle country in the USA'. Home. 30 May 1947

D.83 Travel Talks. 'With the Masai'. Dramatic. Home. 26 September 1947

D.84 Commonwealth and Empire. 'The Overlanders'. With Lewis Hastings. Home. 14 October 1947

1948

D.85 'The war against the locust'. Belgium. Overseas. 16 April 1948

D.86 'The war against the locust'. Trans. Swedish. Overseas. 20 May 1948

D.87 'The war against the locust'. Trans. Portuguese/Spanish. Overseas. 21 May 1948

D.88 'The war against the locust'. London calling Europe. Overseas. 24 May 1948

D.89 'The war agianst the locust'. Trans. Norwegian. Overseas. 2 June 1948

D.90 The Brains Trust. 7th series. No.16. Home. 19 July 1948

D.91 Any Questions? Home, West. 21 December 1948, repeated Home 16 January 1949 and 19 January 1949

1949

D.92 New Books and Old. *The Sorcerer's Apprentice*. Light Programme. 29 January 1949

D.93 Enterprise and Achievement. No.5. 'What next in the Colonies? East Africa'. With Geoffrey Nunn. Home. 7 February 1949

D.94 Meet the Commonwealth. 'What next in the Colonies?' General Overseas. 17 February 1949

D.95 London Forum. 'Colonial Policy – Is Britain advancing self-government at the right speed?' General Overseas. 28 February 1949

D.96 Calling East Africa. 'Talk for Kenya Arbor Day'. General Overseas. 1 May 1949

D.97 Designed for Women. Interview on aspect of 'Colonial Month'. BBC TV. 23 June 1949

D.98 Calling East Africa. 'Christmas Day Talk'. General Overseas. 25 December 1949

1950

D.99 'The Colour Bar: Why are there colour bars today?' With Learie Constantine, Dr. E. J. Dingwall and Professor L. S. Penrose. Third Programme. 9 June 1950, repeated 21 March 1981.

D.100 The Critics: rev/d *The House by the Medlar Tree* (Giovanni Vega). Home. 24 September 1950

D.101 The Critics: rev/d *Such Darling Dodos* (Angus Wilson). Home. 1 October 1950

D.102 The Critics: rev/d *Noble Essences* (Osbert Sitwell). Home. 8 October 1950

D.103 The Critics: rev/d *Huckleberry Finn* (Mark Twain). Home. 15 October 1950

D.104 The Critics: rev/d *Traveller's Prelude* (Freya Stark). Home. 22 October 1950

D.105 The Critics: rev/d *Shaw as a man of letters*. Home. 6 November 1950; repeated 10 November 1950.

D.106 Taking Stock. 'Whither Africa?'. Home. 23 November 1950

D.107 County Championship. Took part in the Wiltshire team. West. 17 November 1950

D.108 County Championship. Wilts team. West. 8 December 1950

D.109 County Championship. No.10. Hants v. Wilts took part in the Wilts team. West. 29 December 1950

1951

D.110 County Championship. No.14. Wilts v. Somerset. West. 26 January 1951

D.111 For your Bookshelf. Home. 7 February 1951

D.112 County Championship. No.18. Glos. v. Wilts West. 25 February 1951

D.113 County Championship. No.20. Cornwall v. Wilts West. 5 March 1951

D.114 History 11. (1) 'The Suez Canal'. Home, Schools. 19 April 1951

D.115 Town Forum. Midland. 24 April 1951, repeated 30 April 1951

D.116 History 11. (2) 'Sir Samuel Baker and the Slave Trade'. Home, Schools. 26 April 1951

D.117 History 11. (3) 'The Opening of Africa: Cecil Rhodes'. Home, Schools. 3 May 1951

D.118 The Critics: rev/d *The Lost Childhood and other essays* (Graham Greene). Home. 20 May 1951

D.119 The Critics: rev/d *The Strangers in the House* (Georges Simenon). Home. 20 May 1951

D.120 Citizenship. No.2. The Colonies Today. 'Kenya'. Forces Educational Broadcast, Light Programme. 21 May 1951

D.121 The Critics: rev/d *Ronald Firbank* (Jocelyn Brooke), and three novels – *Inclinations, Caprice, Vainglory* (Ronald Firbank). Home. 27 May 1951

D.122 The Critics: rev/d *The Day before Yesterday* (W. Robertson Scott). Home. 3 June 1951

D Radio and television appearances by Elspeth Huxley   161

D.123   The Critics: rev/d *Maura* (Huthi Singh). Home. 10 June 1951

D.124   The Critics: rev/d *A Land* (Jaquetta Hawkes). Home. 17 June 1951

D.125   The Critics: rev/d *English Life and Leisure* (B. Seebohm Rowntree and G. R. Lavers). Home. 24 June 1951

D.126   Travel Talks. Children of other lands. 'At a village school in Central Africa'. Home, Schools. 26 October 1951

D.127   Question Time. No.5 from Manchester. Younger generation in race relations at the International Club. Light Programme. 7 November 1951

D.128   Constitutional Experiment. 'Empire to Commonwealth'. Chinese, Far Eastern. 4 December 1951

1952

D.129   The Critics: rev/d *The Youthful Queen Victoria* (Dormer Creston). Home. 6 April 1952

D.130   The Critics: rev/d *Crime in America* (Senator Kevauver). Home. 13 April 1952

D.131   The Critics: rev/d *Mrs. McGinty's Dead* (Agatha Christie). Home. 20 April 1952

D.132   The Critics: rev/d *A Touch of the Sun* (William Sansom). Home. 27 April 1952

D.133   The Critics: rev/d *King Solomon's Mines* (Konrad S. Lorenz). Home. 4 May 1952

D.134   The Critics: rev/d *The Equation of Love* (Ethel Wilson). Home. 11 May 1952

D.135   Travel Talks. In the hot lands. 'Fighting the Tsetse Fly'. Home, Schools. 31 October 1952

D.136   The Critics: rev/d *Arnold Bennett* (Reginald Pound). Home. 14 December 1952

D.137   The Critics: rev/d *The Cardboard Crown* (Martin Boyd). Home. 21 December 1952

D.138   International Commentary. 'Gold Coast'. BBC TV. 22 December 1952

D.139   The Critics: rev/d *The Producer* (Richard Brooks). Home. 28 December 1952

D.140   The Critics: rev/d *R. S. Surtees* (Leonard Cooper). Home. 4 January 1952

1953

D.141　The Critics: rev/d *For the Term of his Natural Life* (Marcus Clarke). Home. 11 January 1953

D.142　The Critics: rev/d *Letters to his Wife* (Thomas Carlyle). Home. 18 January 1953

D.143　International Commentary. 'A Summing-up'. BBC TV. 2 February 1953

D.144　Chronique de l'Empire. 'Pourquoi les Mau-Mau?'. Script in English. Overseas, French. 26 June 1953

D.145　The Critics: rev/d *Reflections on a Marine Venus* (Laurence Durrell). Home. 16 August 1953

D.146　The Critics: rev/d *The City beyond the River* (Hermann Cusack). Home. 23 August 1953

D.147　The Critics: rev/d *Steele's Tatler* (Sir Richard Steele). Home. 30 August 1953

1954

D.148　The Critics: rev/d *Go tell it on the Mountain* (James Baldwin). Home. 28 March 1954

D.149　The Critics: rev/d *Turgenev* (David Magarshack). Home. 6 April 1954

D.150　The Critics: rev/d *Reach for the Sky* (Paul Brickhill). Home. 11 April 1954

D.151　The Critics: rev/d *The Bridge on the River Kwai* (Pierre Boulle). Home. 18 April 1954

D.152　The Critics: rev/d *Don Quixote de la Mancha* (Cervantes). Home. 25 April 1954

D.153　The Critics: rev/d *The Spanish Temper* (V. S. Pritchett). Home. 2 May 1954

D.154　The Critics: rev/d *The New Men* (C. P. Snow). Home. 9 May 1954

D.155　Woman's Hour. 'A writer reads for pleasure'. Light Programme. 18 May 1954

D.156　English Writing. Just Published. London calling Asia. Overseas. 12 October 1954

D.157　The Critics: rev/d Penguin edition of Oscar Wilde. Home. 17 October 1954

D.158　Travel Talks. Round the Commonwealth. 'Farming in Kenya'. Home, Schools. 22 October 1954

D.159   The Critics: rev/d *The First Night of Twelfth Night* (Leslie Hotson). Home. 24 October 1954

D.160   The Critics: rev/d *The Cornerstone* (Zoe Oldenbourg). Home. 31 October 1954

D.161   The Critics: rev/d *Riot* (John Wyllie). Home. 7 November 1954

D.162   English Writing. Just Published. *Lewis Carroll* (Derek Hudson). London Calling Asia. Overseas. 9 November 1954

D.163   The Critics: rev/d *This Country was the World* (Charles Beatty), and *General Gordon* (Lord Elton). Home. 14 November 1954

D.164   The Critics: rev/d *Ionia* (Freya Stark). Home. 21 November 1954

D.165   English Writing. Just Published. *The Old Wives' Tale* (Arnold Bennett). London Calling Asia. Overseas. 7 December 1954

1955

D.166   'Books for You'. Colonial. 21 March 1955

D.167   Michael Blundell – Personal Portrait. General Overseas. 3 April 1955

D.168   'A Journey in Kenya'. Extract read from *Race and Politics in Kenya*. Home. 19 April 1955

D.169   The Critics: rev/d *The Private Diaries of Stendhal* (ed. Robert Sage). Home. 19 June 1955

D.170   The Critics: rev/d *A Rose for Winter* (Laurie Lee). Home. 26 June 1955

D.171   Calling East Africa. Points of View: The Dow Report on East Africa. Unscripted discussion with James Johnson MP. Colonial. 26 June 1955

D.172   The Critics: rev/d *Officers and Gentlemen* (Evelyn Waugh). Home. 3 July 1955

D.173   The Critics: rev/d *Over the Bridge* (Richard Church). Home. 10 July 1955

D.174   The Critics: rev/d *Hogarth's Progress* (Peter Quennell). Home. 17 July 1955

1956

D.175   Calling East Africa. Points of View. Unscripted discussion on the Coutts Report with Colin Legum. Colonial. 22 January 1956

D.176   Speke of the Nile. Speaker – a European View. West. 30 January 1956

164   D   Radio and television appearances by Elspeth Huxley

D.177   Calling East Africa. Points of View. 'Regionalism in Africa'. Discussion with Colin Legum. Colonial. 26 February 1956

D.178   The Critics: rev/d *The Flight from the Enchanter* (Iris Murdoch). Home. 25 March 1956

D.179   The Critics: rev/d *Letter to a Friend* (M. R. James) ed. Gwendolen McBryde. Home. 1 April 1956

D.180   The Critics: rev/d *A Dance in the Sun* (Dan Jacobson). Home. 18 April 1956

D.181   The Critics: rev/d *Sir Robert Walpole: The Making of a Statesman* (J. H. Plumb). Home. 15 April 1956

D.182   The Critics: rev/d *Canaille* (Kathleen Sully). Home. 22 April 1956

D.183   The Critics: rev/d *I Presume* (Ian Anstruther). Home. 29 April 1956

D.184   Weekend Away. Two Bridges, Dartmoor. West. 20 July 1956

D.185   Dear to my Heart. Speaker. Home. West. 29 October 1956

1957

D.186   The Critics: rev/d *The Merchant of Prato* (Iris Origo). Home. 24 February 1957

D.187   The Critics: rev/d *Women in a Village* (Louise Rayner). Home. 3 March 1957

D.188   'Masai of East Africa'. Adaptation of 'With the Masai'. Home. 8 March 1957

D.189   The Critics: rev/d *Without Love* (Gerald Hanley). Home. 10 March 1957

D.190   The Critics: Home. 17 March 1957. [No details available]

D.191   The Critics: rev/d *The Spiked Heel* (Richard Marsten). Home. 24 March 1957

D.192   The Critics: rev/d *There is a Happy Land* (Keith Waterhouse). Home. 31 March 1957

D.193   The Critics: rev/d *The Ordeal of Gilbert Pinfold* (Evelyn Waugh). Home. 21 July 1957

D.194   The Critics: rev/d *Close to Colette* (Maurice Goudeket). Home. 28 July 1957

D.195   The Critics: rev/d *Taine's Notes on England*. Home. 4 August 1957

D.196   The Critics: rev/d *The Company She Keeps* (Mary McCarthy). Home. 11 August 1957

D   Radio and television appearances by Elspeth Huxley   165

D.197   The Critics: rev/d *A Father and his Fate* (Ivy Compton-Burnett). Home. 18 August 1957

D.198   The Critics: rev/d *Dickens at Work* (John Butt and Kathleen Tillotson). Home. 25 August 1957

1958

D.199   'A Real Issue (the future of the small farmer)'. Light Programme. 2 June 1958

D.200   Just Published. Home, West. 6 July 1958

D.201   The Brains Trust. Team. BBC TV. 6 July 1958

D.202   The Brains Trust. TV team. Home. 11 July 1958

D.203   Calling East Africa. Discussion on the Serengeti National Park. With two other speakers. Overseas, African. 23 August 1958

D.204   The Critics: rev/d *Our Man in Havana* (Graham Greene). Home. 12 October 1958

D.205   The Critics: rev/d *Australian Accent* (John D. Pringle). Home. 19 October 1958

D.206   The Critics: rev/d *Mountolive* (Laurence Durrell). Home. 26 October 1958

D.207   The Critics: rev/d *Kitchener* (Philip Magnus). Home. 2 November 1958

D.208   At Home and Abroad. 'The Political Situation in Kenya'. Home. 7 November 1958

D.209   The Critics: rev/d *The Bell* (Iris Murdoch). Home Service. 9 November 1958

D.210   The Critics: rev/d *The Lost World of the Kalahari* (Laurens van der Post). Home. 16 November 1958

D.211   Calling East Africa. A study of the contemporary scene in Britain by means of quotations from novels published in 1958. Overseas, African. 20 December 1958

1959

D.212   Woman's Hour. Serial reading by Fay Compton of *The Flame Trees of Thika*. Light Programme. Daily 4–8 May 1959

D.213   Calling East Africa. Unscripted discussion on fauna conservation. Overseas, African. 23 May 1959

D.214   The Critics: rev/d *Edward Marsh: A Biography* (Christopher Hassall). Home. 14 June 1959

166   D   *Radio and television appearances by Elspeth Huxley*

D.215   The Brains Trust. English talks for Asia. General Overseas. 16 June 1959

D.216   The Brains Trust. Panel. BBC TV. 21 June 1959

D.217   The Critics: rev/d *Summer in the Greenhouse* (Elizabeth Mayor). Home. 21 June 1959

D.218   The Critics: rev/d *The Siege at Peking* (Peter Fleming). Home. 28 June 1959

D.219   The Critics: rev/d *A Passage to England* (Nirad Chaudhuri). Home. 5 July 1959

D.220   The Brains Trust. English talks for Asia. General Overseas. 7 July 1959

D.221   Woman's Hour. Guest of the week. 'African Animals'. Light Programme. 8 July 1959

D.222   The Critics: rev/d *Sorrows, Passions and Alarms* (James Kirkup) and *A Company of Strangers* (John Rosenberg). Home Service. 12 July 1959

D.223   The Critics: rev/d *The Nine Guardians* (Rosario Castellanos) and *A Book of South African Verse* (edit. Guy Butler). Home Service. 19 July 1959

D.224   Ou va l'Afrique noire? 'L'Afrique occidentale et ses voisins de l'Est'. Script in English. French. 5 November 1959

1960

D.225   Woman's Hour. 'Echoes of Guests of 1959'. Light Programme. 6 January 1960

D.226   The Brains Trust. Panel. BBC TV. 21 January 1960

D.227   The Brains Trust. Team. Home. 24 January 1960

D.228   Calling Rhodesia and Nyasaland. 'Serengeti Shall not Die'. Film review. Overseas, African. 11 February 1960

D.229   The Critics: rev/d *Casanova's Chinese Restaurant* (Anthony Powell). Home. 26 June 1960.

D.230   The Critics: rev/d *Escape to an Autumn Pavement* (Andrew Salkey). Home. 3 July 1960

D.231   The Critics: rev/d *Alexander the God* (Maurice Druon). Home. 10 July 1960

D.232   The Critics: rev/d *A Bundle of Sensations* (Goronwy Rees). Home. 17 July 1960

D.233   The Critics: rev/d *The Cheerful Day* (Nan Fairbrother). Home. 24 July 1960

D Radio and television appearances by Elspeth Huxley   167

D.234   The Critcs: rev/d *A Kind of Loving* (Stan Barstow). Home. 31 July 1960
D.235   Focus on Africa. Interview with Mark Dodd on the Monckton Commission. Overseas, West African. 12 October 1960
D.236   BBC Overseas Christmas Programme. EH reviewed *Border Country* (R. Williams). 5 December 1960

1961

D.237   The Critics: rev/d *A Burnt-out Case* (Graham Greene). Home. 15 January 1961
D.238   The Critics: rev/d *Bayonets to Llasa* (Peter Fleming). Home. 22 January 1961
D.239   The Critics: rev/d *Portrait of an Officer* (Pierre-Henri Simon). Home. 29 January 1961
D.240   The Critics: rev/d *Lady Gregory – a literary portrait*. (E. Coxhead). Home. 5 February 1961
D.241   The Critics: rev/d *The Atom Station* (Halldor Laxness). Home. 12 February 1961
D.242   The Critics: rev/d *The Characters of Love* (John Bayley). Home. 19 February 1961
D.243   The World of Books. Review of crime fiction. Home. 9 June 1961
D.244   Wednesday Review: rev/d *Water Bailiff*. Midland. 28 June 1961
D.245   *Frankly Speaking. EH interviews Sir Hugh Foot. Home. 2 July 1961
D.246   The World of Books. Review. Home. 18 August 1961
D.247   The Critics: rev/d *The Prime of Miss Jean Brodie* (Muriel Spark). Home. 20 October 1961
D.248   The Critics: rev/d *Unconditional Surrender* (Evelyn Waugh). Home. 5 November 1961
D.249   The Critics: rev/d *The Forest People* (Colin M. Turnbull). Home. 12 November 1961
D.250   Fisherman's Forum. Took part in discussion. Midland. 15 November 1961
D.251   The Critics: rev/d *The Citizen-King: the Life of Louis-Phillipe* (T. E. B. Howarth). Home. 19 November 1961
D.252   The Critics: rev/d *The Loved and the Lost* (Morley Callaghan). Home. 26 November 1961
D.253   The Critics: rev/d *The Death of Tragedy* (George Steiner). Home. 3 December 1961

D.254 The World of Books: rev/d *Memoir of Thomas Bewick*. (ed. M. Weekley). Home. 16 December 1961

1962

D.255 Woman's Hour. Points from the Postbag. 'Revenge and the Law': discussion. Light Programme. 21 February 1962

D.256 Woman's Hour. Serial reading by Adrienne Corri from *The Mottled Lizard*. Light Programme. 19 April, then daily 24–27 April 1962

D.257 Woman's Hour. Guest of the Week. Light Programme. 6 June 1962

D.258 Signpost. 'Avon Navigation'. Interviewed. Midland. 6 June 1962

D.259 The World of Books: rev/d *Hours to Kill* (Ursula Curtis); *Come Home and be Killed* (Jennie Melville); *The Dog it was that Died* (H. R. F. Keating). Home. 9 June 1962

D.260 The World of Books. Interviews Sir Lawrence S. Jones. Home Service. 30 June 1962

D.261 *Frankly Speaking. Asking questions. With Patrick Keatley. Interviews Margery Perham. Home. 6 July 1962

D.262 The World of Books: rev/d *Gilligan's Last Elephant* (Gerald Hanley), and *Act of Destruction* (Ronald Hardy). Home. 18 August 1962

D.263 Outlook from Africa. 'The White African'. Overseas. 18 August 1962. Repeated 22 August 1962 and 24 August 1962

D.264 Any Questions. Reminiscences of 'Any Questions' programmes. Home. 25 December 1962

1963

D.265 Woman's Hour. 'Born in July'. Interviewed by Mollie Lee. Light Programme. 9 July 1963

D.266 *Frankly Speaking. Questioned Armand Denis. Home. 29 July 1963

D.267 Woman's Hour – Home for the Day. 'How to travel, and the seeing eye: noticing things'. Light Programme. 31 July 1963

D.268 Woman's Hour. 'You ask for it – the most rewarding part of work: as a magistrate (adoption)'. Light Programme. 6 August 1963

1964

D.269 The World of Books: rev/d *Harama* (Wilfred Fowler). Home. 4 January 1964

D.270 Woman's Hour. 'My place in the sun: Africa'. Light Programme. 23 January 1964

D.271 Tonight. Interviewed about her book *Forks and Hope*. BBC1 TV. 11 February 1964

D.272 The World of Books. Interviewed re *Forks and Hope*. Home. 22 February 1964

D.273 The World of Books: rev/d *Verdict on Schweitzer* (Gerald Knight). Home. 30 May 1964

D.274 'The Return of the Hoe: returning to a farm in Kenya'. Home. 29 June 1964

D.275 The World of Books: rev/d *The Philosophy of Albert Schweitzer* (Henry Clark). Home Service. 8 August 1964

D.276 Home this afternoon. 'For your library list'. Home. 10 August 1964

D.277 The World of Books: rev/d *A Night at Sea* (Margaret Lane). Home. 29 August 1964

D.278 *Tonight. *Suki*. BBC1 TV. 22 October 1964

D.279 Interview on Granada (&TWW). 19 November 1964

1965

D.280 The World of Books: rev/d *The Road to Gundagai* (Graham McInnes). Home. 12 June 1965

D.281 Holiday Books: rev/d *A Favourite of the Gods* (Sybille Bedford). Home. 28 July 1965

D.282 On Your Farm. From *Brave New Victuals*. Interviewed. Home. 13 November 1965

1966

D.283 Meeting Point. 'Reverence for Life – man's dominion over animals and his responsibility to them'. BBC1 TV. 28 August 1966

1967

D.284 Twentieth Century Focus – EH's reminiscences of time she spent in Kenya as a young girl. BBC1 TV. 23 January 1967

D.285 The World of Books. Interviewed about her book *Their Shining Eldorado*. Home. 16 May 1967

D.286 Woman's Hour. *Their Shining Eldorado*. Interviewed by Marjorie Anderson on her visit to Australia to get material for this book. Light Programme. 21 June 1967

D Radio and television appearances by Elspeth Huxley

1968

D.287 Christian Focus. Who are the others? The web of life. *The Flame Trees of Thika*. Schools, Radio 4. 14 June 1968

D.288 Home this Afternoon. 'Swaziland' Speaker. Radio 4 Talks. 6 September 1968

D.289 Woman's Hour. *Love among the Daughters*. Talks to Marjorie Anderson. Radio 2. 18 September 1968

1969

D.290 Woman's Hour. Serial reading by Prunella Scales of *Love among the Daughters*. Radio 2 daily 12–21 March (except 15,16) 1969

D.291 Late-night Line-up – interviewed by Sheridan Morley about *Love among the Daughters*. BBC2 TV. 12 September 1969

1973

D.292 Home Country – EH talks about the area in which she lives. BBC TV West. 20 March 1973, repeated 16 October 1973

1974

D.293 The Book Programme – interview. BBC2 TV. 12 September 1974

1975

D.294 Woman's Hour. 'A Giant of the 19th Century' with Teresa McGonagle. Radio 4. 26 March 1975

D.295 Kaleidoscope. Interviewed by James Kellen about *Florence Nightingale*. Radio 4. 1 April 1975

1978

D.296 *Storytime. *The Flame Trees of Thika* abridged by P. M. Wilson, read by Virginia McKenna. Radio 4, daily 27 February 1978 to 10 March 1978 (except 4,5 March).

D.297 'A Name on a Map'. Interview with J. Knox Mawer about her early years in Thika. Radio 4. 8 December 1978

1980

D.298 Kaleidoscope. Interviewed re *Nellie: Letters from Africa*. Radio 4. 6 March 1980

D Radio and television appearances by Elspeth Huxley   171

D.299   *'The Tale Bearer – the life of Karen Blixen and the art of Izak Dinesen'. Took part in group discussion. Radio 3. 22 December 1980

1981

D.300   *John Dunn – interview about 'The Whipsnade Idea'. Radio 2. 27 April 1981

D.301   You and Yours. Interviewed by Bill Brecon about *Whipsnade*. Radio 4. 22 May 1981

D.302   *Desert Island Discs. Radio 4. 17 October 1981

D.303   'The Flame Trees of Thika – The Promised Land'. Thames Television. 1 September 1981, repeated 19 April 1983

D.304   'The Flame Trees of Thika – Hyenas will eat Anything'. Thames Television. 8 September 1981, repeated 26 April 1983

D.305   'The Flame Trees of Thika – Happy New Year'. Thames Television. 15 September 1981, repeated 3 May 1983

D.306   'The Flame Trees of Thika – Friends in High Places'. Thames Television. 22 September 1981, repeated 17 May 1983

D.307   'The Flame Trees of Thika – A Real Sportsman'. Thames Television. 29 September 1981, repeated 23 May 1983

D.308   'The Flame Trees of Thika – Safari'. Thames Television. 6 October 1981, repeated 31 May 1983

D.309   'The Flame Trees of Thika – The Drums of War'. Thames Television. 13 October 1981, repeated 7 June 1983

1982

D.310   'The Flame Trees of Thika – The Promised Land'. WGBH Boston, Masterpiece Theater series. 3 January 1982, repeated 14 August 1983

D.311   'The Flame Trees of Thika – Hyenas will eat Anything'. WGBH Boston, Masterpiece Theater series. 10 January 1982, repeated 21 August 1983

D.312   'The Flame Trees of Thika – Happy New Year'. WGBH Boston, Masterpiece Theater series. 17 January 1982, repeated 28 August 1983.

D.313   'The Flame Trees of Thika – Friends in High Places'. WGBH Boston, Masterpiece Theater series. 24 January 1982, repeated 4 September 1983

172   D   Radio and television appearances by Elspeth Huxley

D.314   'The Flame Trees of Thika — A Real Sportsman'. WGBH Boston, Masterpiece Theater series. 31 January 1982, repeated 11 September 1983

D.315   'The Flame Trees of Thika — Safari'. WGBH Boston, Masterpiece Theater series. 7 February 1982, repeated 18 September 1983

D.316   'The Flame Trees of Thika — The Drums of War'. WGBH Boston, Masterpiece Theater series. 14 February 1982, repeated 25 September 1983

1985

D.317   *Bookshelf. Interviewed about *Out in the Midday Sun*. Radio 4. 3 November 1985

1987

D.318   *Woman's Hour. Interviewed about her travels and Mary Kingsley's book *Travels in West Africa* which EH abridged and introduced. Radio 4. 30 April 1987

1990

D.319   *The Gloria Hunniford Show. EH interviewed by Gloria Hunniford about her life in Kenya and her book *Nine Faces of Kenya*. Radio 2. 20 September 1990

1991

D.320   'The Flame Trees of Thika — Happy New Year'. WGBH Boston. (this one episode repeated during 20th Anniversary Season). 20 January 1991

E. Miscellanea

1. Articles (date or provenance not established)
2. Essay Competition
3. Radio and Television (transmission uncertain)
4. Paper for Malinowski's Seminar
5. Report on setting up of East African Literature Bureau
6. Introduction to book as yet unpublished.

E.1   ARTICLES: (date or provenance not established)

Polo articles

(a) McMillan Cup – Results of Polo Tournament at Makuyu. *East African Standard*. January 1922
(b) The Polo World – The American defeats the British Army. *East African Standard*. November 1923
(c) Nairobi Polo – L.S.T. Cup. *East African Standard*. January 1924
(d) Nairobi Polo Week – Details of First Round of Connaught Cup. *East African Standard*. January 1924
(e) Polo Week Opens in Nairobi. *East African Standard*. January 1924
(f) Nairobi Polo Week – The Connaught Cup. *East African Standard*. January 1924
(g) Makuyu Polo Week – Opening Matches of the Tournament. *East African Standard*. January 1924
(h) Makuyu Polo Week – Njoro wins the Ridley Cup Final. *East African Standard*. January 1924
(i) Polo in Kenya – Cup Winners during the Past Year. *East African Standard*. January 1924

Empire Marketing Board

(j) 'Fishy Butter' – article on research into butter at National Institute of Dairying Research, Reading. (special to *The Daily News*). *Sun-Herald* (Australia?). 10 November 1928
(k) 'Seeds from Australia'. *The Sun*. (Australia?). 6 February 1930
(l) 'Insect Menace Fight'. *Trinidad Guardian*. 1931
(m) 'B.C. Professor helps English Research in Cheese Bacteriology'. *Vancouver Sun*. 1931?
(n) 'Chocolates that Bloom' – article on research into sugar and jam trades. 14 March 1932?

174   E   Miscellanea

- (o) 'Calf TB Vaccine held Practicable'. *Edmonton Journal*. No date.
- (p) 'Plant Doctors fight Bugs of the Empire'. *Ottawa Journal*. No date.
- (q) 'Canadian Explorers wanted to look for Grass'. *The Globe*, Toronto. No date.
- (r) 'Keeping a Watch on the World's Storms'. *Eastern Province Herald*, Port Elizabeth, S.A.

Others

- (s) Weekly Radio Letter on Best Sellers for USA. 1941.
- (t) 'If I were Education Minister'. Talks with Eminent Contemporaries by R. L. Megroz – 5. Elspeth Huxley. *Schoolmaster & Women Teachers' Chronicle*. 1948/9.
- (u) 'The Rhodesian Fiasco' – article on Ian Smith (Rhodesia) with cartoon-style illustration of Harold Wilson. 1967/8?
- (v) 'Earth Bubbles. The Rising Tide of Malnutrition'. Article in magazine about intensive farming. Written before 1980.
- (w) My Weekend. 'On the Prowl – Africa style'. *Daily Mail? Evening Standard?* 1981?

E.2   PRIZE

The **Essay Competition** – was initiated in 1913 and was set by the Royal Colonial Institute, awarding prizes and medals to pupils in the Empire. In 1924 Elspeth Grant won the prize in Class A (for over 16's) for her essay 'Improved Communications as a Factor of Imperial History' by Praesentia Confer Praeteritis, extracts from which were published in the *East African Standard*. Now known as the Royal Commonwealth Society Essay Competition, it continues very successfully under the Commonwealth Trust with 6000 entries last year reaching the International level, these having been chosen from within their own countries from many more applicants: much of this organisation is done by voluntary help. Information on this competition can be obtained from the Royal Commonwealth Society, 18 Northumberland Avenue, London WC2N 5BJ.

E.3   RADIO AND TELEVISION (Contributions to programmes written by EH but not necessarily transmitted – dates may indicate time of recording).

- (a) 'War against Superstition'. Home and Forces. 12 June 1943.
- (b) 'K.U.R.' Calling Africa. Home and Forces. 16 June 1943.
- (c) 'Mass Education in Africa' supplied for inclusion in various Home News Bulletins. 13 January 1944.
- (d) Senior History 1. On Charles Darwin. Home, Schools 1945.
- (e) Freedom Forum. 'Problems of Empire'. 7 August 1946.

(f) The British Overseas. 'Lord Delamere'. General Overseas. 22 November 1951.
(g) 'They Found Fame: Lord Delamere'. 17 February 1953.
(h) The Nigerian Broadcasting Corporation had 5 readings of extracts from *Flame Trees of Thika* in 1959/60: exact dates not known.
(i) Talk on Henry Morton Stanley. 1964.
(j) *The Flame Trees of Thika*. Thames Television. Besides the transmissions indicated in Section D., this production was also shown on many other PBS stations in the USA and was sold to many other countries overseas including Argentine, Australia, Hong Kong, New Zealand, Jordan, Ireland, Greece, Gibraltar, The Netherlands, Belgium, Iceland, Canada, Sweden and Germany.

E.4 SEMINAR

Paper on the Kikuyu entitled 'The Influence of Environment on Land Tenure with special reference to the Kikuyu' for Malinowski's Seminar at the London School of Economics. 1937, see A.6.

E.5 REPORT ON SETTING UP OF EAST AFRICAN LITERATURE BUREAU

Literature for Africans: Report 1946. (Printed in Nairobi by cyclostyle). EH was commissioned to write a report on the desirability of setting up an East African Literature Bureau. Her survey lasted three months, covering Kenya, Tanganyika and Uganda. This extract from *Focus on International and Comparative Librarianship*, Vol. 26, No. 1 of 10 May 1995 sums up EH's conclusions and is reprinted with their kind permission.
(a) Demand for simple books in all languages far exceeds supply.
(b) There is an almost complete absence of vernacular books of special interest to women.
(c) The religious category is at present the best served of all.
(d) Swahili literature is well served but there is still a shortage of books of general interest to adults.
(e) Vernacular editions of official reports are seldom published but often wanted. On the issue of what books Africans needed most, the survey revealed that Africans wanted books that made them literate, so that they could acquire skills to improve their standard of living. This could be followed by books of knowledge about history, geography and recreation. Consequently, the East African Literature Bureau was formed, as an organisation of the East African High Commission in 1948. The Bureau was established with its headquarters in Nairobi, Kenya, and with branches in Dar es Salaam, Tanzania and Kampala respectively.

176   E   *Miscellanea*

Mr. Charles G. Richards became the first Director of the East African Literature Bureau in 1948 after 12 years publishing and bookselling as a member of staff of the Church Missionary Society (CMS). Mr. Richards was kind enough to send me the following information by letter:

> Mrs Huxley was asked to advise the Governments whether the normal development and investments of publishing concerns in East Africa, and other bodies such as local government bodies would provide the reading material, and encourage local growth in its provision (this would include libraries) or whether the Governments should take action. Her advice was that they should do so. This was in 1945, and the cost was, I understood, met by the Colonial Office in London. In 1947 the CO asked what the Governments were going to do. I was not at that time fully aware of the notice that was being taken by people in government of my own efforts in literature provision, though I remember attending one of the meetings held with Mrs Huxley at which I showed a list of manuscripts by local authors that I'd publish if I could find the capital. However, the response of the Governments to the CO question was to ask me to follow up Mrs Huxley's study and make a detailed plan. The CMS was asked to allow me time to do this, and Government would meet half my allowance and pay costs.
>
> Over about 6 months, I spent time in all 3 countries and produced a very detailed plan and estimates for an East African Literature Bureau. A Publishing Fund was included, to be run on business lines. For Libraries development and Periodicals development funds were asked for staff to produce detailed plans. The Colonial Office accepted the plan. The CMS was asked to release me to start the EALB and finally to run it. This I did from 1948 to 1963, when I retired, leaving the Bureau to be run by East Africans. I did submit later plans, prepared by professional librarians, for libraries and the training of local librarians, and for a popular magazine. Libraries did grow, slowly. The magazine had a short and difficult life but had a powerful effect on periodicals develoment.

Mr. Richards' memoir, *No Carpet on the Floor* can be seen at the Bodleian Library and the SOAS Library.

E.6   INTRODUCTION to book not yet committed to a publisher: *The Elephant of Tsavo* by Noel Simon. Introduction by EH – book being submitted to publishers, 1995.

Index

Sections A., B. and E. are fully indexed. Sections C. and D. are only indexed by name of periodical or radio or TV Station.

ACAC Journal, C.522
Abruquah, J.W., B.8
Adamson, Joy, B.11
Adprint, London, A.6
Africa, A.1
Africa and Asia (see THE CHALLENGE OF AFRICA)
African Home Library, (see Sheldon Press)
African Affairs, C.267, C.288, C.291, C.295
AFRICAN DILEMMAS, A.15
AFRICAN POISON MURDERS, THE, (see DEATH OF AN ARYAN)
Africana, C.707, C.718, C.719
African Sketchbook, An, B.18
Aird, Holly, A.24
Aldus Books (London) (including Aldus Encyclopaedia of Discovery and Exploration) A.35,
Allen Lane, A.24
Amaryllis Press (New York) A.45
America, A.25
Americana (Chicago) A.35
Amin, Mohamed, B.14, B.17
Ampersand, A.21
Anderson, Marjorie, A.34
Animals, C.615
Apollo Edition (see William Morrow) A.24(*d*)
Aragon Reproductions, A.24
Arcata Graphics (Fairfield) A.2, A.5
Asantehene, The, A.18
Atheneum (New York) A.41
Atlantic Monthly, A.24, A.33
ATLANTIC ORDEAL, A.8

Attenborough, Sir David, A.48
Australian, The, A.38
Australian Library for the Blind, A.24
Australasian Publishing, A.33

BACK STREET NEW WORLDS, A.31
Background Books, (see Batchworth Press)
Bader, Douglas, A.10
Baines, Thomas, A.37
Baker, Denys, A.28
Baltimore Sun, C.107
Banta, George, Co. (Harrisonburg) A.24
Barzun, Jacques, A.5
Bastei-Lubbe, A.3, A.22, A.24, A.26, A.46
Batchworth Press, The, A.21
Bawden, Edward, A.13
Baylis, Ebenezer, Trinity Press (Worcester) A.13, A16, A.17, A.19, A.22, A.24–9, A.34
BBC Home Midland, D.115, D.244, D.250, D.258
BBC Home Schools (including National) D.1–10, D.11–13, D.15, D.18, D.30, D.31, D.37–9, D.52, D.53, D.60, D.69, D.72, D.75, D.114, D.116, D.117, D.126, D.135, D.158, E.3(*d*)
BBC Home West, D.80, D.91, D.107–110, D.112, D.113, D.176, D.184, D.185, D.200
BBC Colonial, D.166, D.171, D.175, D.177, E.3(*e*)
BBC Light Programme, D.92, D.127, D.199

177

178 Index

BBC Home 'Critics' (including Radio 3) D.100–105, D.118, D.119, D.121–125, D.129–134, D.136, D.137, D.139–142, D.145–154, D.157, D.159–161, D.163, D.164, D.169, D.170, D.172–174, D.178–183, D.186, D.187, D.189–198, D.204–207, D.209, D.210, D.214, D.217–219, D.222–223, D.229–234, D.237–242, D.247–249, D.251–253

BBC Home Service and Radio 4, D.40–46, D.54, D.55, D.59, D.62–65, D.73, D.78, D.79, D.82–84, D.90, D.93, D.106, D.111, D.168, D.188, D.208, D.244, D.260, D.264, D.266, D.274, D.276, D.281, D.282, D.287, D.288, D.294–298, D.301, D.302, D.317, D.318, E.3(c)

BBC Home, Woman's Hour and Radio 2, A.30, D.212, D.221, D.225, D.255–257, D.265, D.267, D.268, D.270, D.286, D.289, D.290, D.294, D.318

BBC Home 'World of Books', D.243, D.246, D.254, D.259, D.262, D.269, D.272, D.273, D.275, D.277, D.280, D.285

BBC Forces, D.14, D.16, D.17, D.20–29, D.32, D.35, D.36, D.57, D.61, D.67, D.120, E.3(a)–(b)

BBC Overseas Africa (including West and East Africa) D.48, D.57, D.68, D.70, D.74, D.76, D.77, D.203, D.211, D.213, D.228, D.235, E.3(h)

BBC Overseas, D.71, D.94, D.95, D.96, D.98, D.167, D.214, D.236, D.263, E.3(f)

BBC Overseas Empire Eastern, D.33, D.51

BBC Overseas European, D.85–89, D.144, D.224

BBC Overseas Near East, D.66

BBC Overseas Pacific and Far Eastern, D.49, D.50, D.128, D.165

BBC Overseas South Africa, D.48

BBC Third Programme, D.99

BBC TV Blue Peter programme, A.8
BBC TV Brains Trust, D.201–2, D.216, D.226
BBC TV International Commentary, D.138, D.143
BBC1 TV (including BBCTV) D.97, D.271, D.278, D.283, D.284, D.292
BBC2 TV, D.291, D.293
Bell, Simon, A.39
Billing and Sons (Guildford), A.7, A.9, A.10
Birmingham Post, A.42
Black Lechwe, C.618
Blackwood Magazine, C.536
Bliven, Naomi, A.24
Blixen, Karen, B.12
Bloemfontein Friend, C.173
Blundell, Michael, A.23
Bodley Head, A.21, B.17
Book Society, The, A.13, A.17–19, A.22, A.24
Books on Tape, A.1–3, A.5, A.16, A.18, A.24, A.26, A.33, A.37, A.38, A.41, A.46
Boston Globe, A.22, A.24
Bounty Books, (see Chancellor Press)
Bradbury Agnew Press, A.31
Bradford, Grant, A.41, B.18
BRAVE DEEDS OF THE WAR, A.10
BRAVE NEW VICTUALS, A.32
Bray, Thomas, Rev., A.7
Brepols (Turnhout), A.45
Briant, Edward, A.2
Brickell, T. H. & Son, A.44
'Britain in Pictures', A.6
British Broadcasting Corporation, A.10
British Commonwealth Affairs Series, (see Longmans Green)
BRITISH COMMONWEALTH AND EMPIRE, A.6(b)
British Council, A.9
Buckley, Paul, A.47
Building Materials, C.614
Butler & Tanner (Frome), A.4, A.33, A.42

Cahill and Co. (Dublin) A.9
Calgary Daily Herald, C.94, C.164
Calvocoressi, Peter, A.29
Cambridge University Library, A.15
Cambridge University Press, A.12
Cape, Jonathan, A.39
Cape Argus, C.102, C.174, C.190
Cape Times, C.92, C.93, C.136, C.138, C.145, C.156, C.167, C.183, C.203
CAPITAN SCOTT: LA ODISEA DEL ANTARTICO, A.41
Cargoes of the East, B.10
Carrier Corps, The, B.15
Catechist, The, B.8
Central African Examiner, C.478–9
Central African Federation, A.27
Century Hutchinson, A.39
Cesam Media (Oslo), A.24
Ceylon Observer, C.149, C.166, C.182
C. G. S. Studios (Cheltenham), A.2, A.3
Chancellor Press, A.38
Charlton, Michael, A.22
Chatto & Windus, A.1, A.4, A.8, A.13, A.16–19, A.22, A.24–34, A.44, A.46
Cheltenham Press, A.15
Chicago Tribune, C.643
Christian Herald, A.24
Christian Science Monitor, A.1, A.4, A.13, A.24–26, A.28, A.33, A.34, A.37, A.47
City of Benares, A.8
Clark, Dora, A.4
Clark, R. & R. (Edinburgh), A.1, A.8
Clarke, Doble & Brendon, A.21
Clarke and Sherwell, A.6
Clarke, Irwin & Co. (Toronto), A.1, A.4, A.16–19, A.22, A.24–34, A.44
Clays Ltd. (St. Ives), A.26, A.46, A.48
Clay, Richard (Bungay), A.4, A.18, A.22, A.27, A.39, A.40
Clendening, Alfred, A.39
Clio Press, (see Isis Large Print)
Cloete, Stuart, A.24
Cohen, Anthony, A.38
Collins, William, Sons, A.6, A.43, A.45
Collins Harvill (see Harvill Press)

COLONIES: A READER'S GUIDE, A.12
Constable, T. & A. (Edinburgh), A.32
Cooke, Alistair, A.24
Corona (Journal of H.M's Colonial Service), C.309, C.318, C.325
Country Life, A.42, A.48
Cox & Wyman (Reading), A.2, A.29, A.37, A.41
Crankshaw, Edward, A.42
Crestwood Publishing Inc., A.3
Curtis, Arnold, B.13, B.16

Daily Mail, A.13, A.34, A.48, C.120–6
Daily Express (Scottish edition), C.142
Daily Telegraph (including Magazine), A.13, A.34, A.42, C.96, C.195, C.321, C.336, C.338, C.341, C.355, C.407–8, C.421–2, C.523, C.525–528, C.533, C.542, C.548, C.549, C.606, C.653, C.654, C.670, C.672, C.693, C.694, C.729, C.731–739, C.741–746, C.748, C.749, C.751, C.754, C.755–758, C.762
Dalton, Liz, A.5
Danquah, J. B. Dr., A.18
Davey, Patricia, A.29
Davies, Granville, A.46
Day Lewis, C., A.13, A.28
DEATH OF AN ARYAN, A.5
de Gex, Jenny, A.24
DE LAATSTEN IN DE HOF VAN EDEN, A.45
Delamere, Lady, A.1
Delamere, Lord, A.1
Delderfield, Delia, A.39
Dent, J. M. & Sons, A.2, A.3, A.5, A.21, A.40
DER EIDECHSENFAD, A.26
DER FELSEN VON BAMILI, A.22
Dickson Carr, John, A.5
DIE FLAMMENBÄUME VON THIKA, A.24
DIE STUNDEN DES LEOPARDEN, A.3

180 *Index*

Dominion (Wellington, N.Z.), C.153, C.207, C.209
Donnelley, R. R. & Sons (Harrisonburg), A.46
Doolittle and Dalley (Kidderminster), A.44
Doubleday, A.24, A.35
Douglas-Menzies, Lucinda, A.47
Dutton, E. P. (see Saturday Review Press)

Eames, John, B.17
EAST AFRICA, A.6
East Africa Literature Bureau, including E.H.'s report, A.14, E.5
East Africa Womens' League, B.13, B.16
East African Observer, C.19, C.22, C.25, C.29, C.30, C.32, C.35, C.38, C.39, C.41–47, C.54, C.59
East African Standard (Nairobi), A.1, A.23, A.34, C.1, C.18, C.20, C.21, C.23, C.24, C.26–28, C.31, C.33, C.34, C.36, C.37, C.48–53, C.55–58, C.60–62, C.64–77, C.95, C.109, C.192, C.197, C.214, C.220, C.236, E.1(*a*)–(*i*), E.2
East African Wildlife Journal, C.541
Eastern Province Herald, E.1(*r*)
Economist, A.18, A.41
Editions de Seuil, B.2
Edmonton Journal, E.1(*o*)
Elephants of Tsavo, The, E.6
Elm Tree Books, B.10
Empire Essay Competition, E.2
Encounter, C.499, C.502
ENGLISH WOMEN (including Swahili edition), A.9
Euston Films, A.24
Evans Brothers, B.13, B.16
Evening Standard, A.1, A.16, A.34, C.159, C.387, C.391, C.402, C.433, C.441
Everyman Classics, (see Dent, J. M.)

Faber and Faber, A.11, A.48, B.3
Farley, Malcolm, A.2

Farm and Home (Vancouver), C.101
Farmer and Stockbreeder, C.146
Farmers Weekly (Bloemfontein), C.141, C.157, C.172, C.175, C.177, C.205
Field, The, A.1, A.48, C.3, C.4, C.40, C.63, C.85
Financial Times, A.44, A.46, A.48
Finlay, C. K., B.6
Flag-Wagger, The, B.9
FLAME TREES OF THIKA, THE, A.24, A.26
FLAMMETRAEERNE I THIKA, A.24
FLORENCE NIGHTINGALE, A.38
Foges, Wolfgang, A.6, A.35
Folio Society, A.40, B.12
Fordham, David, A.24
Foreign Affairs, C.308, C.501
Foreign Office (IRD), A.21
FORKS AND HOPE, A.28
Fountain Press, B.18
FOUR GUINEAS, A.13, A.18
Four Square Book, A.26
Foyle's Quality Book Club, A.26
Fredriksson, Christer, A.47
Freeman, Irving, A.46
Friend, Donald, A.33
Fryer, Joan, A.24
Fuchs, Sir Vivian, A.37
Fulcrum Publishing (Colorado), A.48

GALLIPOT EYES, A.39
Gee Graphics, A.2
Geer, Charles, A.22
Gentlemen, Scholars and Scoundrels, A.8
Geographical Magazine, A.33, C.231, C.235, C.239, C.240, C.242, C.243, C.248, C.254, C.301, C.303, C.330, C.339, C.482, C.516
George Allen & Unwin, A.36, A.46, B.8
Giffard, Ingaret, A.4
Gilchrist Brothers, A.45
Glasgow Evening Times, C.201
Glassman, Leda, A.26
Glenn, Burt, Magnum Photos, A.47

Winchester Bibliographies of 20th Century Writers

ELSPETH HUXLEY
A Bibliography

Robert Cross read English Literature at Cambridge in 1945. He was an enthusiastic book-collector from childhood and at twelve he bought at auction the Cabinet Edition of George Eliot's Works for 10s, not realising that it was accompanied by 48 plant pots and 10 tennis nets with posts. In 1957 he gave up farming and became personal assistant to Michael Sadleir, thus starting 37 years in publishing. His publications, as a young man, were *Death in Another World, A Portion for Foxes* and *Pai Naa*.

Michael Perkin was formerly Curator of Special Collections, Liverpool University Library, and a founder and sometime Secretary of Liverpool Bibliographical Society. He is now working part-time at Reading University, in the Library and in the Department of Typography, in Winchester Cathedral Library, and on freelance bibliographical and editorial work. His publications include *Abraham Cowley: a Bibliography* (1977) and *The Book Trade in Liverpool to 1850: a Directory* (1981 and 1987). He is at present working on a revision of *The Parochial Libraries of the Church of England*, published in 1959.

I. Elspeth Huxley CBE